WHAT WE MEAN BY EXPERIENCE

WHAT WE MEAN BY EXPERIENCE

Marianne Janack

STANFORD UNIVERSITY PRESS

STANFORD, CALIFORNIA

Stanford University Press
Stanford, California

Library of Congress Cataloging-in-Publication Data

Janack, Marianne, 1964– author.
  What we mean by experience / Marianne Janack.
    pages cm
  Includes bibliographical references and index.
    ISBN 978-0-8047-7614-1 (cloth : alk. paper)
    ISBN 978-0-8047-7615-8 (pbk : alk. paper)
    1. Experience. 2. Knowledge, Theory of. 3. Psychology and philosophy. I Title.
B105.E9J36   2012
128'.4—dc23

2012006397

To Al and Florence Janack, Marilyn Thie, and Linda Martín Alcoff

Contents

Preface

When I told people that I was writing a book about experience, I found that many of them had ideas about it: what it is, who has it, what counts as experience. For philosophers, this everyday word has a very particular meaning, however, which does not always carry over to other disciplines, and is significantly different from its ordinary language use. The term seems to have as many definitions as there are people, which has made writing this book a bit of a challenge. Not everyone will find a story here about what they think we mean by experience, but I think that the narrative line I try to draw through several of these seemingly disparate senses of the term will help illuminate some of the primary problems that have plagued feminist theory, philosophy of science, and epistemology.

And now about that narrative: because the topic of experience is potentially so vast, I have worked very hard to maintain a narrative line that can carry readers through the variety of discussions I touch on in the book. But I couldn't address all the different discussions of experience. The feminist theory chapter was particularly troublesome in this respect. In trying to maintain some textual and narrative integrity, I had to eschew the usual approach to a literature review of the area, focusing instead on selected authors and on particularly important contributions to the discussion. I regret that I was not able to discuss the whole range of attempts to redefine or resuscitate the concept of experience. I suspect that everyone will find someone they think should have been discussed in these pages but isn't—I apologize in advance for that, and ask the reader simply to bear in mind that I am interested in following a particular narrative thread, and that some topics and authors, while interesting, needed to be left out of the narrative so that I could focus on a larger picture of what we mean by experience. The book is a story not just about experience, but about the chasm between experience and discourse that opened up in twentieth-century accounts of experience as a result of the dominant accounts of human nature and the social-natural relationship that seemed to be forced upon all right-thinking people by advances in empirical psychology, on one hand, and by more sophisticated theories of discourse, on the other. The chasm mirrored an even more fundamental divide: that between a conception of human beings as cultural products and the equally coercive conception of ourselves as information-processing systems or primates with sophisticated theory-building tendencies. Each of these conceptions of human beings arose as the product of more naturalistic approaches to accounting for human nature as well: as ways of taking seriously discourse theory, sociology, history, linguistic anthropology, and cognitive science, among other fields. Talking about experience is ineluctably a way of talking about human nature and human cognitive projects, and the story I tell in the following chapters is about the ways in which our conception of human nature and human cognitive projects changed over the course of a hundred years of philosophical, psychological, social scientific, and political territorial shifts.

Acknowledgments

This book has been a long time in the writing and has had a number of different incarnations along the way. Its present form was most directly influenced by a year I spent as a fellow at the Pembroke Center at Brown University in 2000–2001. I'd like to thank all the participants in that seminar, but especially Monique Roelofs and Mimi Long, who pushed me to think about the critique of experience offered by Joan Scott. I also wish to thank my institution at the time, Worcester Polytechnic Institute (WPI) in Worcester, Massachusetts, for granting me the leave I needed to accept the Pembroke fellowship. The work on this project benefited immensely, too, from time I spent in a summer NEH seminar on feminist epistemologies run by Shannon Sullivan and Nancy Tuana. The research and the first draft writing were supported by the National Science Foundation (NSF award SES-0824133), and I am very grateful both to the NSF and to Hamilton College, where I now teach, for their investment in this project.

I have been especially fortunate to have found colleagues generous with their time and willing to read and comment on my work. Meurig Beynon and Steve Russ of the Computer Science Department at the University of Warwick; Ruth Smith, Roger Gottlieb, and Tom Shannon at WPI; Maude Clark and Georgia Frank at Colgate; and Katheryn Doran, Kirk Pillow, Bob Simon, and Rick Werner at Hamilton have all helped me think about these issues. I'd like to give special thanks to Rick, for allowing me to hold on to his books for so long and for his comments on a paper I wrote on William James that helped me think about some of these issues differently, to Bob for reading the book proposal, and to Katheryn, who had her classes read some of these chapters and also made very careful and useful comments on drafts.

Students in my senior seminar on objectivity in the spring of 2011 were a great audience on which to try out some of my ideas about John McDowell, and the students in my senior seminar on mind and body in the spring of 2010 helped me work through some of the readings that went into the last and penultimate chapters. I thank them especially for being willing to dive into this material, while also knowing that I didn't really have a good sense of whether the readings I proposed were going to take us anywhere, or whether we might finally come up against some dead ends. Their trust in me, and their willingness to play a large role in helping me to formulate my thoughts, was a gift of incalculable value. Those students reinforced my conviction that I have the best job in the world.

My friends Heather Buchman and Lydia Hamessley always asked how the work was going and helped buoy my spirits when I felt overwhelmed. Kim and Oran at Café Domenico, in Utica, New York, offered me the perfect table and lots of caffeine on Saturdays, and provided an outlet and adaptor when I needed them. Nick Stagliano, my invaluable editorial assistant, did much tedious work that helped me get the manuscript done, and he was also a great cheerleader along the way. I can't thank him enough. My daughter, Madeleine Adams, recognized my need to write in the afternoons when she came home from school, and she was a great companion as we sat together in our house doing our respective academic work. She also did the illustrations of optical illusions in chapter 2, for which I am very grateful as well. My husband, John Adams, cheered me on and helped me think about the rhetorical aspects of appeals to experience. I also appreciate the feedback I got from Lorraine Code and an anonymous reviewer for Stanford University Press, both of whom made very constructive comments. Libby Potter invited me to present my work at the Bay Area Feminism and Philosophy Colloquium, and I appreciate immensely the seriousness with which the participants engaged with my work. Libby deserves special mention, because she's now read this both when it was a proposal to the NSF and in its final manuscript state, and she has continued to be a good critic and supportive colleague. All of these people stand, in my mind, as representatives of what's best in peer review. Emily-Jane Cohen, my editor at Stanford, was very supportive and very prompt with her replies and advice. I'm grateful for her enthusiasm for the project and her willingness to work with me.

Books often begin before the writer has actually even found her voice, and this is so with this book. Marilyn Thie and Linda Martín Alcoff helped me find my philosophical feminist voice, and I am immensely grateful to them. My parents, Florence and Al Janack, gave me more than I can ever possibly repay: college tuition, loans, and faith that whatever I was studying was valuable if I loved it, even if they had no idea what it was. I am lucky to have had parents who were willing to invest so much in my education and my hopes. I wish all daughters could be so lucky. I dedicate this book to Marilyn, Linda, and my mother and father.

Introduction

THE AUTHORITY OF EXPERIENCE:
REALISM, EMPIRICISM, AND THE
PROBLEM OF THEORY

Does experience have any authority to confirm or undermine our worldviews, theories, or value commitments? Those who think that it does usually trace that authority to its status as a way in which "the world" gets to have its say about the acceptability of our theories. And yet such authority seems to pose its own problems: if the world that is supposed to have its "say" is understood as brute nature, how can it make itself understood to us? What kind of language can it speak? When it comes to brute nature, the idea of speaking is metaphorical at best, incoherent at worst.

Furthermore, the intelligibility of our experience depends on its meaningfulness, and this seems to depend on its expression in terms of concepts, which, in turn, seems to depend on its propositional expression—or, at least, the possibility of capturing experience in propositional terms. But if concepts are themselves intelligible only in terms of a complex web of inferential relationships that they have with other concepts, and this web of relationships constitutes something like a "theory" or "worldview," then the contact with the world that experience is supposed to supply seems to slip away, to become merely a vaporous we-know-not-what. As a result, any say that the world might have had about the acceptability of our theories seems itself to disappear, since presumably it can have no say without our (perhaps unconscious) collusion. Experience must show up in the form in which we allow it to show up, laced up in our conceptual schemes, or in our theories about the world and what it includes.

Anecdotal evidence seems to reinforce skepticism about the extent to which experience is independent of "worldviews" or expectations, and this anecdotal evidence seems to be confirmed by experimental evidence. Thomas Kuhn cites an example of selective perception in *The Structure of Scientific Revolutions* in which subjects in an experiment with playing cards cannot see anomalous cards, such as red cards in the suit of spades or black cards in the suit of hearts. Kuhn takes this to be evidence that sense experience is dictated to a large extent by our expectations, which come out of our worldviews. The subjects cannot see red spade cards because their theory of playing cards or their entrenched worldviews do not include the possibility of the existence of such cards. Similar "change-blindness" experiments show the same thing. In one, observers charged with counting the number of passes that occur in a slow-paced basketball game fail to notice a person dressed in a gorilla suit who walks right through the middle of the game. In this case, as well as in the playing-card example, it seems that interpretation and projection shape perception and sometimes undermine its accuracy.

But the idea that interpretation and the constructive work of the mind count as distortion depends on "the idea that 'the world' is there once for all and immutably," as Jerome Bruner (1986, 105) puts it in his discussion of Nelson Goodman's work; or that there is what Bernard Williams (1978) has called an "Absolute Conception" of the world—a way the world is independent of our attempts to come to know it. If we give up on this conception of the world, then the interpretive and constructive work of the mind is not distorting, since there is no original it is charged with representing accurately. Psychological experiments like those mentioned above operationalize the assumption that there is some way that the world is, independent of observers who come to know it: whether there is a person dressed in a gorilla suit walking through a basketball game, for instance, is a state of affairs that the mind should be able to represent accurately. There is a right answer to the question: "Was there a person in a gorilla suit on the court?" But for psychologists like Bruner and philosophers like Goodman, the assumption that we can judge what counts as accurate representation and what counts as distortion can only carry so much weight when we try to apply it to our on-the-go, laboratory-free attempts to grapple with the world. The Absolute Conception is itself a construction or a stipulative premise that we adopt for certain purposes, according to Bruner; it counts as the real, uninterpreted "given" world only through convention. In his summary of this point, Goodman says, "[T]he world is as many ways as it can be truly described, seen, pictured, etc. . . . there is no such thing as the way the world is."[1] Thus there is no single answer to the questions we have about the way the world is. The idea that the playing-card experiment or the change-blindness experiment could tell us something important about our experience of the world assumes that these experimental contexts are sufficiently analogous with our everyday cognitive endeavors to allow us to extrapolate to those from these experimental conditions. Goodman and Bruner are skeptical about the extent to which that analogy is apt.[2]

Yet most of us have a sense that good epistemic hygiene requires that we recognize that some descriptions of the world are more basic than others—less distorted, perhaps, or less embellished, and it is this intuition that the experiments capture. While this might not make our accurate descriptions interpretation-free, they would seem to constitute a more stripped-down ontology—a thinner interpretive veneer perhaps, or, as in the case of the psychological tests above, simply The Way Things Are. This conception of The Way Things Are serves the purpose of allowing us to identify the mistakes the subjects in these studies make, and in our everyday cognitive tasks, it allows us to eliminate some descriptions or interpretations of the world as distortions or errors.

The concept of a Way Things Are, or perhaps less tendentiously, facts of the matter or descriptions that are more basic than other descriptions, is a metaphysical commitment to some extent, but it has been given a naturalistic interpretation as well. In a fairly lengthy debate between Paul Churchland and Jerry Fodor, we find a discussion of the extent to which the modules of the brain that are responsible for sense perception are permeable to the modules that are involved in, for instance, astronomical theory. Fodor argues that the persistence of certain visual illusions even in the face of a conscious belief on the part of the subject that they are illusions shows that observations can be impermeable to theory, while Churchland argues that actual studies of brain physiology show that there is no such encapsulation. But while they may disagree on the topic of whether observation can be independent of theory, as naturalists they think it is an empirical, not a metaphysical, problem, answerable by appeal to psychology.

In a parallel discussion, we also find that the authority of experience to make deliverances about political theory is a subject for debate. In these instances, the experience in question is less like sensory observation and more like "lived experience," but the challenges to the authority of experience in the domain of political theory have the same contours. Appeals to experience in this domain are taken to be an invocation of a mode of knowing the world that is less distorted and more immediate, and "experience" in these discussions is usually contrasted with "theoretical knowledge" or "theory." According to critics, however, appeals to experience imply that experience is a "no interpretation" zone, and that such appeals constitute an invocation of a "view from nowhere."[3] In these discussions, the authority of experience seems to depend on its naturalness, or the extent to which it is untutored. Critics of appeals to experience in political discourse are skeptical of the opposition between experience and theory, believing either that a commitment to the priority of experience over theory is misguided or that the atheoretical "lived experience" is a myth—and perhaps a dangerous one at that. Terry Eagleton pithily summarizes this concern: experience cannot be a corrective to ideological structures, since experience is "ideology's homeland" (2006, 15). That is, ideological structures are grounded and nurtured in experience. Experience and ideology are tied up together, so lived experience is far from authentic. It cannot serve as a corrective to ideology, because it is, rather, the source of ideology. If experience is theory-dependent and ideologically structured, its authority, granted on the basis of its independence and authenticity, would seem to be undermined.

Yet in some cases, it is the extent to which experience is not untutored that gives it its authority. In some areas, the authority of experience depends on the fact that it is embedded in virtuosity or expertise. While the appeal to experience is sometimes a democratic move, insofar as it is an appeal to evidence that is accessible intersubjectively, or requires no special hermeneutical skills, not all appeals to experience have this leveling effect.

Wine connoisseurs, art critics, radiologists, and musicians are just some of the people whose refined abilities of perception and skilled observation are essential to the authority granted to their descriptions. My daughter, who has been studying music and playing the harp for ten years, can hear things that I cannot, and I take her descriptions of things to carry an authority that mine do not, and should not. If she tells me that the F string on her harp is sharp, or that the singer in the school musical sang flat the whole time, I take her description to be the right one, even if I cannot hear the sharpness or the flatness. We might conclude, on the basis of these kinds of examples, that virtuosos might have more refined—and more accurate—experiences of the world that make their descriptions more authoritative, precisely because they have been refined and educated by learning. Thus, in some instances, experience gains authority by its valida-tion intersubjectively, and in some instances, it gains authority because it is grounded in a process of education and discernment that characterize connoisseurship and virtuosity. The idea that an experienced mechanic is preferable to one who is inexperienced, for instance, implies that experi-ence is a learning process, leading to the accumulation of know-how and the refinement of judgment.

But then the question arises: how do we determine the extent to which a putative description is grounded in a more refined experience of the world, and is thus rightly considered to be a detection of elements of the world, and when a putative description is a projection of a worldview or a theory of the world that has, to a large extent, decided in advance what the world must be like? We are thus back to the question raised by Bruner. Most experience of the world does not occur in the controlled environment of a psychological experiment, in which the experimenter already knows the right answer to the question "What should the person be seeing here?" The experimenter knows both that the subject is being asked to see anomalous cards and which cards they are, and wants to find out whether the subject can also see the anomalous cards. There is an independent standard for accuracy in perception that the experimenter can use to measure the subject's reports in experimental contexts. But outside the psychology lab, in our everyday cognitive tasks, we must deter-mine, without any such measure, the extent to which our experiences and those of others are properly given authority and the extent to which they are biased by our upbringing, our theoretical commitments, our hopes or our fears. The problem of the authority of experience is a problem that brings together discussions of realism with the theory of the subject of experience.

With so many different and competing storylines in the discussion of experience, we might be tempted to say, with Karl Popper, "if we consider how infinitely problematic the concept of experience is . . . enthusiastic affirmation is far less appropriate in regard to it . . . than the most careful and guarded criticism."[4] And, indeed, the present attitude toward experience in philosophy and in political theory is a decidedly skeptical one, if experience is considered at all. In some quarters, it is not even thought worthy of discussion. This constitutes a major shift in American philosophy in particular.

Reversal of Fortune

Hailed at the beginning of the twentieth century as the well-spring of knowledge and the weapon to vanquish metaphysics and Cartesianism, the concept of experience subsequently underwent a major reversal of fortune. In contemporary philosophy and political theory, it has come to be equated with the metaphysics of seventeenth-century empiricism and the Cartesian model of mind.

The most famous—or perhaps infamous—use of experience as a philosophical tool is probably that of the logical positivists, who used it as a methodological scalpel to sort metaphysical "pseudo-questions" from the questions of what they termed "positive science." Moritz Schlick expresses this methodological caveat as the command that the philosopher, like the scientist, always "abide in the given," by which, he says, he does not mean "appearances" as philosophers usually understand that term, but only "what is simplest and no longer open to question" (1991, 38).

The given—that which is simplest and no longer open to question—is, according to Schlick, to be understood as the circumstances that hold when a certain claim is true. This is determined, Schlick says, on the basis of sensory experiences. If the truth or falsity of a claim makes no difference in the ways in which one experiences the world—if it makes no observable difference whether the claim is true or false—the claim is literally meaningless, Schlick says. Meaning is a function of verification: the meaning of a statement is captured by confirming or infirming experiences. With this methodological move, he jettisons the metaphysical debates about realism and skepticism. Since our experience of the world would be no different from what it is now if an evil demon were producing our experiences, and the external world were unreal, Schlick argues, claims that "the external world is real" and "the external world is unreal" are equally vacuous, since their truth would have no bearing on our experience. We cannot formulate an empirical test that would allow us to determine which of these claims is true; more than that, we cannot even specify what these claims mean, since they cannot be sorted or defined in terms of what our experiences would deliver if one of them were true and the other false. This and other perennial problems of philosophy, like the question of whether two different people have the same qualitative experience when they see a green object, are, according to Schlick, questions whose answers are logically impossible to verify. For Schlick and other positivists, the use of appeals to experience was meant to help philosophers dispatch those questions that were mere pseudo-questions, while focusing attention on the criteria for acceptable answers to real, scientific questions.

William James was also impatient with what he saw as the vacuity of some traditional philosophical debates. Like the positivists who came after him and the philosophical ancestor he and they identified with, David Hume, James argued that experience was essential to knowledge. But James's "radical empiricism" rejected the atomistic version of experience bequeathed to philosophers and psychologists by Hume. James thought that Hume's account of experience was too thin, and that it actually gave rise to the trends in philosophy that James thought had been most objectionable—including the problem of skepticism and its equally troublesome purported solutions. One of James's primary targets in advocating radical empiricism was transcendental idealism, which he thought had too little connection to the complicated and superabundant "temperament of life" (1977, 194). Transcendental idealism's approach to philosophical debate was too abstract and academic, he charged; it let the world "wag incomprehensibly" (195). In James's view, the emphasis that transcendental idealism (among other schools in philosophy) placed on logical rigor and formal purity was purchased at the price of leaving the world in which people lived largely dark and inscrutable, and as a result it lacked the ability to help us better understand that life. In Charlene Haddock Seigfried's words, "James's criterion for philosophy is an engaged understanding and transformation of the human condition" (1990, 1). Transcendental idealism could not provide this understanding; it had no resources for improving human life. As a result, in James's estimation, it was not good philosophy; its claims had no bearing on lived experience.

But while James allied himself to some extent with Humean empiricism against transcendental idealism, he added the term "radical" to signal the difference between his empiricism and Hume's. Hume's empiricism, like radical empiricism and unlike transcendental idealism, was a "mosaic philosophy" of "plural facts" that were not accounted for by the idea of substances in which they inhere or an Absolute Mind that creates them, according to James. The mosaic quality of this approach was part of its appeal for James. Nevertheless, he thought that Humean empiricism failed to recognize the ways in which relations like causation, conjunction, similarity, and unity could themselves be experienced. According to James's radical empiricism, these connective relations did not need to be added to experience by an act of association; Hume and his followers ignored the fact that our experiences actually did include such relations, and that "any kind of relation experienced must be accounted as 'real' as anything else in the system" (James 1977, 195). The parsimonious account of experience that Humean empiricism offered prompted rationalists to correct the problems that arose out of this account of experience about conjunction, causation, and so on, by adding "transexperiential agents of unification" (195), such as substances and intellectual categories. Thus Humean empiricism carried with it the seeds of the idealism and skepticism that empiricism set itself against. Since radical empiricism took experience of the world at face value, however, it did not need the transexperiential agents to do the work of unification and conjunction.

But James's ecumenical approach to experience had its own problems, of the projectionist type. James's conviction that the philosopher was obliged to take account of all the varieties of experience was a direct result of his radical empiricism: religious, hallucinatory, and ecstatic experiences were not to be excluded from consideration; they were to be taken at face value, just like garden-variety sense experience. This, of course, led James into some strange places: he experimented with nitrous oxide, which, he said, gave him a sense of what Hegel had gotten right;[5] he became very interested in spiritualists who claimed to be able to communicate with the dead, and, along with a number of other philosophers, tried to examine these claims scientifically; and he famously worked out a treatise on religious experience that took at face value the accounts of visitation, vastation, and mystic vision offered by a variety of people. Radical empiricism meant that none of these could be eliminated a priori as unimportant, illusory, or deceptive. An emphasis on experience, James believed, would allow philosophy to speak better to the concerns that occupied people, rather than addressing itself to dry, lifeless, and abstract scholastic concerns. And the content of experience could not itself be stipulated, as Humean empiricism tried to do, but was instead to be taken as it was, including connections that Hume thought were added only by the mind. For James, the problems of projectionism and ontological pluralism were a small price to pay if the effort to give a fuller account of experience could give philosophy more relevance to the problems of human life. He thought that, like life itself, a relevant philosophy would be a sloppy, imprecise, asystematic affair. And, indeed, many of his critics charged him with being asystematic and sloppy.

When James is pursuing his goal of rescuing philosophy from itself, he can sometimes sound like a logical positivist. He announces, for instance, that "the only things that shall be debatable among philosophers shall be things definable in terms drawn from experience" (James 1885), making him seem to be trying to police the boundaries of philosophical discussion like the positivists.[6] The emphasis on experience is clearly meant to express a departure from an arid scholasticism that James disliked in philosophy, but that departure seems to be motivated as well by a concern to make philosophy more relevant to everyday life. This marks one of the major differences between James's pragmatism and the positivist project.[7] James's primary targets in advocating radical empiricism were transcendental idealism and an anemic conception of the contents of experience, but he was no less troubled by a form of scientism that he thought threatened inquiry into questions of value and meaning.

The democratic urge that drove James's radical empiricism meant that kinds of experiences that philosophers had traditionally dismissed, such as religious, mystical, and pharmaceutically induced experiences, could not so easily be pushed aside as illusory or too marginal to be worthy of serious consideration. This is one of the important differences between James's emphasis on experience and that which the logical positivists placed on it. James did not mean by "experience" simply scientific experimentation or sense perception—his concept of experience was more capacious, more like "lived experience" than like sense data or sense experience. This had much to do with James's idea of what the subject of experience was like. Not only are subjects of experience sensing and perceiving: they are agents and evaluators as well. They care about values and morality, and these are not simply emotional or affective states (though James would never have used the trivializing term "simply" for emotional or affective states). James shows clear concern for practical knowledge and questions of spirituality and morality, whereas A. J. Ayer and subsequent logical positivists like him excluded moral claims from the realm of statements that could have truth values. This points to a rather important point of disagreement with the positivists—a disagreement that is rooted in James's thicker and more nuanced account of experience. The positivists essentially took Hume's version of empiricism and elaborated it with an eye to capturing the insights of twentieth-century science, using it to argue against the meaningfulness of metaphysical debates. But James rejected the Humean starting point, arguing that it led to either skepticism or transcendental idealism. In addition, such a conception of experience was not even very empirical, according to James—it was not true to the ways in which human beings experienced a world of meaning and value, a world of things and events in which the subject of experience and the object of experience were woven together. In this sense, James argued, experience is a "double-barreled" concept, pointing both toward the consciousness of a subject and toward the world, entwining them.

James's empiricism and his model of science differed from the empiricism and scientificity that the logical positivists advocated. Whereas the invocation by logical positivists of science and empirical method was usually a turn toward eliminativism and reductionism, for James, it was a turn toward something more like "naturalism."[8] James's naturalism was not eliminativist or reductive, however, as we see in the fact that he took the marginal experiences of religious ecstasy and spiritualism quite seriously, nor was it an embrace of a metaphysical commitment to physicalism or materialism. James thought that a naturalistic philosophy that embraced real empiricism, rather than a prescriptive notion of the contents of experience, should be able to say something about the questions of fundamental meaning and value that present themselves to human beings. James was a natural scientist, and he believed that the practical consequences of a theory, claim, or belief were of ultimate importance. Those practical consequences included the way a particular person would conduct her life as a result of adopting a certain theory. They were not limited to sensory perception, but included the ways in which theories or beliefs led to practices. John Dewey saw James as a humanist and educator above all: James had not sought to displace philosophy from its traditional province by paying attention to the physiological aspects of human cognition and experience; rather, he had hoped that study of these would complement the study of humanistic problems.

James's influence on Dewey was, according to Dewey himself, quite significant.[9] This is clearest in the ways in which Dewey understood the goal of philosophy and in his adoption of James's conception of experience. Dewey wrote three books with the word "experience" in their titles during the first half of the twentieth century: *Experience and Nature*, *Experience and Education*, and *Art as Experience*, and, like James, he privileged experience in his discussions of philosophy's tasks. He offered as a test for any philosophy the following list of questions: "Does it end in conclusions which, when they are referred back to ordinary life-experiences and their predicaments, render them more significant, more luminous to us, and make our dealings with them more fruitful? Or does it terminate in rendering the things of ordinary experience more opaque than they were before, and in depriving them of having in 'reality' even the significance they had previously seemed to have?" (1981, 256). Dewey, like James, objected to the theory of experience that had been handed down to philosophers and psychologists from the British empiricists, partly because of the poverty of the resources it made available for discussions of knowledge. Experience in the hands of the British empiricists was a veil through which human beings groped toward a representation of the world—it was not part of nature, but was, instead, a filter through which the world could be dimly perceived. The problem with this, Dewey thought, was that the qualitative aspects of the ways in which "the organism"[10] experiences the world were thought to be irrelevant, or worse, misleading.

This problem was exacerbated by what Dewey took to be the primary vice of philosophy: an "arbitrary intellectualism" that expressed itself as "the theory that all experiencing is a mode of knowing, and that all subject-matter, all nature, is, in principle, to be reduced and transformed till it is defined in terms identical with the characteristics presented by refined objects of science as such. The assumption of 'intellectualism' goes contrary to the facts of what is primarily experienced. For things are objects to be treated, used, acted upon and with, enjoyed and endured, even more than things to be known. They are things had before they are things cognized" (Dewey 1981, 265).

This vice, Dewey argues, and the thin theory of experience that the British empiricists peddled, "accounts for the belief that nature is an indifferent, dead mechanism" (265), which in turn gives rise to the problem of value and desire: why do we value some things and despise others, since, the story goes, "in reality" they are all inert and neutral. The problem, Dewey suggests, should be the other way around: why do things that are experienced primarily as affective or conative become transformed into neutral and inert things to be known and represented, in which the affective, aesthetic, and volitional aspects are seen as secondary, or illusory? Experience is cut off from nature in this transformation, Dewey argues— and this, he thinks, must be remedied.

While Dewey thinks that the kind of reflection on experience that this intellectualism provides is valuable, he worries that it becomes an end in itself for philosophers, and that the products of that reflection fail to make their way back to ordinary experience, becoming, instead, "curiosities to be deposited, with appropriate labels, in a metaphysical museum" (Dewey 1981, 264). In both James and Dewey we see that the emphasis on experience is meant to make philosophy less technical and abstract, and that this sometimes expresses itself in grumblings against metaphysics— another characteristic that they share with the logical positivists. But the scientific approach that the logical positivists advocated was, for Dewey and James, something more like "scientism": while they agreed that the methods of the natural sciences were the right methods for investigating questions of import to human beings, their conception of what counted as the methods of the natural sciences differed from that of the positivists. While physics was the scientific enterprise par excellence for the logical positivists, Dewey and James did not single out a particular science as representative of all sciences. They thought that the methods of the natural sciences were captured by empiricism, but the broadened conception of experience they used meant that the contours of that empiricism were radically different from those of the empiricism of the positivists. Verifiability, testability, an experimental approach—these were essential aspects of the method of the natural sciences, but the conditions of verification and testability were not limited to simple sensory experience in Dewey's and James's understanding of empirical method.

For James and Dewey, projects, activity, and agency are the central organizing features of experience and cognition; the subject of experience is understood to be engaged in a broad array of inquiries and activities. It is here that we see the significance of Dewey's insistence on using the term "organism" in his discussions of inquiry. Dewey's choice emphasizes the ways in which a particular living being interacts with, responds to, and acts upon its environment. But this environment does not consist solely of inert physical objects; the human organism is engaged in social and political life, and seeks meaning, value, beauty, and enjoyment. Furthermore, Dewey emphasizes the essential place that artistic, productive activity plays in the life of the human organism. According to Dewey, "the history of human experience is the history of the development of the arts" (Dewey 1981, 322), and by this he means that the history of human experience is the history not just of the development of poetry, music, architecture, and so on, but of the wide array of activities, including science, aimed at the delightful enhancement of perception or appreciation. This skillful and intelligent activity that allows natural things to show their meanings, or to take on greater or more nuanced meanings, is what Dewey thinks of as artistic activity, and it is exemplified, not only in the traditional fields we consider the arts, but in the pursuit of science as well. Science, like the arts, is skillful intervention and crafting, and it aims at the enhancement of perception and action. According to Dewey, this activity is a natural aspect of human life. It is not derived from some supernatural force (which might be one way of understanding reason), but rather constitutes a continuation of the kind of informed and skillful activity aimed at "intensifying, purifying, prolonging, and deepening the satisfactions that [natural things] spontaneously afford" (323). Natural things spontaneously offer us satisfactions and delight, but human activities can be targeted to making new connections, or deepening our appreciation of phenomena and things. In this respect, Dewey says, science is another form of artistic endeavor, since it involves the production of meanings, the arrangement and transformation of natural things that enhance and deepen human satisfaction and understanding.

Dewey's account of science as art is given its foundation in a story about the natural development of human societies. The history of human beings begins as the story of animals reacting to things on a strictly physical level, "pulled and pushed about, overwhelmed, broken to pieces, lifted on the crest of the wave of things, like anything else" (Dewey 1981, 311). The move from the level of brute animality to humanness is achieved when things can be understood as having meanings, as opposed to having only effects, and can be experimented with reflectively, imaginatively, and with enjoyment. This, Dewey says, is the fruition of human life in the artistic: the refinement of experience through reflection, and the initiation of experience on the basis of enjoyment and meanings.

Whereas James emphasizes the extent to which experience gives us access to causation, connection, and so forth, Dewey makes a similar point by emphasizing the fact that experiences have a structure, a plot: they have a determinate beginning and end; they can be distinguished from other experiences; and they have a meaning of their own. While to some extent experience is continuous because it constitutes the interaction of a living organism and its environment, some experience remains inchoate, while other experiences are singled out. Some experience remains inchoate, Dewey says, because our attention is diverted or we are interrupted, but a real experience will have a culmination in the mutual adaptation of "self" and environment: we try to pick up a rock to use to build a stone wall, and the rock is too heavy, too big, or not the right shape; we put it down and pick up another rock, until we find the right one (Dewey 1981, 562). In this way, a human being building a wall adapts to the environment, and adapts the environment to her own needs.

Philosophical reflection, Dewey believed, should aim at the improvement of the lived experience of human beings. Here he picks up a Jamesian theme, but he also expands it in his discussion of the aesthetic. Experience, for Dewey, is not merely a conduit for information—it is an end in itself, since an essential part of experience is its aesthetic and affective qualities. Science, rightly pursued, could also be used to enhance lived experience. For James and Dewey, philosophical and scientific inquiry could both benefit from an appropriately understood empiricism, but the methodological appeal to experience was meant more as an arbiter of applicability to human life than as a divining rod to track "real science" and eliminate metaphysics, which was the methodological goal of the positivists. The problem with the philosophical orientations of many of their contemporaries, for James and Dewey, was the centrality of a priori reasoning, which blocked inquiry and deformed philosophy, making it unsuitable for the project of improving human life.

This short summary of the appeals to experience that populated analytic and Anglo-American philosophy in the early twentieth century might leave one thinking that pragmatists like James and Dewey and logical positivists like Moritz Schlick were not really talking about the same thing in their invocations of experience. For the positivists, the term is a stand-in for observation or sense perception; for the pragmatists it has a broader connotation, more like the experience of living through something. One might object that grouping these disparate notions under one term—"experience"—is a source of confusion, that the positivists and the pragmatists were attempting to appeal to very different things.

Yet the similarity is not just in the word; the positivists and the pragmatists reached for the concept of experience to capture something that was more quotidian than theoretical. And it seems to be an attempt at tying philosophical thought to outcomes and to an embodied existence of some sort. The invocation of experience by philosophers in the pragmatist and analytic traditions in the early twentieth century was, essentially, an attempt to reconstruct philosophy. Logical positivists wanted to get beyond the metaphysical issues that seemed to bog down progress in the sciences; the attempt to use experience and possible experience as a methodological tool was an explicit rejection of the Cartesian problem of skepticism as a challenge to the legitimacy of science. The positivists offered, not a solution to the skeptical problem, but rather a rejection of it, a way of saying that epistemologists and philosophers of science need not have a solution to that "perennial" problem. The positivists saw themselves as staking out new territory, formed by a new rupture of boundaries between philosophy and empirical science. The perennial problems of philosophy, like the problem of the reality of the external world, would not be harbored there. If the answer to a particular question could not be framed in terms of the experiences that would serve to verify or falsify that answer, then the question itself was simply a pseudo-question: questions without verifiable answers were not bona fide questions.

The invocation of experience by pragmatists like James and Dewey was also a rejection of the traditional problem of skepticism, but this was mostly because of that problem's status as one of the arid and Scholastic exercises that could not contribute to the goal of improving human life. James's requirement that "the only things that shall be debatable among philosophers shall be things definable in terms drawn from experience" (James 1885) was his expression of impatience with what he saw as useless debates, fostered for the simple sake of debating them. This was, of course, an impatience that the logical positivists shared.

The appeal to experience was an attempt to make philosophy accountable to other domains of inquiry and other aspects of human life. The appeal to experience was also a shift in "philosophical style." If we understand approaches to philosophizing as embodied in the difference between "naïve" and "sophisticated" approaches, where the former are characterized by a distrust of theory and a prioricity and a more thorough-going naturalism (in the broad sense of that term), and the latter by an emphasis on theory, a skeptical attitude toward that which is thought to be "given" or primary, and distrust of the deliverances of common sense, then the stance of the logical positivists and the pragmatism of James and Dewey count as naïve approaches. The appeal to experience captured by these naïve approaches was the hallmark of a new way of philosophizing, and the early twentieth century was its heyday.

By the late twentieth century, however, "experience" had been demoted, if not completely displaced from the realm of philosophical concern. In Quine's story about science and epistemology, "experience" is just shorthand for the stimulus input to our sensory faculties.[11] In the move toward inferentialism, this Quinean redefinition of experience allowed Robert Brandom to say that when he speaks of experience, he is "speaking with the vulgar: 'Experience' is not one of my words" (Brandom 2000, 205n7). The situation was little different among those who rejected epistemology entirely: "experience," Rorty argued, was a term better left behind, abandoned for the term "discourse" (which, he implies, is synonymous with experience), or left on the side of the nondiscursive, where it could only refer to meaningless causal prompts: "Think of human minds as webs of beliefs and desires, of sentential attitudes—webs which continually reweave themselves so as to accommodate new sentential attitudes. Do not ask where the new beliefs and desires come from. Forget, for the moment, about the external world, as well as about that dubious interface between self and world called 'perceptual experience'" (Rorty 1991a, 93).

The advice Rorty has to offer, if we want to overcome the problems bequeathed to us by Descartes, as the early pragmatists and logical positivists did, is as follows: give up on the concept of experience, and on the concept of a self as anything more than a mechanism that reweaves these beliefs and desires. The idea that there is need of an interface between self and world called "experience" is a relic of the Descartes-Locke-Kant tradition and the idea of the mind as mirror that animates that tradition. The faith in the therapeutic role that experience could play in bringing philosophy back from the brink of arid scholasticism, a faith that was alive and well in the early twentieth century, was apparently lost by the end of that century, replaced by a new vision of the human mind and the self that had no place for the concept of experience.

A similar romance and breakup with "experience" was playing out, albeit in a more compressed time frame, in feminist theory and in other disciplines in which the question of racial, sexual, or gendered identity was a central concern in discussions of politics and knowledge. Discussions of women's experience and the experiences of marginalized others populated the discourses of identity politics in the 1960s and 1970s, but by the 1990s, Joan Scott was putting "experience" in scare quotes to signal that the term was intellectually and politically suspect.

Consciousness-raising, a method for analyzing the interplay of the personal and the political that was almost synonymous with feminism and political enlightenment in the 1970s, used personal experience as the springboard for political analysis, often emphasizing the commonalities in women's experience that were thought to cut across class and race lines.

In discussions of racial identity, consciousness-raising drew on the experiences of racism that were thought to cut across class and gender lines. Thus, in 1977, the Combahee River Collective gave the following analysis of the growing black feminist movement:

There is . . . undeniably a personal genesis for black feminism that is the political realization that comes from the seemingly personal experiences of individual black women's lives. Black feminists and many more black women who do not define themselves as feminists have all experienced sexual oppression as a constant factor in our day-to-day existence.

. . . In the process of consciousness-raising, actually life-sharing, we began to recognize the commonality of our experiences and, from that sharing and growing consciousness, to build a politics that will change our lives and inevitably end our oppression. (Nicholson 1997, 64)

There are experiences that black women share, and this reservoir of shared experiences can be used as a political tool aimed at dismantling racist and sexist institutions and practices.

The experience of the oppressed was also put forward as a starting point for feminist epistemologies by advocates of standpoint epistemology. The standpoint of the oppressed and the marginalized, and the experiences that marked that standpoint, were advanced as a superior alternative to the idea of objectivity as a "view from nowhere" and of knowledge as best pursued from a position of neutrality. Standpoint epistemologies and consciousness-raising understood appeals to experience as correctives to traditional epistemological approaches, as well as to abstract theory and to ideology. Experience as a concept represented a phenomenon at the nexus of the individual, the world, and the political structure: it seemed to present the possibility of something that was both a result of the forces of racism and sexism and a resource for discovering the ways in which those forces could be undermined. The project of making visible the experiences of marginalized members of society was taken to be a defining characteristic of the new fields of women's history, African-American history, and queer studies, among others.

By the late 1980s, however, this faith in experience was beginning to give way to skepticism. Experience is always ideological, carrying with it the "worldview" that was part of the oppressive political system, critics argued, so it could not constitute the check on ideology that its champions had been assuming it to be capable of. We can only see what we are taught to see, these critics argued, and insofar as what we are taught to see is a function of the political and social system in which we are raised, we can only see what that system thinks is important or relevant.

Furthermore, critics claimed that appeals to experience relied on a model of experience as nondiscursive, authentic, and innocent access to the-way-the-world-is that is prior to (both conceptually and causally) linguistic expression. Appeals to experience valorized the model of seeing as knowledge, a process that is in its essence representational and passive. But since no vision is without a history or a shaping perspective, such a model of knowing obscured the forces that made certain kinds of knowledge possible. Appeals to experience were suspect, amounting to a return of a repressed foundationalism, since the experience in question was taken to be given, rather than a product of interpretation. The critique of occularcentrism led to a critique of experience.

Finally, critics argued that the appeals to women's experience, which had been the lifeblood of political organizing and solidarity in the 1970s, depended upon an outmoded and politically regressive model of an autonomous subject of experience who could simply "mirror" and then report her experiences, a position that failed to take into account the discursive construction of identities as well as experience. According to the skeptics, the autonomous subject of traditional epistemology, as well as that traditional epistemology itself—foundationalism—were both smuggled in with the appeals to experience that earlier feminist theorists had set such store by.

It might seem that these are different, and not necessarily connected, trends in the humanities and social sciences. After all, one might argue, the discussion of the extent to which observation sentences can be theory-independent—the dominant theme in Anglo-American philosophy of science—is not the same as the discussion about whether personal experience can constitute evidence for social theories, or whether it can be suitably revelatory to play the role it is supposed to play in identity politics. The Kuhnian-inspired claim that experience is theory-dependent is different from Joan Scott's claim that experience is discursively constructed, one might object. In this book, I aim to show that the two discussions are actually not as unrelated as they might seem initially; that the theories of the subject that animate both trends share commitments that make the problem show up in the particular guises that it does. The problem of experience as it manifests itself in these seemingly disparate intellectual trends is made intractable by the gap that opens up between a naturalistic understanding of ourselves and an understanding of ourselves as cultural entities. But it also arises in both philosophy of science and in critiques of appeals to experience as a result of something that both methodologies share: a retreat from the first-person perspective and the concepts of agency, intentionality, and subjectivity that are tied to it.

CHAPTER I

The Linguistic Turn and the Ascendancy of Anti-foundationalism

The concept of experience went from being the most useful concept for philosophical purposes to being one of the most neglected or vilified concepts over the course of the twentieth century. This is attributable to two dominant intellectual developments: the ascendancy of the theoretical trend known as "the linguistic turn," and the growth of anti-foundationalism (see below) in the humanities generally, and in Anglo-American philosophy in particular. When the linguistic turn was paired with anti-foundationalism, there was little left for the term "experience" to do. Discussions of the concept "experience" were replaced by linguistic analysis and discourse theory, or by empirical psychology and linguistic behaviorism, and bifurcated into "discourse" and "stimuli." This division introduced new versions of the problem of realism and new challenges to the theory of mind and philosophical psychology more broadly, even as it appeared to offer new solutions to those problems. Anti-foundationalism, as it was worked out by figures like Popper, Kuhn, Rorty, and Quine, branched off in two different directions, with those who were less concerned with problems of realism and objectivity arguing that "discourse" could substitute for the concept of experience, while anti-foundationalists like Quine, who were more willing to treat experience as a purely psychological event, turned to "stimuli" or "input" to try to close the gap between theory and the world that seemed to open up as a result of the displacement of "experience" from the epistemological story. This chapter examines the different challenges to experience that we find in the key writings of the anti-foundationalists and advocates of the linguistic turn that led to the reversal of fortune for the concept of experience. Popper, Kuhn, Rorty, and Quine represent the variety of challenges to experience that arose out of these intellectual movements; their primary target was the idea of the "observation" or "observation sentence."

The philosophers who challenged the value of appeals to experience focused on the question of the possibility of "observation sentences"—that is, simple, basic observational reports like those that the positivists argued could serve the purpose of verifying a claim, and thus limn the border between the scientific and the metaphysical. Some philosophers—in particular, Karl Popper—called into question the appeal to experience in order to show that metaphysics could not be so readily dismissed, and to save philosophy from "psychologism." But the attack on observation sentences went well beyond that, challenging the very possibility of empiricism. The role that was claimed for them in theory-choice in general by garden-variety empiricists was also imperiled by the attack on experience and observation, as we see in Thomas Kuhn's controversial discussions of scientific revolutions.

Since James and Dewey used a very different concept of experience, one might wonder why the attack on observation would extend to their use of the term, as it did. Skepticism about observation sentences does not seem to apply to their use of experience, or so it would seem. Nevertheless, the linguistic turn and general skepticism about the role that experience could (or should) play as "contact with the world" undermined the appeal to experience that marked the early pragmatists' philosophical project as well. The idea that there was some way in which experience could count as contact with a real world and as a corrective to our theories, which characterizes both pragmatists' version of empiricism and the more narrowly circumscribed methodology of empiricism in philosophy of science, was also caught up in the skeptical attitude toward observation. This debate, of course, continues as the debate about realism and objectivity.

Anti-foundationalism and the Problem
of Observation Sentences

The critique of experience in the philosophy of science that dominated the middle and late twentieth century seems to have had very
wide-reaching effects. We see it not only in the traditional philosophical debates; echoes of it also appear in political theory, testifying to the
power, most centrally, of one book: Thomas Kuhn's *The Structure of Scientific Revolutions* (1962). Kuhn himself, however, drew on earlier work
by N. Russell Hanson, whose book *Patterns of Discovery* (1958) offers a
detailed argument supporting the claim that observation is theory-dependent, and cannot play the confirming or infirming role that empiricists
claimed for it. Empiricism is, in its most general outline, a story about
the source of knowledge (properly so called). All knowledge, according
to Hume, begins with the senses, and empiricists are so called because
they privilege sensory experience in their accounts of justification and
knowledge. In the account of empiricism that comes from the British
empiricists, sense impressions give rise to ideas, which are the functional
equivalent of copies of impressions. This form of empiricism has a ready
ally in foundationalism: the way of characterizing our epistemic practices
in which some beliefs are immediately justified. For the empiricist foundationalist, that immediate justification arises for those beliefs that have
their basis in experience.

Anti-foundationalism is characterized by two different tenets: the
idea that the source of our beliefs is not relevant to their justification; and
the idea that sensory experience-cum-observation is theory-dependent.
The first is a straightforwardly philosophical point, based on the idea that
there is a difference between causes and reasons, and that no story about
causes (that is, sources) can, by itself, be a story about reasons. The second
claim can be taken to be a philosophical point as well, but it becomes
something more like a hybrid of an empirical and philosophical point in
its development by people like Kuhn and Hanson. These tenets, in combination or singly, raise the question of the evidential role that experience
is capable of playing. But they also jeopardize the grounding function that
the early pragmatists attributed to experience as a way of tying philosophy to real-world problems. As a result, the anti-foundationalist program

opened the prospect for redefining traditional philosophical problems about language, mind, and knowledge.

The idea that the source of our beliefs is irrelevant to their justification follows from the idea that justification is a logical notion, while experience is a quasi-psychological and causal notion. Karl Popper blamed the confusion of justification (a normative and discursive concept) with the causal, anormative process of sensory experience on the British empiricists of the seventeenth and eighteenth centuries. He called these philosophers (along with Russell and Popper's logical positivist contemporaries) "belief philosophers."

According to Popper, the epistemology and philosophy of science produced by the belief philosophers is marked by a confusion of justification with empirical psychology, leading to subjectivism and the introduction of irrelevant considerations into the theory of scientific knowledge (Popper 1972, 108). Only claims (propositional entities) can justify other claims, and the essence of the justification of scientific knowledge is the inferential relationship between these claims: the intellect is essentially discursive, Popper argues, and psychological states (which are what Popper takes experience to be) are too subjective and private to do the rational work of justification. Thus one strand of anti-foundationalism is critical of the elision of the distinction between sensory experience and rationality.[1] For Popper, the main objection to British empiricism and its successor subject, logical positivism, is that it is a form of psychologism: the replacement of philosophical and normative problems by psychology.

The British empiricists and the "belief philosophers" whom Popper saw as their heirs confused psychological claims with justificatory claims in their characterization of knowledge as a state that one could be in as a result of having certain kinds of sensory experiences, and tying justification to a foundation in such experiences. In order to show the difference between justifications and causes, Popper argued that the physiological state that follows from a causal interaction with particles (Locke's story of corpuscles and the way in which they literally bombard our sensory organs) can be caused in many ways. If that is so, then there are many ways that one might end up with a particular belief without having any reason for having it. So the question of justification, Popper argued, is independent of the question about how I came to have certain impressions.

Furthermore, according to Popper, the British empiricists and their associationist models of knowledge confused psychological questions with philosophical questions, preparing the way for the eventual replacement of philosophical questions by psychological questions. In response to the positivists' efforts to eliminate metaphysical problems, labeling them "pseudo-problems," critical rationalists like Karl Popper took it upon themselves to defend the importance of philosophy:

Time and again, an entirely new philosophical movement arises which finally unmasks the old philosophical problems as pseudo-problems and which confronts the wicked nonsense of philosophy with the good sense of meaningful, positive, empirical science. And time and again do the despised defenders of "traditional philosophy" try to explain to the leaders of the latest positivistic assault that the main problem of philosophy is the critical analysis of the appeal to the authority of "experience"—precisely that "experience" which every latest discoverer of positivism is as ever, artlessly taking for granted. . . . "Experience" for him is a programme, not a problem (unless it is studied by empirical psychology). (Boyd et al. 1991, 102)

In posing the problem as the problem of the authority of experience, Popper gave the problem a distinctly Kantian cast in an attempt to fend off the dangers of psychologism that he saw lurking in the positivists' naïve appeals to experience. Only claims, which are propositional entities, can justify other claims—this is the point that Popper pursues in framing the question as about the authority of experience. Thus, having a certain experience is not the end of the discussion. The important question is: what kind of authority can and should experience have in determining our scientific theories? The essence of the justification of scientific knowledge is the inferential relationship that holds between claims, Popper argued, and so the question of the authority of experience is not answered by simply stating that one has had an experience of a certain type. Rather the question is: what kinds of inferences are licensed by that experience? What are the claims that one can be said to be entitled to on the basis of a particular sensory experience? The intellect is essentially discursive, Popper argues, and psychological states (which are what Popper takes experience to be) are too subjective and private to do the rational work of justification. Thus one strand of anti-foundationalism, represented by Popper, is critical of attempts to undermine the distinction between sensory experience and rationality. For Popper the main objection to the epistemology of the British empiricists and their successors, the logical positivists, is that they are guilty of psychologism: the replacement by psychology of philosophical and normative problems. This exemplifies the first tenet of anti-foundationalism: that a purely causal process like sensory experience is irrelevant to the question of justification. Rationality is discursive, which is to say it has an inferential structure that admits of evaluation. Sensory experience is a psychological event, so this argument goes, but rationality is normative. While nonhuman animals have sensory experience, they do not have rationality—the ability to justify and critically evaluate their beliefs (if they can even be said to have them). This objection is a philosophical point about the conceptual difference between causes and reasons.

The second objection to foundationalism, however—that sensory observation is theory-dependent—actually relies, in some of its versions, on the results of empirical psychology for its persuasiveness. I will begin with a discussion of this aspect of the anti-foundationalist critique of experience, and return to the claim that justification is essentially discursive after that discussion.

Challenges to Experience: The Data of Psychology and the Attempt to Replace Epistemology with Empirical Psychology

There Is No Innocent Eye: Experience Is Theory-Dependent

I begin with the challenge to experience that arises out of post-Kuhnian philosophy of science, not because it is the first, but because in Kuhn, we find the problem put most pointedly. In "Revolutions as Changes in World View," chapter 10 of *The Structure of Scientific Revolutions*, Kuhn remarks that the history of scientific revolutions seems to demand a rather radical interpretation: that not only do scientists "adopt new instruments and look in new places" during revolutions, they also "see new and different things when looking with familiar instruments in places they looked before. It is rather as if the professional community had been suddenly transported to another planet where familiar objects are seen in a different light and are joined by unfamiliar ones as well" (1996 [1962], 111). But, of course, scientists are not bodily transported to a new world, Kuhn says. Nevertheless, he says that insofar as the only recourse that practicing scientists have to the world is "through what they see and do" (111), they are, in a sense, transported to another world: their research world is transformed by means of scientific training in a new paradigm. This training involves teaching scientists to see differently by taking old situations and reorganizing them into a new gestalt.

The idea that perception is of a situation—that is, elements or entities configured in relation to one another such that the situation is more than simply the sum of its constituent elements, but is rather a meaningful arrangement of those elements—is a cornerstone of Kuhn's claims about the ways in which scientific education teaches scientists in the making to see. Observation is literally theory-dependent, because the process of seeing requires such an education. The claim that scientists working in different paradigms work in different worlds goes back to Kuhn's claim, which he advances on the basis of psychological experiments, that what one sees depends both on what one looks at and what one's "previous visual-conceptual experience has taught" (113) one to see. Kuhn cites the playing-card experiment, mentioned in the Introduction above, as well as cases in which subjects are fitted with goggles with inverting lenses.

The inverting-lens experiment, originally performed at the end of the nineteenth century, showed that, while the subjects who were wearing the goggles were initially completely disoriented, "after the subject has begun to deal with his new world, his entire visual field flips over, usually after an intervening period in which vision is simply confused. Thereafter, objects are again seen as they had been before the goggles were put on. The assimilation of a previously anomalous field has reacted upon and changed the field itself" (112). Kuhn uses this example to support his claim that we cannot isolate "raw data" of sense experience, because the candidates for such a role in sense perception cannot really explain how we see things. While the inverting-lens experiment shows that two people with different retinal images (i.e., one who is wearing the goggles, one who is not) can see the same thing, Kuhn points out that the duck-rabbit gestalt, in which a picture can be seen either as a duck or a rabbit, but not both at the same time, shows, conversely, that two people with the same retinal images can see different things (127). In effect, Kuhn argues that the idea that we could isolate a neutral stimulus input like retinal images that could serve as a given of sensory experience is undermined by these different experimental results.

Kuhn connects these empirical data to the history of failed attempts to identify a "language of observation"—a language comprising only percepts and logical terms to which the logical positivists aspired. The failure of these attempts was due, Kuhn argues, to the fact that meaningful terms are embedded in a theory of nature that involves a "host of expectations about nature and fails to function the moment these expectations are violated" (127). Attempts to identify a language of observation show that paradigms are essential to perception, because the most successful such attempts have usually involved areas of discourse in which a paradigm is already operative, or a small bit of everyday discourse. The alternative to some paradigm-informed observation is not a more basic "fixed" vision but only "vision through another paradigm" (129). The search for an observation language—a purportedly theory-neutral description of the world— or the attempt to identify retinal images (the physical stand-in for theory-neutral data) can only begin after experience has been determined by paradigms, Kuhn argues. This is because it is only with a paradigm that our experience of the world can be experience under a description. But more important, the questions about which descriptions are more basic than others can only be answered by invoking other theory-informed descriptions: "it is . . . only after experience has thus been determined that the search for an operational definition or a pure observation-language can begin. . . . Therefore, though they are always legitimate, and are occasionally extraordinarily fruitful, questions about retinal imprints or about the consequences of particular laboratory manipulations presuppose a world already perceptually and conceptually subdivided in a certain way" (129). An artificial language, or a language of sense data must include in its specifications an ontology—the kinds of things that are possible subjects of description—and thus are themselves theory-dependent. Our designation, then, of a more basic description does not mean that we have stripped away the theory; it means only that we have opted for a particular version of the world. This gives rise to the diagnosis of incommensurability, for which Kuhn is notorious. The fact that scientific paradigms are incommensurable, Kuhn says, means that it is misleading to characterize one paradigm as a correction to an earlier paradigm. Scientific theories do not progress through accretion, but through radical rupture, in which the world is reconfigured each time. There is no theory-free, basic, or primitive description of the world that could serve as the corrective for, or touchstone of, theories and paradigms.

Kuhn has been charged with making choice of scientific theory an agonistic and wholly rhetorical exercise. The ontological pluralism that seems to follow from his claim that observation is always theory-dependent, and that no one ontology is more "real" than any other, allegedly makes choosing a theory at best arational, at worst irrational. The challenge to the rationality of scientific theory choice arises because, if there are no common observations that can serve as the arbiter between competing theories, then it is not clear that there is any evidence that could be invoked to justify the choice of one theory rather than another; incommensurability and the claim that paradigms determine "large areas of experience" (129) means that there is no theory-independent evidence. In William James's words, this seems to leave the world wagging; our theories do not seem to be constrained in any important way by the world. We might have a completely consistent theory, but this leaves open the possibility that there might be a number of internally consistent, but mutually inconsistent, theories. How should we choose among them?

This problem is even more difficult when we realize that according to Kuhn's analysis, a scientist only "sees" the evidence that would falsify a paradigm if she has already developed an allegiance to a competing paradigm. Similarly, she only has access to the evidence that would corroborate a particular theory if she already accepts the paradigm of which that theory is part. This would seem to be the worst kind of data-mining and confirmation bias, but is, according to Kuhn, exactly how science works.

Kuhn describes the process that leads to a scientist's allegiance to a new paradigm as a "conversion," fully recognizing, and even self-consciously drawing upon, the term's connotation of an enthusiastic embrace of a moral stance or religious commitment.[2] Kuhn's adoption of this form of narrative, perhaps more than anything else in his theory, provokes concerns on the part of his critics and his sympathizers alike about the extent to which scientific revolutions could be said to be rational and constrained by the world. If, that is, scientific revolutions involve a process of persuasion that is not dependent on facts or observations about which the competing accounts agree, and if the changes in scientists' allegiances are due as much to faith as to evidence, then it seems that scientific theories are no different in their evidential bases than are religious dogmas.

In subsequent years, Kuhn tried to make the claims about the extent to which paradigms are prerequisite to experience and the related claim that scientific revolutions involve gestalt switches seem less radical by appealing to uncontroversial examples of education and to examples of computer programming. In the postscript to *The Structure of Scientific Revolutions* that he included in the 1969 edition, Kuhn makes his case by explaining the role of "know-how" in theorizing:

One of the fundamental techniques by which the members of a group, whether an entire culture or a specialists' sub-community within it, learn to see the same things when confronted with the same stimuli is by being shown examples of situations that their predecessors in the group have already learned to see as like each other and as different from other sorts of situations. These similar situations may be successive sensory presentations of the same individual—say of mother, who is ultimately recognized on sight as what she is and as different from father or sister. They may be presentations of the member of natural families, say of swans on the one hand and of geese on the other. Or they may, for the member of more specialized groups, be examples of the Newtonian situation, of situations, that is, that are alike in being subject to a version of the symbolic form $f = ma$ and that are different from those situations to which, for example, the law-sketches of optics apply. (Kuhn 1996 [1969], 194)

Exemplars of this type are the bedrock on which paradigms rest, and the process of being initiated into a given community involves agreement in "forms of life"—the processes of judging, categorizing, and, ultimately, seeing. Seeing rightly is a form of know-how in which theory is tethered to the world, and the world is made intelligible. Experience, to be intelligible, must be organized, and this organization is made possible through the acquisition of a theory of nature. Seeing cannot be seeing without this theoretical backdrop, and, Kuhn argues, the acquisition of the know-how of seeing comes about in the quotidian exchanges between parent and child.

In *The Essential Tension* (1977), Kuhn tries to give this process of education a physiological explanation and suggests that he has come close to being able to replicate it with a computer program. Kuhn asks us to consider the situation in which a child ("Johnny," as Kuhn baptizes him) is taught, on a visit to the zoo, to discriminate swans, geese, and ducks. In this exercise, generalizations (e.g., "all swans are white") might play a role, but the lesson need not rely on them. The parent simply points to a bird and names it for the child, giving examples rather than general rules of classification. When Johnny mislabels a bird, the parent corrects him, and Johnny learns, through this process of ostension, practice, and correction, to label the birds correctly in a relatively short period of time. Kuhn's explanation for this is that, during this exercise, Johnny has been "reprogrammed": "When he began his walk, the neural program highlighted the differences between individual swans as much as those between swans and geese. By the end of the walk, features like the length and curvature of the swan's neck have been highlighted and others suppressed so that swan data match each other and differ from goose and duck data as they had not before. Birds that had previously all looked alike (and also different) are now grouped in discrete clusters in perceptual space."[3]

The invocation of the child, the computer program, and sometimes the two of them together is a common trope of philosophical discussions of experience and the education of experience, and I will have more to say about this later. It suffices to note here that Kuhn takes himself to be relying simply on an empirical hypothesis about information processing, not on an a priori argument about how we learn to organize the world. He is making an empirical claim, not a philosophical one. This distinction is important because it means that Kuhn's claim amounts to the descriptive point that this is just the way we carve up the world. Don't blame me if it seems irrational, he implies. It's just what we do.

Experience as Stimuli: Quine's Attempt to Block the Relativity of Observation Sentences

It is "tempting," Kuhn says, to describe this acquired ability to organize the world into meaningful relationships as an effect of learning to apply rules, but he rejects this account of the process: "Our seeing a situation as like ones we have encountered before must be the result of neural processing, fully governed by physical and chemical laws. In this sense, once we have learned to do it, recognition may also be involuntary, a process over which we have no control" (Kuhn 1996 [1962], 194). If we are applying rules, Kuhn implies, they can be understood as rules only secondarily—they are primarily neural programs. The idea that learning to perceive the world is the process of learning rules and applying them assumes that perception is an interpretive process (195), and this gets perception wrong in a fundamental way. Perception is not an interpretive process, Kuhn says, since there is no "given" that is then interpreted—there is no principled way of making the distinction between any such given and its interpretation. A theory that posits an uninterpreted given gives us no way to understand what would appear to be a two-step process: taking in stimuli, and subsequently applying rules. Rather, Kuhn argues, perception involves a process in which "past experience is *embodied in the neural apparatus* that transforms stimuli to sensations" (195 [my emphasis]). Past experience is written into the brain, changing what are essentially physically instantiated processing programs. We thus have something that is both "hardware" and "software"—the neural apparatus is physical, yet it contains instructions or information that change stimuli into sensations. Stimuli are, however, theoretical posits; we have access to sensations, which are objects and situations. We do not have access to stimuli, Kuhn argues, except as posits of a scientific theory of perception. Our experience of the world is experience of a conceptually articulated world, a world of chairs, books, cats, and cars. Insofar as groups share language, culture, and education, "[w]e have good reason to suppose that their sensations are the same. . . . But where differentiation and specialization of groups begins, we have no similar evidence for the immutability of sensation. Mere parochialism, I suspect, makes us suppose that the route from stimuli to sensation is the same for the members of all groups" (193). Different groups of people might well have different sensations; the world might contain different conceptual fault lines and divisions. Chairs, books, cats, and cars might not be objects for other people, but rather very slow events. The possibility that their neural programming is different from ours is always there. Thus, the question of whether Aristotle saw the same thing when he saw a rock swinging at the end of a string as Galileo saw when he saw a rock swinging at the end of a string can be answered only this way: maybe they did, but we have no evidence of it. Galileo saw a pendulum, an example of constrained fall; Aristotle did not, since the pendulum is an object that has a particular meaning, given by its scientific context, and that context only arises after Aristotle.

Hanson, on whom Kuhn draws extensively, addresses this question with, among other examples, a discussion of an X-ray tube, seen from the cathode (1969, 15). While the layperson and the trained physicist might, in some sense, see the same thing—that is, they have the same sense data, the same visual input—in another sense they do not, Hanson argues. The trained physicist sees an instrument, and that instrument is understood in terms of electrical circuit theory, thermodynamics, and a whole host of other aspects of contemporary physical theory. The layperson sees only an odd-looking metal and glass contraption. To the objection that the layperson and the trained physicist see the same thing, but interpret it differently, Hanson, like Kuhn, questions what sense of "interpretation" can be meant here.

If we take seriously the idea that the layperson and the trained physicist have the same retinal images, but they just interpret that data differently, we lose the ability to distinguish interpretations from simple descriptions, according to Hanson. Hanson cites the following use of "description" and "interpretation" to show what the move to explain perception as a form of interpretation costs: "Thucydides presented the facts objectively; Herodotus put an interpretation on them. The word [interpretation] does not apply to everything—it has a meaning. Can interpreting always be going on when we see? Sometimes, perhaps, as when the hazy outline of an agricultural machine looms up on a foggy morning, and, with effort, we finally identify it. Is this the 'interpretation' which is active when bicycles and boxes are clearly seen?" (1969, 10). Rather than stretch the concept of interpretation to fit the case of vision, Hanson argues that the problem lies with our paradigm cases of seeing. The attempt to preserve a theory in which sense data (or some other kind of intersubjectively accessible "raw material") is the "grist" going into an "intellectual mill" is an instance of ad hoc reasoning that Hanson thinks points to the weakness of the sense-data theory. Furthermore, the attempt to identify the raw material of sense perception is an artifact of the fact that our paradigm cases of seeing are "the visual apprehension of colour patches" (1969, 16)— that is, sense-data language, and the stripped-down model of vision that sense-data language assumes.

Better candidates for paradigmatic instances of seeing, according to Hanson, would be " seeing what time it is, seeing what key a piece of music is written in, and seeing whether a wound is septic" (1969, 16). To see is not simply to have a visual representation present in one's visual field; rather, "seeing" is an achievement term. While the characterization of seeing in terms of color patches, shapes, lines, and so on, might be appropriate for an ambiguous scene—or what Hanson calls the unsettled experimental situation (1969, 20)—it does not capture the ways in which seeing and knowing are connected. Seeing is ineluctably about knowledge: "Robots and electric eyes are blind, however efficiently they react to light. Cameras cannot see" (1969, 20). This is because to see something is to know that it will behave in certain ways, or that doing something in particular to it (dropping it, for instance) will have certain consequences. It is to recognize the type of thing it is, and its relationship to other things or possible events. Seeing is a skilled enterprise that has a complicated connection to what we know. It is not the learned application of rules or a two-step process of making observations and then "casting about for knowledge of them" (1969, 20). All observation is theory-dependent to the extent that to see things, in Hanson's use of the term, is to recognize them and to see what they can do, what they have done, or what their possibilities are. This is why the trained physicist and the layperson do not see the same thing when they look at the object that the trained physicist knows as a cathode ray tube and the layperson only knows as an odd-looking metal and glass contraption.

Quine (1993) argues that in their attempts to establish the relativity of observation sentences, Kuhn and Hanson have gone too far: "I agree that the notion of a phenomenalistic conceptual scheme, ready and waiting for the positing of a physical world, is perverse. What are in fact noticed and remembered are usually physical things and events. These we capture in words and retain in memory, forgetting most sensory aspects of the scene" (Quine 1993,107). This sounds much like Kuhn, but Quine thinks that he can avoid the relativistic conclusion he objects to in Kuhn and Hanson by appealing to the physical and behavioral processes he sees as sufficient for establishing the possibility of "pure observation." The possibility of pure observations is secured, Quine thinks, by childhood language learning: "Our channel of continuing information about the world is the impact of molecules and light rays on our sensory receptors; just this and some kinaesthetic incidentals. The protocol sentences should be sentences most closely linked causally to this neural intake: most closely linked not in respect of subject matter, but physically, physiologically, neurally. They should be sentences like 'It's cold,' 'It's raining,' 'That's milk,' 'That's a dog', to which we have learned to assent unreflectively on the spot if we are queried when certain associated sensory receptors are triggered."[4] Such sentences are the kinds of sentences that represent something approaching conceptual purity, reaching back to that time when the child, as proto-theorizer, was either a blank slate or perhaps a minimally programmed information system.

And while Quine acknowledges that the trained scientist will develop more sophisticated sentences that will count as observation sentences, since they are the sentences that she will "assent to outright on the strength of appropriate neural intake" (Quine 1993, 108), we can still distinguish pure cases of observation sentences, which are those that we acquire early on, as children, before we have become too immersed in theory: "Observation sentences in this pristine purity are the child's port of entry to cognitive language, for it is just these which he can acquire without aid of previously acquired language" (109). These sentences are acquired through simple conditioning.

Kuhn's elaboration of the initial learning of the sentences that Quine takes to be our best examples of "pure observation sentences" is meant to illustrate his claim that paradigms determine large areas of experience all at once. When a child learns the correct application of the word "Mama," he claims, she learns a dense and interconnected system of classifications as well, so that language learning is part and parcel of what it is to learn to divide up the world into meaningful categories. Quine's account can accommodate this point to a certain extent, but he thinks nonetheless that even if we do not in fact have introspective access to those stimuli, but only to sensations, these pure observation statements are tied to stimuli that undergird the sentences.[5]

Thus, in the debate over the status of observation sentences, we find that Quine tries to block the relativism about observation sentences that he sees as objectionable in Kuhn's and Hanson's accounts of the theory-dependence of observation by appealing to a form of linguistic behaviorism. In this account, basic observation sentences come about as a result of the conditioning in which certain sets of stimuli are paired with certain simple utterances in early childhood language learning. And while the trained scientist might come to assent as unreflectively to "That is a cathode ray tube" as she does to "That's a dog," Quine tries to make a case for the observational status of the latter that sets it apart from the former by appealing to the idea that a child can learn the latter types of sentences when she is a blank slate: she does not need any other language to acquire them, and so they are not really theory-dependent. They are connected to the world through a process of simple conditioning, so no theory is required for the child to grasp them or use them. The conditioning process simply pairs up stimuli with utterance, and correct utterances are reinforced positively. This, he thinks, distinguishes pure observation sentences from sentences like "This is a cathode ray tube" because, even though the scientist might come to assent to the latter statement unreflectively, its acquisition depends on a more elaborate theory and linguistic repertoire. Quine tries to evade the metaphysical question—the question of whether some aspects of the world are more fundamental, less interpretive, than others—by making the question into a question about how sensory input gets hooked up with linguistic utterance. Hanson and Kuhn, on the other hand, draw not only on gestalt psychology, but also on philosophical points about concept use and acquisition. According to Quine, the term "experience" can be replaced by "the stimulation of our sensory receptors," a phrase that is agnostic about the events or entities that cause this stimulation, and that puts the question squarely in the field of psychology and linguistics.

Kuhn and Hanson, however, tie experience and observation to meaningfulness: to acquire a concept is to have at hand a large background of theory, even when the concept is as simple as the child's recognition of "Mama." The correct application of concepts, and the process of making true statements, is grounded in practical activity and in intelligibility—in using those concepts. The emphasis on use and meaning opens up the prospect of the replacement of "experience" by "discourse." The most enthusiastic advocate of this project is Richard Rorty.

Challenges to Experience: The Linguistic Turn

Richard Rorty appeals to the work of Quine and Kuhn in his own attack on the concept of experience and the theory of mind he thinks it harbors, but Rorty has no use for appeals to stimuli or even sensations. These are beside the point—they are only that which human beings share with computers and other animals. And while Rorty identifies his project with that of the pragmatists of the early twentieth century, he parts ways with them on the issue of experience. Much of Rorty's work either implicitly or explicitly calls for the substitution of the term "discourse" for "experience," appeals to which, he contends, are misguided, even regressive. Dewey himself, he contends, seemed willing to replace "experience" with "discourse."[6]

Beginning with *Philosophy and the Mirror of Nature* (1979), and continuing through the rest of his writings, Rorty argues that a "representationalist" approach to mind frames problems about knowledge as a question about the extent to which our ideas accurately represent objects or states of affairs in the external world. The epistemological partner of a representationalist model of mind is, according to Rorty, a "foundationalist" epistemology in which experience is taken to be the nondiscursive "foundation" on which reliable knowledge is based.[7] But such a model of knowledge seems to present insuperable problems: what could this nondiscursive foundation possibly be? And how could it do the work of justifying our beliefs—a process that seems to require, not merely a causal interaction with the world, but rather the kind of thing that can do the work of justification: a reason. Reasons are discursive, and so cannot be identical with the nondiscursive "happenings" of sense experience.

Furthermore, Rorty argues that for experience to be intelligible, it must be conceptualized in some way (Rorty 1972). But if it is conceptualized—that is, if it is meaningful in virtue of its conceptual structure—then it is not unmediated or pure access to the world, since the process of conceptualization is essentially a process into which human interpretation has been injected. And if human interpretation has been introduced, the experience is no longer input from the brute world of nature, but is instead some admixture of the subjective world of the mind and the objective world of brute nature. Yet, insofar as the objective world of brute nature provides we-know-not-what to this formula, there is nothing to be said about it, except to point to it as the causal prompt that begins a physiological sequence of events. Thus, Rorty argues, the foundational role of experience is a will o' the wisp. The appeal to experience cannot get the foundationalist what she wants: contact with the world as it is, independently of human beings.

Given the conundrum that arises as a result of the commitment to the essentially discursive nature of justification, and the related point that the world of brute nature is unintelligible if it is understood as nondiscursive or unconceptualized content, it is easy to see why Rorty prefers "discourse" to "experience." We now also have some sense of why he thinks that "experience" and "discourse" are synonymous: if experience is essentially conceptualized, the reasoning would go, then it is essentially propositional and so, at least in principle, linguistic. If we think, as Rorty does, that our linguistic practices shape our conceptual repertoire, then experience is, to some extent, a myth, since the purely subjective and private mental content that the term "experience" seems to signify is merely an artifact of a bad metaphysics of mind and a worse epistemology.

Rorty argues that giving up this representational model of mind, in which the mind is conceived of as a mirror in which the world is reflected, either correctly or in distorted fashion, means that "perennial problems of philosophy" such as the question of how we come to know the external world cease to be problems. So, for instance, if we give up the representational model of mind, we can abandon the question of whether our ideas are true to the way the world is, independently of us. Similarly, we can give up on the question of what makes our claims true, since this problem in its usual form also goes back to an assumption about the role of language in representing our ideas and reality, and the function of nondiscursive truth-makers. Finally, we can give up on referring to experience, opting, instead, for "discourse." If, however, we insist on appealing to experience, we should understand it as a term that refers only to "the non-inferential judgments caused by changes in the physiological condition of sense-organs" (Rorty 1998, 123).

Although this substitution of "non-inferential judgments caused by changes in the physiological condition of sense-organs" for "experience" sounds a lot like Quine's attempt to replace epistemology with cognitive psychology, there are subtle differences. First, even though Rorty will accept this translation of "experience" into the language of a causal chain of events that starts with sensory stimulation, that causal chain puts into play a series of events that lead to judgments, whereas for Quine the chain leads to an utterance. The difference here may well be one of emphasis, but for Quine the emphasis on utterances rather than on judgments aligns his cognitive psychology with his linguistic behaviorism. For Rorty, the judgments are taken up in discursive practices that make it possible for changes to our sensory organs to jump the chasm that divides causes from reasons. Human "programming" via the acquisition of discursive practices is essential to this process, according to Rorty. As we become initiated into a language community, we are also initiated into a form of life in which we learn the practices of reason-giving and conversation.

And, indeed, the idea that discursive practices prepare human beings to "output" certain kinds of responses to sensory stimulation is exactly the right metaphor to explain this process, according to Rorty:

One can restate this reinterpretation of "experience" [as the ability to acquire beliefs noninferentially as a result of neurological, causal transactions with the world] as the claim that human beings' only confrontation with the world is the sort that computers also have. Computers are programmed to respond to certain causal transactions with input devices by entering certain program states. . . . We humans program ourselves to respond to causal interactions between the higher brain centers and the sense organs with dispositions to make assertions. There is no epistemologically interesting difference between a machine's program state and our dispositions, and both may equally well be called "beliefs" or "judgments." There is no more or less intentionality, world-directedness, or rationality in the one case than in the other. (Rorty 1998, 141–42)

Human beings are "programmed" via the acquisition of a language, which in turn transmits a culture and a way of interpreting the world. Experience is the input that triggers changes of program state, but it is not itself more philosophically significant than that. It has a functional definition, but nothing more.

These nondiscursive changes in sense organs are not very interesting, Rorty thinks, since they are no more than biological and neurological processes. It is only discourse that holds out hope for edification, and Rorty thus argues that the project of epistemology should be abandoned, along with the metaphysical problems of truth and realism. In place of epistemology, discussions of realism, and appeals to experience, Rorty urges us to take up hermeneutics, edifying conversation, and the poetry of prophecy. He regards hermeneutics as a search for understanding, rather than for solid foundations for our knowledge, and he therefore proposes it as an appropriate successor subject to epistemology. It is, in its orientation, more interested in interpretations than in foundations or reality. In his appeal to hermeneutics, Rorty argues that there is no sense in talking about some vocabularies as truer than others; some vocabularies are simply better suited to certain tasks than others. In this sense, Rorty hopes to put to rest problems about accurate representations of a mind-independent world, or representations that enjoy a certain kind of privilege because of their sources in sense perception, preferring to look at the ways in which linguistic forms offer alternative, albeit not necessarily true (or false), descriptions or redescriptions. The linguistic turn focuses attention, not on experience, but on vocabularies, statements, and discursivity.

This understanding of experience also serves as the background for Rorty's claim that changes in language are the essential element in bringing about social, political, and even philosophical changes: by changing the language, we essentially change the programming instructions for the computers that we are. But here it is important to note it is we who change experience; it does not change us. The causal chain of sensory stimulation, while an impetus to judgment, is still barred from playing a robust explanatory role in how we come to make certain judgments, and ultimately, Rorty argues, we cannot be accountable to a nonhuman world or reality. Insofar as we account for our judgments, we do so to other human beings, other members of our community of discourse. The invocation of "facts"—be they "moral facts" or "empirical facts"—are equally empty feints in that accounting.

But if both Quine and Rorty translate "experience" into sensory stimulation and neurological events, why doesn't Rorty, like Quine, advocate for the replacement of epistemology by psychology? Why, instead, does Rorty want to replace epistemology with conversation and hermeneutics? Part of the answer has to do with the relative priority Quine extends to scientific psychology, but the other difference is Quine's commitment to maintaining something like "contact with the world"—if only a very thin contact—and Rorty's rejection of that commitment.

The difference between Quine's and Rorty's evaluations of scientific psychology, or science in general, can be summed up in Quine's claim that the sciences are our best going theories and Rorty's claim that there are no important differences between science and other kinds of literature. Rorty, like Quine, sees himself as a naturalist (Rorty 1991a, 113), but he rejects the assumption that naturalism requires the privileging of scientific accounts of human behavior over humanistic, literary, or artistic accounts. Scientific accounts are vocabularies that serve a particular purpose, Rorty argues, and he rejects Quine's commitment to the vocabularies of the sciences as superior to the vocabularies of poetry or evaluation. For certain purposes, it may be useful to explain things in the language of physics, but for other purposes, poetry might be more useful, Rorty points out. Similarly, talk of mental events and their ilk—beliefs, desires, judgments—can cohabit with talk of physical events and their ilk—neural states, sensory stimulation, physiological states. Neither description need displace the other, since vocabularies are tools, according to Rorty, rather than true or false ways of representing a world of brute nature.[8]

Both Rorty and Quine characterize experience in terms of sensory stimulation, but Rorty does not see that as relevant to the discursive practices he focuses on in his advocacy of hermeneutics. Experience only enters the picture in Rorty's characterization of the training or programming that members of particular communities undergo, but this, like Quine's linguistic behaviorism, is merely the process according to which language is learned: it enters as a form of programming, or reprogramming. The purposes to which we put language take center stage in Rorty's account, and experience drops out of the story, unless it is understood as human beings' ability to acquire beliefs as the result of certain kinds of neurobiological responses to stimuli. For Quine, however, because experience is best understood as a neurobiological process that connects to theory by way of conditioned utterances, the project of epistemology goes on as a branch of experimental psychology. The observation sentence is salvaged, to a certain extent, as the bedrock which can adjudicate among competing theories, as the logical positivists hoped. Yet its status is not that of a theory-free or neutral statement—it is simply a statement that is the primitive link between language and theory, on one side, and "the world" (stimuli, really), on the other.

While Rorty abandons empiricism, Quine tries to put it on what he thinks is more like the right path. According to Quine, although we cannot reduce observation statements to sensory states, as the positivists hoped, we can focus instead on how scientific theories are actually confirmed—and, in turn, on how observation sentences are confirmed. But what this process yields is not an epistemological insight, but rather an account of the psychological processes and linguistic conditions that we link up when we construct scientific theories. For Rorty, language is not merely the conditioned response that follows a particular sensory event—it has the power to remake worlds. Not, of course, the world of brute nature—that is itself only a linguistic token we put forward in our pyrrhic attempts to make our theories accountable to something grander than human communities. Rorty's naturalism amounts to a rejection of this need to find some nonhuman thing to which human knowers can be accountable.

Sensory Stimulation, Naturalism, and the "Thin Input" Premise

Rorty's naturalizing move is, like Quine's, a rejection of the search for a priori grounds for knowledge and the enthronement of epistemology as the arbiter of discourses that are well-founded, as opposed to those that are not. In addition, for both Quine and Rorty, the naturalistic approach follows from our understanding of human beings as natural entities and their lives as the subject of naturalistic inquiry. And while, for Quine, that naturalistic inquiry is natural science traditionally understood, Rorty's emphasis on the priority of linguistic practices leads him to embrace instead something like "discourse studies" as the appropriate naturalistic approach. Rorty turns to hermeneutics to replace epistemology; Quine sees epistemology as continuing, albeit as a department of psychology.[9] Both reject the assumption that motivates the Cartesian project in epistemology: that the sciences cannot provide justification of their own methods without succumbing to a vicious circularity, and are thus in need of philosophy. Rorty sees the sciences as having their own rules of evidence and justification, like all discourse communities. But he also thinks that the privilege accorded the sciences as a form of knowledge is a relic of representationalist approaches to knowledge. Quine, like Rorty, rejects the assumption that epistemology must first legitimate the sciences before the sciences can themselves be said to give us knowledge, and particularly knowledge about our own attempts to come to know. We should use the methods of the sciences to explain how we come to have scientific knowledge, according to Quine, since the sciences are our best going theories. We have no better candidates for a proper methodology than the sciences, Quine claims. And, given that science is something that human beings, as natural entities, engage in, and that it seems to be our best going methodology, epistemology would be best conducted as the scientific study of science.

Quine reframes epistemology as a discipline concerned with a natural phenomenon: the process whereby human beings, a primate species that receives only "the impact of light rays and molecules upon our sensory surfaces" (Quine 1975a, 68), or "certain patterns of irradiation in assorted frequencies" (Quine 1969, 82), produce the "torrential output of a theory of nature" (Quine 1969, 83) that dramatically outstrips the meager input allotted them. The idea that the goal of epistemology is to understand how we get from this stimulus input to science is the basis for Quine's willingness to hand epistemology over to empirical psychology.

By contrast, Rorty argues that the important project is to understand, not sentience, which we share with other animals and with computers, but what is characteristic of our sapience: our cultural and linguistic practices, our attempts at redescription, our practices of giving and asking for reasons.[10] He agrees with Quine that an epistemological approach that gives a central role to experience focuses on the part of our nature that aligns us with animals and computers, and while Quine approves of this way of seeing human beings and their knowledge projects, Rorty rejects it in favor of a way of seeing human beings that emphasizes that which distinguishes us from those other beings or from things.

This, it seems to me, inevitably raises the question of how we ought to understand ourselves, and the stories about human beings that Rorty and Quine present seem to point to a bifurcated account of human beings that is mirrored in the bifurcation of experience into stimuli and discourse. If, in Robert Brandom's terms, we are characterized by both sapience and sentience, how does experience fit into this picture? Sapience, Brandom and Rorty argue, is what is distinctive about us and sets us apart from other animals; in this respect, experience, as an aspect of our sentience is less relevant to an account of our ways of making sense of the world.[11] Quine, on the other hand, pays no attention to this invocation of that which distinguishes us from computers and other animals—we, like all other primates, are simply trying to cope with our world, to make sense of it and control it. This is all there is to epistemology and theory construction. Language use is just another tool that our particular species of primates has at its disposal for those purposes. The conception here of human beings and their cognitive, epistemic, and cultural activities is an important issue that deserves more extended treatment. I shall take this up in subsequent chapters.

It is worth noting that Rorty and Quine agree on a substantial body of theory, even though they disagree on the status of science and on the appropriate role of empirical psychology in an explanation of the move from meager input to torrential output. They agree that "experience," in the sense in which the British empiricists meant it and the logical positivists invoked it, cannot do the serious justificatory work that foundationalism demanded of it. Quine's attack on the distinction between a priori and empirical statements means that the distinction between claims that are true in virtue of experience (the empirical statements that the foundationalist claims are immediately justified), those that depend upon other claims for their justification, and those that are true independent of experience is a pragmatic, rather than truly epistemic, distinction. We can hold any claim true, come what may, Quine says, by changing enough of our other beliefs. Similarly, the role played by empirical statements as the immediately justified foundations of theories is a role that can be filled by any statement. Particular statements are foundational by virtue, not of their content, but of our epistemic practices. For Rorty, the idea of a claim that is immediately justified—in the sense that the foundationalist needs empirical statements to be justified—ignores the fact that justifications are discursive, communicative acts—even if the interlocutor to whom one justifies one's beliefs is only an internalized "other." Justifications are made in a social and cultural context, so Quine's claim that we distinguish "foundational" from other claims pragmatically is taken up by Rorty as the idea that in our actual practices of giving and asking for reasons, we can treat some claims as open to challenge and others as less so. Again, this is not a function of their content as much as of the role they play in a given cultural practice of justification.

Both Quine and Rorty assume, however, that human beings' access to the world is pretty much as the British empiricists envisioned it: the world is understood as fairly niggardly in the resources it provides human beings who try to understand it, and human beings are understood as interacting with the sensorial world much as computers accessorized with scanning optical equipment do, taking electrical impulses provided by the stimulation of our sensory receptors and turning them into claims and theories. But whereas, for Quine, this input from the world is, to a certain extent, informational (although its informational content is minimal), for Rorty, the physical and neurological events that coincide with our ability to acquire beliefs noninferentially are mostly beside the point. They are the prompt for our judgments, but they have no information value.

Thus, for Quine, what we mean by experience is, essentially, the stimulus input that grounds observation sentences. "Experience" is just the nonscientific term for what we now know to be stimulus input to our sensory system. And while observation sentences do not wear their status on their semantic sleeves, and are community-dependent to some extent, we do have an absolute standard for them: the sentences uttered by early language users when presented with quotidian situations and objects. Thus, "experience" is not an interesting philosophical topic, and its role in accounts of our theory construction is relatively limited. For Rorty, what we mean by experience is rather beside the point; we undergo certain kinds of physical changes, prompted by our environment, but these changes are simply the causes of our judgments, rather than the source of our "contact with the world." Since we share "experience" with computers and nonhuman animals, it has no interesting role to play in accounts of the peculiarly human enterprises with which philosophy concerns itself. Discourse is where the action is. In essence, in Rorty's view, if we're talking about experience, then we aren't really talking about experience.

The causal connection established by sensory stimuli is, for Quine, a guarantee that we are not merely spinning a web that is untethered from the world—the boundary conditions of our web of belief are established by the meager input of sensory stimuli. In contrast, the causal chain of sensory stimulation is, for Rorty, merely the prompt for noninferential judgments; other than that, nothing meaningful can be said of experience.

Anti-foundationalism ends up with this rather unsatisfying concept of experience, then: either experience is meaningful, in which case discourse studies can better fill its conceptual role, or it is simply physical goings-on that are the proper province of cognitive science. Thus, experience either evaporates into language or it evaporates into stimuli—it becomes the province of either literature or discourse studies; or if it is just physical goings-on, it belongs to psychology.

In addition, the role that experience can play as a corrective to theory seems to be undermined in this account. The idea that experience could be an avenue by which the world has its say in our theory construction or choice, or as a touchstone of reality, seems hopelessly compromised, at best, or, at worst, an inappropriate criterion that only the benighted could expect to find met. Some might argue that the move away from the early pragmatists' valorization of experience as a way of driving out intellectualism and idealism might seem to be progress of a sort. After all, one might say, the redefinition of experience by a more thoroughgoing critique of foundationalism might be an example of what philosophy does best—refine concepts, try to give them more content, or, if they are hopelessly muddled, give them up. The paeans to experience that we find in James and Dewey might be understood as the hangover of romanticism, or the unfortunate relic of an unsophisticated empiricism that had yet to confront all the problems of realism, idealism, and theory-dependence that would arise as a result of science studies and a more rigorous epistemological examination. While the problem of experience might not be solved, it might at least be said that the problem has been improved.

The issue of "contact with the world"—and whether we need a more robust theory of experience than that with which Rorty and Quine, the paradigmatic anti-foundationalists, provide us—is addressed in chapter 4, as is their shared premise of the thinness of the input we have to go on in our attempts to understand that world. But before I leave the issue of observation and experience, I would like to address just one more issue that seems to be an artifact of the anti-foundationalist skirmishes over the theory-dependence of experience. This arises as a result of introducing to the problem the added complexity of the question of the status of scientific evidence, and the issue of moral observations. This is an issue that arises more pointedly for Quine and Kuhn, who are more troubled by the problems of relativism and the role of scientific evidence in our accounts of experience and observation, so I will leave Rorty behind here—he will enter the discussion again in my discussion of models of mind, and when I discuss the twentieth-century feminist critiques of experience—but at this point, I would like to focus on how this discussion of experience in the philosophy of science leads us into other problems.

Observations and Theory

One of the virtues Quine sees to giving epistemology over to the domain of psychology is the prospect this opens for resolving the issue of what counts as an observation sentence and how these sentences are confirmed—a problem that, as we have seen, plagued the logical positivists. Citing Hanson's work on scientific observation, Quine poses the problem as one about the variability of sensory reports relative to background knowledge. A trained physicist may look at an apparatus and see an X-ray tube, whereas someone who lacks that training sees a glass and metal instrument with a lot of odd accessories. Hanson implies that neither of these descriptions can be unproblematically disqualified as observation sentences, even though the untrained observer cannot see what the trained specialist can see when looking at exactly the same item. According to Quine, a naturalized approach using both empirical psychology and linguistics can settle the issue. Observation sentences are those "in closest causal proximity to the sensory receptors," that is, those that as we learn language are "most strongly conditioned to concurrent sensory stimulation rather than to stored collateral information" (Quine 1969, 85). But of course, as Quine points out, the learning of a language seems to constitute just such collateral information, and if we are trying to identify observation sentences, we cannot very well exclude language from our purview. And while he recognizes that specialist communities might identify more detailed claims as observation sentences (i.e., "That is an X-ray tube" versus

"That is a glass and metal doohickey"), Quine denies that this entails that there are no pure or absolute observation sentences. Quine responds to Hanson's attempt to show that observation sentences are, to some extent, in the eye of the beholder, by arguing that we can in fact determine an "absolute" standard for an observation sentence by appealing not only to the sentences that a child first learns, but also to those that "most of the speakers of a language" (Quine 1969, 88)—with the exclusion of "deviants" such as "the insane or the blind" (88n7)— would assent to unreflectively. Empirical psychology and linguistic observation, according to Quine, can solve a problem that plagued many philosophers of science of the twentieth century: what counts as an "observation" and what counts as an "interpretation," where the latter involves a substantial body of theory.

What might be troubling to anyone trying to reconstitute a distinction between "observation sentences" and "theoretical sentences" on the basis of this psycholinguistic behaviorism, however, is that some odd kinds of sentences might turn out to be observational sentences. For instance, certain evaluations of states of affairs, such as "That is mean," or "That is disgusting," would clearly seem to be candidates for such a status. They might well turn out to enjoy a level of agreement comparable to simple empirical claims like "That's a dog." Quine's appeal to an absolute standard in which the earliest sentences a child learns constitute such a standard will not block such an outcome, and in fact invites it, unless the appeal is supported by a fairly robust but limited ontology, such as that which we find in Mackie (1991).[12] With the tools of linguistic behaviorism, which gives us the idea that observation sentences are those most closely linked causally to the unreflective utterances of untutored new language users and to which the majority of competent speakers unreflectively assent, the exclusion of these types of thick descriptions would seem arbitrary. Indeed, Judith Lichtenberg (1994) has argued that moral claims often admit of a greater level of commitment—measured as certainty and consensus—than do some empirical claims.

Gilbert Harman (1977) asks us to compare two different instances of putative observation: in one, a scientist sees a vapor trail in a cloud chamber and takes himself to have seen a proton; in the other, an observer sees children pouring gasoline on a cat and setting the animal on fire and takes herself to have witnessed an act of cruelty—an immoral act.

Harman argues that both observations are theory-dependent: the scientist would not see a proton but for her acceptance of a particular scientific theory; the observer who witnesses the cat burning would not see an act of cruelty without accepting a particular theory of sentient beings, harm to them, and how that can constitute cruelty.

Harman, however, makes use of a distinction between the explanatory resources provided by the observer's "psychological set" and the explanatory resources provided by the actual occurrence of a physical event to distinguish these two putative cases of observation. Even if we grant that scientific observation is a kind of skillful perception, as Hansen and Kuhn argue, Harman argues that the moral "observation" in the case of the cat-burning need not appeal to an objectively perceivable moral property for us to explain its occurrence, whereas the observation of scientific phenomena requires that a particular event in the external world (i.e., as distinct from the internal world of the subject) actually occur, and it further requires that the terms used in true observations refer to real properties of objects. According to Harman, we can explain the moral "observation" without remainder by reference to the observer's "psychological set"—which seems to be the observer's disposition to feel certain things in certain circumstances (McNaughton 1991, 101). We do not need to invoke perceptible moral properties to explain that observation. But in the case of the vapor trail and the cloud chamber, we must invoke the occurrence of a particular physical event to explain that observation. Thus, even though only a person trained to "read" cloud chambers and vapor trails could observe the proton, and only a person trained in the appropriate moral theory could see the situation in which a cat is burned alive as cruel, nevertheless, Harman argues, there is an important distinction that should not be overlooked here: in the case of the scientific observation, there is a physical event that occurs—a physical entity causally interacts with an observer—without which the observation would not occur and the postulation of which must be invoked to explain the observation. But in the case of the moral observation, no such causal chain is required to explain the observer's experience. We need only invoke the observer's "psychological set" to explain it.

The attempt to block certain statements from the category of observation statements, and the corresponding worry that the theory-dependence of observation risks allowing us to see almost anything—an appropriately trained observer would seem able to see such things as "God's grace and impending doom," in Simon Blackburn's words (2006, 210)—arises again and again in the literature on empiricism and anti-foundationalism. The Quinean move of "democratizing" observation sentences draws on the idea that certain observations are more basic than others. But some of our most "basic" statements, in some sense of the term "basic," are moral or evaluative claims. Harman's attempt to block that outcome involves an appeal to causation, and, we might conjecture, on an account of perception that assumes the truth of Quine's characterization of it as "patterns of irradiation and the impact of light rays and molecules on our sensory surfaces" (Quine 1975a, 68). Thus, it is the external world of objects that causes us to observe scientific objects (via this biological/cognitive route), even if that observation is tied up with and imbued with scientific theory. Our moral "observations" are not so caused, the response might go—at least not so simply.

But Harman's account runs into a different problem: the question of how causal events can constitute epistemic justification. That is, we run into the problem that Rorty identifies and resolves by relegating causal events to a realm of meaninglessness. Causation might differentiate the moral observation from the scientific observation, but it cannot play a justificatory role in this story about empirical knowledge. We are left with a distinction between moral observations and scientific observations that is essentially trivial. It does not establish an epistemic difference. We are returned to Rorty's account of the self-reweaving web: "don't ask where the beliefs come from." There are some pingings and bangings that inexplicably prompt us to say things. But don't look behind the curtain.

The Disunity of Psychology

Harman and Quine both appeal to psychology in their accounts, and the resources for halting this ontological slide might be found here. Quine appeals to psychology because that is the scientific discipline concerned with correlations between the thin input of sensation and the torrential output of science and linguistic behavior. The stimulus input that scientific psychology posits surely does not include evaluative properties;

in fact, for Quine, it is not clear to what extent even the "thing language" of physical-object theory is necessary for science.[13] Yet we can at least see how one might be entitled to physical objects like protons without being entitled to posit moral properties by appealing to causation—itself a relationship licensed by scientific theory. Physical-object theory can at least be accommodated within the confines of theories of causation, while a realistic theory of moral properties cannot. Thus, we might say that the ontology of the sciences can license the attribution to physical objects of causal properties that it cannot license to moral or evaluative properties. I will have much more to say about this in chapter 6.

There is a certain ambiguity here, though, in the different senses of "psychology" to which Quine and Harman appeal. In his reference to the observer's "psychological set," Harman seems to mean the folk psychological categories of beliefs, desires, and dispositions that make up the subject's mental states, although, truth be told, Harman's invocation is rather vague.[14] Quine remarks that Harman shows "a tolerant concern for mental entities" and that, in Harman's view, mental states can still be identified as "hypothetical states of the nervous system" (Quine 1975b, 296). But while Quine embraces behaviorism, Harman keeps it at arm's length. In fact, it seems that Harman's attempt to circumscribe the realm of observation by appeal to causation arises only because Quine's attempt to find "behavioristic substitutions" for "outmoded notions" like observation sentences (Harman 1975, 23, 26n4) itself gives rise to the ontological relativism that Harman seeks to block by appealing to causation.

While Harman tries to salvage something like observation sentences in science without appealing to behaviorism, Quine does not seem to want to be saved from charges of behaviorism: "I am not sure I know what philosophical behaviorism is, but I do consider myself as behavioristic as anyone in his right mind could be," Quine remarks, distinguishing his position only from a "doctrine too absurd to admit to," which, he suspects, the pejorative use of "philosophical behaviorism" is meant to refer to. "But in that sense no one is a philosophical behaviorist," he adds (Quine 1975b, 296), leaving the reader to puzzle over just what kind of behaviorism he has excluded.

Quine appeals to "psychology" to establish that some sentences can count as observational in an absolute sense because it is the scientific discipline concerned with correlations between behavior and sensory input. In contrast, Harman's appeal to "psychology" seems to be less an invocation of psychology as a science than a term that refers to the private mental states of an observer. But Quine's story of how we come to have accounts of the nature of the external world assumes behavioristic methodology in its formulation (contrary to Harman's attempts to sidestep that methodological commitment), and thus seems to be incapable of evading the relativism that Harman worries about, and that Quine himself attributes to Hanson and Kuhn. Quine's attempt to block the relativistic conclusions that he thinks follow from Kuhn's and Hanson's analyses of observation is an appeal to science itself: "Science tells us that our data regarding the external world are limited to the irritations of our bodily surfaces" and "asks how it is that people manage from those data to project their story about the external world—true though their story is. 'Posit' is a term proper to this methodological facet of science. To apply the term to molecules or wombats is not to deny that these are real; but declaring them real is left to other facets of science, namely physics and zoology" (Quine 1975b, 294). It would seem, then, that the only reason we might have for thinking that moral evaluations, even if they are some of the earliest statements a child makes, are barred from being observation sentences is that moral properties are not the kinds of things that could give rise to "the irritations of our bodily surfaces." In addition, there is no science that is committed to the reality of evaluative properties.

However, Quine's invocation of stimuli is vague, and the attempt to identify them with irritations of our bodily surfaces means that they could still be keyed to moral utterances as readily as they are keyed, in Quine's account, to purely empirical utterances. The appeal to the consensus of competent speakers of the language makes it even more likely that some statements that are not simple empirical statements will count as observation statements. The fact that there is no scientific enterprise that licenses the ontology of evaluative properties, which is one element of the arsenal that Quine can use to make the idea of stimuli less vague, depends on a particular account of what science is, and I'll have more to say about that later. Minimally, however, it puts this claim in tension with Quine's claim that science is just a more refined version of common sense, since common sense reasoning licenses talk of evaluative and moral properties.[15] Quine's behaviorism leaves open the door to the possibility of moral observations; Harman's attempt to block that outcome seems to rely on having a less vague sense of what could count as a stimulus. But if we take that route out of the dilemma set up by Quine's account, we are left to wonder what epistemic difference is made by drawing this distinction. That is, if we think that the ways in which our beliefs are caused is a story about how we get those beliefs, and that the question of justification, which is the epistemic question, is not answered by a story about causation—or not entirely answered by such a story—then it's not clear that the distinction between evaluative and factual claims on the basis of causal origin is epistemically relevant. Furthermore, the idea that science posits causation by objects is ambiguous. The objects in question may be brute objects or objects in situations, and on the latter interpretation it would seem that moral observations stand a chance of counting as proper observations.

The univocality of "science" that Quine summons in his discussion of the role of posits and attributions of reality to entities disguises some very real and interesting debates in psychology. This is nowhere more apparent than in his use of, and unpersuasive defense of, behaviorism and Harman's criticism of that methodological commitment. The claim that science tells us that the only data we have to go on in our construction of stories about the external world are "surface irritations of our sensory organs" is true only insofar as we do not look too closely at the debates about just what those "surface irritations" constitute, and it is here that we find disunity, not only among the sciences, but even among the different subfields of psychology. If we look carefully at the practices of scientists in different subfields of psychology—for instance, between those working in child development theory, those working in social psychology, and those working in neuroscience—the attempt to pin down a common ontology leads only to triviality. The posits that the neuroscientist uses in her theorizing are different in a number of ways from the posits that the social psychologist and the child development specialist use. The neuroscientist appeals to subpersonal entities, while the other two may sometimes appeal to persons and groups as entities. Quine smuggles in a fairly narrow construal of stimuli and objects, and it is this narrow construal that underwrites both his linguistic behaviorism and his version of naturalized epistemology. As Phyllis Rooney remarks, many naturalist epistemologists assume that scientific descriptions of cognition form (or will form) a relatively coherent uniform account that will converge on, or be reducible to, neuroscience or some other appropriately "foundational" cognitive science; they ignore the fact that there are deep divisions between the methodologies of the "individual" and the "social" cognitive sciences (Rooney 2003). In chapter 2, I show how these deep divisions in the cognitive sciences show themselves in the attempt to frame the question of the theory-dependence of experience as an empirical question. Moreover, as I will be arguing, these disagreements about methodology in the cognitive sciences are symptomatic of tensions in our ways of understanding human subjects.

CHAPTER 2

Cognitive Sciences of Experience

Kuhnian Paradigms Versus Cognitive Modularity: Can Changes in Language and Concepts Change Our Experience of the World?

That there is no firm, nonarbitrary distinction between theory and observation is suggested by empirical evidence, Thomas Kuhn claims.[1] Jerry Fodor argues that the empirical evidence does not support this. Fodor argues that the persistence of certain visual illusions in the face of evidence that they are illusions seems to suggest that some types of perceptual experiences are "encapsulated," or sealed off from higher-level cognition. Experience can thus neutrally arbitrate between theories to the extent that sensory perception occurs in modules that are relatively impenetrable by more abstract theories (Fodor 1984). Paul Churchland, extending and defending the Kuhnian argument, imagines us one day swapping our "Neolithic legacy" for a "conception of reality embodied in modern-era science" (Churchland 1979, 35). In this future, children could be raised to experience the world quite differently from the way we presently experience it; rather than listening to the surf on a beach, for example, they would "'listen to the aperiodic atmospheric compression waves produced as the coherent energy of the ocean waves is audibly distributed in the chaotic turbulence of the shallows'" (30).

This could never happen, Fodor argues, because of the kinds of biological beings we are and the kinds of perceptual and sensory organs we have. The Kuhnian assumption that observation is theory-dependent, running together cognition and perception, is based on a failure to appreciate the modularity of perception and cognitive processes, borne out in the persistence of certain kinds of visual illusions. If our background beliefs and the theories we believe lead us to see only what we already know, Fodor asks, why is it that even though we know that the two lines in the classic Müller-Lyer picture (fig. 1) are the same length, we nevertheless continue to see one as longer than the other? Similarly, why is it that, even though the astronomical theory most of us learned when we were very young tells us that the sun is much larger than a dinner plate, we continue to see it as if it were only the size of a dinner plate? Fodor argues that increasing theoretical sophistication fails to change one's perceptions in these cases, supporting his contention that perception is not synchronically penetrable by just any background beliefs or theories; the empirical evidence only supports the idea of "perceptual plasticity" in some (relatively narrow) cases of perception (Fodor 1988).

Experimental and anecdotal evidence shows us that we can have sensory perception that is not informed by theory, Fodor argues. And while he recognizes that this does not give us a story of objectivity in which perception is completely uninfluenced by our theoretical beliefs, it does mean that we can have experiences that can serve the purposes that classical empiricism sought to apply them to: as objective arbiters of theories. If we accept Fodor's evidence, then, contrary to what Quine and Kuhn argue, there is a strong and relatively inviolable distinction between knowledge based on experience and theoretical knowledge, and that distinction can be made because of the rigid modularity of the brain, which Fodor contends is biological and fixed by nature, not a result of learning. The distinction between knowledge based on experience and theoretical knowledge can be maintained on the basis of our biological/sensory capacities. We are so constituted that our visual processing systems are not subject to our higher-level cognition, which is the source of theoretical knowledge (Fodor 1984). The modularity argument thus undermines the anti-foundationalist claim that experience is dictated by theory, since some experiences are "insulated" from theory, and so can serve as independent arbiters of theories and worldviews.

While the modularity theorist might not be a foundationalist of the classical empiricist school, she can still be a foundationalist in thinking that some experiences are "cleaner" than others. The biasing mechanism is biological rather than epistemic, however. According to the modularity theorist, the observation/theory distinction is grounded in the "general inability of central systems (e.g., reasoning, analogy, perceptual judgments) to feed information back to the brain modules responsible for perception" (McCauley and Henrich 2006, 80). The constraints on perception that arise as a result of the structural aspects of the brain account for the persistence of the Müller-Lyer illusion even when the observer knows that the two lines are the same length. Thus, we can distinguish observation from the fixation of perceptual beliefs, where the first is the "rigid output of the perceptual modules," while the second is "a global process that our central systems carry out by assessing those module's outputs in the light of our relevant knowledge" (81). Thus, the process of balancing theory against observation involves a process of simple perception, and another, different process in which "central systems" assess the output of the perceptual modules and weigh its relevance to our other beliefs.[2]

The data from cross-cultural studies of perception seem, however, to point to a certain amount of variability and malleability that is the result of "forms of life" and training. Fodor's skepticism about the possibility of radical transformations in what we can "see," a skepticism that he thinks is warranted by the facts of human biology, is, by the lights of anthropological psychology, merely a failure of imagination. Indeed, Churchland's examples of learning to see the world through the lens of well-confirmed scientific theories are particularly intriguing, because such learning would not be a distortion, but more accurate than our present modes of perception—themselves equally a function of learning, according to Churchland. Churchland's scenario of a future in which people hear the aperiodic compression waves produced by the ocean's energy rather than the surf is an application of the anti-foundationalist's claim that "linguistic innovation" and conceptual change drive changes in experience.

McCauley and Henrich (2006) take issue with the empirical data that Fodor cites to support his thesis of encapsulation, arguing that cross-cultural studies show that differences in visual experience in different cultures, especially when these experiences occur prior to the age of twenty, lead to different levels of immunity to the Müller-Lyer illusion. Whereas for Fodor, there are certain kinds of things that a normal human being

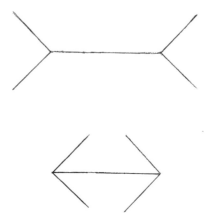

Figure 1. The Müller-Lyer illusion. Sketch for the author courtesy of Madeleine Adams.

just could never see, theorists who argue for the plasticity of perception and its relative penetrability by beliefs and theories cite anthropologically informed studies of perception to support their arguments against modularity and in favor of the plasticity of perception.

Fodor argues that modularity theorists can accommodate the anthropological evidence of cultural differences in immunity to the Müller-Lyer illusion, as well as the evidence of perceptual "recalibration" drawn from the inverting-lens experiment and the "kitten gondola experiment."[3] According to Fodor, "you find specific perceptual plasticity pretty much where you'd expect to find it on specific ecological grounds. Organisms grow, and so must recalibrate the perceptual/motor mechanisms that correlate bodily gestures with perceived spatial positions" (Fodor 1988, 193). Churchland's case thus depends on showing that we find perceptual plasticity where an ecological rationale for such recalibration is lacking: "for example that you can somehow reshape the perceptual field by learning physics (194).

Churchland argues that even if Fodor is right about perceptual modules, this would not give us theory-neutral observation. As Churchland points out, Fodor himself sometimes describes the contents of perceptual modules as "hypotheses" and insists that the processes they carry out are

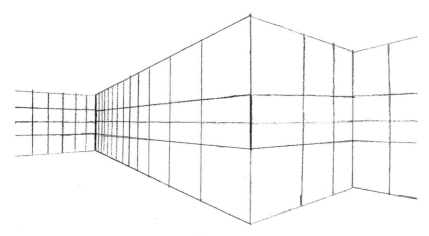

Figure 2. Room and walls in perspective. Sketch for the author courtesy of Madeleine Adams.

inferential (McCauley and Henrich 2006, 88). The fact that these are not conscious inferences does not mean that they aren't a form of theory-informed perception, Churchland points out. Furthermore, Churchland argues, while Fodor might be right about the synchronic case, the fact that, through training and increased experience, we can come to see differently seems to imply that perception is, at least in principle, permeable by theory. The Müller-Lyer illusion exists only because "the relevant processing module is the well-trained victim of some substantial education—that is, of some penetration by cognitive activity" (Churchland 1988, 174)—it arises because of our learning to make automatic adjustments for an object's distance when judging its size or length, and Churchland makes his point by transposing the schematic of the Müller-Lyer illusion into a detailed scene of a room with angled walls, represented according to the principles of perspective drawing (fig. 2).

Churchland argues that, if the Müller-Lyer illusion has its basis in our learned ways of reading perspective, we would expect to find that the illusion could be overridden, although not by a simple act of will (given the extent to which the perception has become automatic). Education and training in a different kind of perceptual environment, with different kinds of perceptual problems to be addressed by the subject, would be necessary. But were such perceptual training to happen, we would expect that subjects could become immune to the illusion, according to Churchland. And, in fact, the empirical evidence seems to point to this: there is a good deal of cross-cultural variation and age variation in susceptibility to the Müller-Lyer illusion, according to studies cited by McCauley and Henrich (2006).[4] Children from the Suku tribe in the Congo were not at all susceptible to the illusion, one study found, while children from Evanston, Illinois (the only American location sampled in the study) were most susceptible; adults from Evanston were likewise the most susceptible among adult test subjects, while South African miners and San (hunter-gatherer) adults from the Kalahari Desert were least susceptible (Segall et al. 1966, cited in McCauley and Henrich 2006, 93). Researchers noted, too, that susceptibility to the illusion decreased between the ages of five and twelve (to a lifetime low) in American test subjects, then rose again from thirteen to twenty, but less than the decrease between five and twelve (McCauley and Henrich 2006, 94).

Churchland cites ear-training and musical training as further evidence for the possibility of theoretically informed and transformed perception, calling ear-training "a straightforward existence proof" of such perception. According to Churchland, this kind of theoretically informed and transformed perception is a way of connecting discursive systems to perceptual activity: the person who can hear pitches and identify chords has learned to connect the conceptual framework of music theory, so that she can "perceive, in any composition . . . a structure, development and rationale that is lost on the untrained ear" (Churchland 1988, 179). Hearing is thus informed by music theory. What such training does, according to Churchland, is allow the trained perceiver to use spontaneous perceptual judgments to "anticipate, manipulate, and exploit" (180) the details of particular perceptual phenomena. The possibility of such training shows that the spontaneity characteristic of mundane, everyday perception can be extended to include "conceptual frameworks radically different from those we learned at mother's knee" (181). We can not only learn to see perspectives, tables, and chairs; we can also come to perceive abstractions like musical notes or chords.

In response to concerns that the thesis of perceptual plasticity or relativism means that there seems to be no limit to what one might be said to "see," Churchland says that not just anything can be observed, since to be observed, the feature in question must "really exist" and the observer's sensory system must have some reliable discriminatory response to the occurrence of that feature: "in sum, my position entails that we can observe many features of the world quite different from the features we are used to observing, and that we might not really be observing some features that we think we are. But it does not entail that we can observe everything" (Churchland 1988, 182). This attempt to avoid a relativistic conclusion is, of course, reminiscent of Quine and Harman, as discussed in chapter 1. But Churchland is essentially arguing that the distinction between observables and unobservables might well turn out to be theory-dependent and so subject to the influence of education itself. And while we can't observe everything—only what "really exists"—there may be many descriptions of that which exists. The world may be dense with description and possible redescription.

But, Churchland claims, simply believing a proposition is not enough to transform perception; the necessary transformation can only happen after "long familiarity with the 'novel idiom,' repeated practical applications of its principles, and socialization within a like-minded group of researchers" (Churchland 1988, 175), or, one might add, socialization within a like-minded group of practitioners. Churchland says that simply holding the relevant beliefs is not sufficient for seeing the things to which the theory in question refers; the newly initiated Copernican scientist, for instance, must also be able to see "the changing heavens as an unfold-ing instance of the Copernican organization, as viewed from our peculiar perspective within it" (176). The observer must be able to see the entities in question in context, and thus understand their meaning. In the case of ear-training, it would mean hearing a particular sound as a musical note of a particular pitch, but also hearing a simultaneous collection of sounds as notes comprising a particular chord—hearing them in the con-text of particular musical intervals, and thus as falling into "an organized matrix of different types (majors, minors, sevenths, ninths, diminisheds, augmenteds, etc.)" (179).

Fodor and Churchland do not really disagree on this front; Fodor does not rule out the possibility that some kinds of education and training might give us access to the background knowledge on which perceptual input systems draw (McCauley and Henrich 2006, 89). Rather, he simply denies that this establishes the claim that beliefs are doing the work of changing our perception in these cases. Churchland argues that the distinction that Fodor wants to draw between uniquely cognitive permeability and other kinds of permeability seems arbitrary, and he argues that Kuhn, in particular, should not be read as claiming that the scientist's perception could be changed by simply accepting a new belief (Churchland 1988, 175). Without the requisite practical applications and socialization, Churchland says, the beliefs would essentially be empty. They could not themselves bring about the necessary change in perception, just as memorizing the rules for making an omelet would not necessarily mean that one could successfully prepare one. Practice is essential.

Churchland does not rest his argument entirely on examples like ear-training, however; he argues that there is neurophysiological evidence for his claim that there is systemic permeability of the "peripheral" perceptual modules by the more central cognitive modules. Not only are there "ascending" pathways from parts of the eye and optical nerve to the higher levels of the information-processing hierarchy of the brain, but we also find, in examinations of the brain, that there are "descending" pathways from the higher levels to the peripheral sensory modules. "Prima facie, the function of these descending pathways is 'centrifugal control.' They allow for the modulation of lower level neural activity as a function of the demands sent down from levels higher in the cognitive hierarchy. . . . In sum, the wiring of the brain relative to its sensory periphery does not suggest the encapsulation and isolation of perceptual processing" (Churchland 1988, 178).

This is a rather odd argument strategy. Churchland seems to be arguing that the circuitry of the brain is evidence that vision and higher-level cognition are not shielded from each other, that the information-processing relationship is represented in the physical layout of the brain and the peripheral sensory modules. But why think that the fact that there are pathways between the parts of the brain thought to be primarily responsible for higher-level cognition (e.g., thinking about epistemology) and the peripheral sensory modules constitutes support for the claim that the higher-level cognitive functions can influence sensory perception? If the information processed were a physical entity like water, and flowed along channels, then this might make sense, but information has semantic content—it is what it is not just because of its physical proximity to, or distance from, some part of the brain. Churchland's argument draws an analogy between physical proximity and semantic proximity; it is as if one said that because a river flows between Texas and Ohio, what happens in Texas cannot be isolated from what happens in Ohio. This may well be the case, but it's not clear that the fact that the river flows between them is what makes it true. Churchland's assumption that brain structure can give us evidence of relevance relations among semantic entities seems to be something like a category mistake.

In a detailed rereading of the studies on which Churchland bases his claims about the neuroarchitecture of the brain, Daniel Gilman (1990, 1992) suggests that they are not all that relevant to answering the questions posed about perceptual plasticity anyway. Churchland's biological evidence is based either on animal studies (in this case, bird studies), cadaver studies, or on examinations of brains and eyes seriously damaged by illness or injury. As a result it is difficult to determine the extent to which conclusions drawn from these studies can be applied to live, real-time human perception and to scientific theory construction and testing (Gilman 1990, 361; 1992, 301–3).

Is perception determined by our received theories? Fodor's evidence, based on the empirical investigations of the Müller-Lyer illusion, implies that there is a limit to how malleable our experience of the world can be, given the way our brains are structured; studies in anthropological psychology imply that Fodor's claims about subjects' susceptibility to the illusion is a cultural artifact, and so cannot be accounted for on the basis of brain structure alone. Churchland, on the other hand, draws on an entirely different body of empirical evidence to support his claims about the plasticity of perception. What the debate seems to show is that the question is not itself one that can be settled by more empirical data. At the moment, the advocates of modularity and the advocates of plasticity seem to be at a stalemate. In the following chapters, I argue that it is, in fact, the theory of mind assumed in this debate that gives rise to the stalemate, as well as to the other versions of the problem of experience.

In sum, what we mean by experience, according to Fodor and Churchland, is sensory experience, produced by the brain's interaction with its surroundings. It is the ways in which our hearing, sight, and touch give us a world. But the story we can tell about experience is most centrally a story about brains and their functions. Brains perceive things; brain centers send out commands, make judgments. This way of understanding ourselves and our experience is fairly widespread. It is not just part of the cognitive scientist's repertoire; it has taken hold in nonspecialist communities as well. The assumption here is that to understand experience naturalistically is to understand it as something that the brain produces. Both Churchland and Fodor recognize that changes in belief are not sufficient to change experience, since practical activity and application are essential to whatever permeability we admit can hold between brain centers that are involved in the processing of sensory stimuli and brain centers that are involved in higher-level theory.

Do Brains Have Experience?

M. R. Bennett and P. M. S. Hacker (2003) object to this approach to experience however, because they argue that talk of brains having experiences, or knowing things, seems to be a confusion of levels. Bennett and Hacker argue that experience and knowledge can only be attributed to persons, not to subpersonal entities like brains or brain modules. According to Bennett and Hacker, this is methodologically suspect and infects discussions like those between Fodor and Churchland. To try to explain experience and knowledge by just talking about the brain is to fail to appreciate that experience and knowledge are not just brain states, but have some claim on our justificatory resources, which are not themselves reducible to brain states.

Perhaps a more damaging criticism comes from Alva Noë, who points out that this approach to cognition implies that the brain secretes experience the way the liver secretes bile. Furthermore, Noë argues that the attempt to study cognition by focusing on brain states exclusively substitutes a "brain in a vat" for Descartes's disembodied mind. We cannot fully understand consciousness and experience of the world if we assume that the brain is the only important element involved. Rather, our experience should be understood as body- and world-involving as well. While the brain is essential to the operations and activities by which an organism accommodates itself to its environment, it is not the only element of that interaction. Interpreting our experience should begin, not with the assumptions of neuroscience, but with those of biology. Moving the frame outward makes it possible to see ourselves as organisms in the world, not just individual brains undergoing brain events. "Consciousness isn't something that happens inside us: it is something that we do, actively, in our dynamic interaction with the world around us," Noë argues—in other words, "you are not your brain" (Noë 2009, 24).

Like Bennett and Hacker, Noë emphasizes the danger of attributing the kinds of states that we usually only attribute to persons to subpersonal entities like brains. The brain-centric approach that animates the traditional methodologies of cognitive science essentially treats the brain as a computational device. But computers don't follow rules and eyes don't see, Noë says, just as watches don't tell time. Our understanding of human beings' cognitive endeavors should recognize that brains, like computers, are tools for achieving certain kinds of goals, but the tool itself is always used in a context in which its functions can be understood. Without the context, the goals and functions are obscured, and we cannot understand what it is that brains help us do, and how experience is related to that.

The brain-centric way of talking about ourselves nonetheless has a peculiar appeal, Noë points out. "You might turn on the radio any day of the week and hear an author blandly state, as a matter of established fact, that language is 'processed' in the left hemisphere of the brain or that it is the neocortex that computes higher cognitive functions" (Noë 2009, 160). Philosophers in the analytic tradition seem particularly drawn to this model, and as we will see in the next chapter, the picture of the brain as information processor is the picture that animates accounts of experience even for those who would urge us to give up on the concept of experience. But Noë argues that the brain-centric approach leads us to scientific mistakes, and that it is indebted to an outmoded model of the mind. He urges us to understand ourselves as biological entities that are always already in a world, and actively engaged in activities. While mechanistic versions of ourselves might serve some purposes, seeing ourselves as living beings actually shows us the poverty of such self-conceptions: "No living being is merely a mechanism, even though every biological system can be viewed as merely physical and so, in some suitable sense, as merely mechanical" (39). Once we start using the vocabulary of action, however, we start to treat the living being as more than just a mechanical system, since an active organism is active as a unity, not as a mere assemblage of mechanical parts.

The question of the adequacy of different models and different disciplinary approaches to the question of experience makes salient this issue: how do we understand ourselves scientifically, and how does that understanding relate to our understanding of ourselves as being in search of self-understanding? This question will arise again in subsequent chapters. What we can conclude from these debates, though, is that a suitably scientific model of ourselves does not seem to dictate that we see ourselves as mechanisms, and that seeing ourselves as organisms, rather than simply as information-processing machines, changes the terms of the debate. Nonetheless, the idea that we are information-processing machines, and that our information processing function is primarily carried out by a brain-optical system, is deeply entrenched, even in philosophical accounts, as we will see.

CHAPTER 3

Children and Other Living Computers

In her discussion of Quinean naturalized epistemology, Lorraine Code remarks on the fact that philosophers seem to have rather strong—yet undefended—ideas about the scientific evidence that is relevant to discussions of knowledge, and we saw evidence of this in chapters 1 and 2. Philosophers working on naturalizing epistemology tend to choose neuroscience as the privileged home for the new epistemology, or, as we saw in Quine's case, some combination of neuroscience and behaviorism, on the basis of those assumptions. Yet, as my discussion of anti-foundationalism shows, many of the discussions of experience, while bifurcating experience into "stimuli" and "discourse," feel the need to bring these back together in some way. For Rorty, the pressure is not as pronounced—experience is just the "non-inferential prompts" that cause us to utter sentences. Beyond that, we cannot say much about what those prompts are. For Quine, the "non-inferential prompts" can be understood as stimuli. In this chapter I would like to delve a little deeper into the accounts of language learning that the representative anti-foundationalists who are the focus of this book offer. The attempts to bring back together the discursive and the nondiscursive we find in these accounts offers us a glimpse into the shortcomings of this bifurcated model.

The particular stories we get from Kuhn and Quine about how children learn to label and classify things, and the process of language acquisition these stories assume, are not simply meant by these authors as illustrations or thought experiments—they actually play an important role in structuring the debate about the possibility of theory-independent observation sentences. In fact, the accounts that Quine and Kuhn give of childhood language acquisition are offered as empirical claims about children's language acquisition, and these empirical claims then function as premises for the arguments about the theory-dependence of observation. The appeal to a form of "physiological programming" by which experience is "educated" recurs in the attempts of anti-foundationalists to address the "no contact with the world" objection leveled at anti-foundationalism. It is also, however, an important element in understanding the way in which the bifurcation of experience into "discourse" and "stimuli" reflects, and depends upon, an idea of the subject in which that subject is understood to be a dualistic entity, divided into a social creature and a natural entity.

In this chapter, I examine in more detail the way in which the anti-foundationalist's treatment of experience gives rise to a model of the mind as a computer, and of experience as the "input" to that computational system. I begin with a detailed analysis of the role that examples of childhood learning, and particularly language learning and classification, play in anti-foundationalists' accounts of experience and its relationship to theory. I argue that the model of childhood learning draws either explicitly or implicitly on the model of the child's mind as a computer to be programmed, and, by extension, that adult minds "learn by experience" insofar as they are also "reprogrammed." These arguments have the appearance of being supported by empirical evidence, and yet the descriptions of childhood learning seem to be based, not on real studies of childhood learning, but on an a priori story about what these philosophers think childhood language learning and classification must be like. Actual work by psychologists working on childhood cognition gives a much more complicated picture of what happens when children learn language and classifications.[1]

The stories of how experience and language get linked up in theory construction and in "initiation into the space of reasons" are central to the plausibility of the picture of experience as bifurcated into "stimuli," or nondiscursive input, and "discourse," or utterances. That the model of mind as computer is useful for solving particular kinds of problems about sensory perception does not mean that human beings are computational devices. That is, the scientific model of the mind that animates computationalism is being treated, not as a model, but as a truth about what minds and selves are. One might argue that Quine is entitled to this ontological assumption because of his commitment to empirical psychology as a replacement for epistemology and philosophy of mind, and his claims about the virtues of ontologies that arise out of the sciences. But, as we shall see, it is not clear that this is the model that is operative in empirical psychology.

More interesting, however, is the fact that Rorty and Kuhn, who are not as eager as Quine to reduce philosophical problems about knowledge and mind to problems in empirical psychology, would also seem to have assumed that the model of mind as computational device is the right account. Even though he rejects Quine's attempt to secure observation sentences by appealing to stimuli, Kuhn seems to think that a computer model can illuminate how children—and by extension, he implies, scientists—learn to divide the world up into categories: they are essentially "reprogrammed." And Rorty, though disagreeing with Quine's assumption that the sciences are the privileged discourse for understanding human cognitive practices, seems to have replaced the model of mind as mirror with a model of mind borrowed from Quine. Rorty's model, like Quine's, emphasizes the mind's function as an information-processor and the disembodied aspect of that process as an input-output relationship.[2] Experience falls on the biological side of our nature, Rorty assumes; it is what the brain does in turning stimuli into utterances. As such, it is not essential to an account of our social practices of justifying, speaking, and making claims, since these happen on the "sapient" side of our nature, while the biological processes of the brain and sensory organs belong to our sentient side—the side we share with other animals.

My contention is that this unnatural story about how children learn language and the complementary story of how experience "reprograms" minds are not genuinely empirical accounts. Thus, this is not really a naturalistic approach. It does not just suffer from being insufficiently naturalistic, however. It also reinforces a particular model of the knower as a disembodied—or minimally embodied—entity. In so doing, the model of mind as computer program misses the essential role of agency and normativity in understanding how language and "the world" come together. I argue, following Jerome Bruner, that this trend in modeling human cognition is due to a distrust of subjectivity that has as its patron a refined behaviorism.

This introduces a related issue, which I take up in chapter 6: the problem with the bifurcation of experience into stimuli and discourse is that the model of the subject it assumes—a computational model—fails to recognize the ways in which children are educated, rather than trained, and this education involves a whole range of activity in the world that is central to the development of cognition.

Quine's Story: Language Learning and Observation Sentences

Let us return to Quine's attempt to resuscitate observation sentences by invoking the sentences a child learns. Quine does not use Kuhn's model of children as computer programs, with "Johnny" learning to categorize swans, ducks, and geese while on a visit to the zoo. Kuhn tries to explain the gestalt switch that results from this learning process by invoking a presumed process by which Johnny is "reprogrammed." The reprogramming process involves ostension paired with labeling and correction when the categories are misapplied. However, while Quine does not explicitly invoke the metaphor of computer programming, his description of the process of developing scientific theories relies on the idea of input and output, which, if not explicitly a computational metaphor, certainly shares a background story with such metaphors.[3] For Quine, the interesting question for epistemology is how we humans get from meager input ("the impact of light rays and molecules upon our sensory surfaces" [Quine 1975a, 68] or "certain patterns of irradiation in assorted frequencies" [1969, 82]) to the "torrential out-put of a theory of nature" (1969, 83). Observation sentences are the connection between sensory stimulation, language, and the world.

For Quine, the process by which a young child learns language is best understood as the process by which he or she acquires dispositions. Through this process she acquires dispositions to utter particular sentences (including one-word sentences, like "Dog" or "Mama") or assent to queries ("See the dog?" "Is that mama?"). The inculcation of these dispositions is accomplished through conditioning and is a fully physiological process. It involves the correlation of particular stimuli with appropriate verbal performances—a simple input-output relationship, established through conditioning as the parent labels things and rewards the child for successfully imitating the parent's and other adults' verbal behavior. But the stimuli are not to be understood in mentalistic terms—they are not sensations or perceptions. The occasion sentences Quine wants to single out as observation sentences are those that require a minimal amount of "collateral information" to acquire—that is, they require little or no language.[4] The child is conditioned to utter them holophrastically. Only later does he or she understand the relationship of reference that is supposed to hold between a particular word and a particular item in the world.

"[O]bservation sentences . . . can be conditioned outright to distinctive ranges of sensory intake, or as physicalists let us say neural intake," according to Quine. "The child can be conditioned simply to assert or assent to the sentence under some distinctive stimulation, and he can come to learn only later that part of the sentence is a term denoting bodies or substances in an articulated external world" (Quine 1993, 108). In this respect, observation sentences are the human counterpart of animal cries: "Birds and apes have repertories of distinctive calls and cries for alerting one another to distinctive dangers and opportunities. Each cry is associated, by instinct or conditioning, to some range of neural intake" (109). Human language learning is achieved through conditioning, and it begins with simple observation sentences that can be keyed to a particular range of neural intake. These sentences can essentially be produced without knowing what they mean—they are simply noises initially made when the appropriate stimuli are encountered. Some sentences are thus relatively theory-independent, Quine argues, because they can be learned when the child is a blank slate, a biological entity that learns to make certain cries when it receives certain input.[5]

Kuhn's Story: Categorizing and Computer Programming

Whereas Quine's story of childhood training begins with the idea of human beings as primates who learn to make certain noises when conditioned to do so by particular kinds of input, Kuhn's story of child-hood language learning begins with the image of Johnny going to the park with a parent, who teaches him to categorize various birds. Kuhn's story is more detailed than Quine's: having learned to recognize birds as a class and to pick out robins from among them, Johnny comes to "learn for the first time to identify swans, geese, and ducks." The primary tool for teaching him these categorizations is ostension:

Father points to a bird, saying, "Look, Johnny, there's a swan." A short time later Johnny himself points to a bird, saying, "Daddy, another swan." He has not yet, however, learned what swans are and must be corrected: "No, Johnny, that's a goose." Johnny's next identification of a swan proves to be correct, but his next "goose" is, in fact, a duck and he is again set straight. After a few more such en-counters, however, each with its appropriate correction or reinforcement, John-ny's ability to identify these waterfowl is as great as his father's. Instruction has been quickly completed." (Kuhn 1977, 309)

Kuhn's explanation of what has happened to Johnny goes like this:

During the afternoon, part of the neural mechanism by which he processes vi-sual stimuli has been reprogrammed, and the data he receives from stimuli which would all earlier have evoked "bird" have changed. When he began his walk, the neural program highlighted the differences between individual swans as much as those between swans and geese. By the end of the walk, features like the length and curvature of the swan's neck have been highlighted, and others have been suppressed so that swan data match each other and differ from goose and duck data as they had not before. . . . A process of this sort can readily be modeled on a computer; I am in the early stages of such an experiment myself. (310)

This process involves the translation of a stimulus into the form of data clusters that are transformed by sets of functions that then allow for different groupings of data. The transformation functions are what Johnny learns when he is programmed to distinguish ducks, geese, and swans—he is being "programmed to recognize what his prospective com-munity knows" (1977, 312). Kuhn asks whether we can say that Johnny knows what the terms "goose," "duck," and "swan" mean, and he says that insofar as Johnny can apply these labels, then it seems that we should say that he does.

Kuhn's account of this transformation of Johnny's way of organizing the set of birds is meant to explain, in a naturalistic way, what happens when scientists come to learn exemplars that constitute the bedrock of paradigms. Responding to the charge that his talk about gestalt switches in the process of paradigm changes makes scientific revolutions irrational, Kuhn tries to provide a scientific account of these gestalt switches. Acquiring a paradigm is like being programmed to transform some data clusters into others: "assimilating solutions to such problems as the inclined plane and the conical pendulum is part of learning what Newtonian physics is. Only after a number of such problems have been assimilated, can a student or a professional proceed to identify other Newtonian problems for himself" (Kuhn 1977, 313). Normal science depends on being able to go on in this way, to assimilate some situations to the exemplars that ground theory. The process of learning to see ducks, geese, and swans in what was once an undifferentiated mass of birds is analogous to the process of scientific training in a paradigm: "Presented to Johnny with their labels attached, they were solutions to a problem that the members of his prospective community had already resolved. Assimilating them is part of the socialization procedure by which Johnny is made part of that community, and, in the process, learns about the world which the community inhabits" (313). Assimilating the exemplars of a particular paradigm is the process by which a prospective scientist is made into a member of a particular scientific community, and is what allows her to solve the problems set by that paradigm. It enables the recognition of similarity and difference relationships that allow for the application of problem solutions to new instances.

Rorty: The Mind as Web of Beliefs

Rorty does not make claims about childhood language learning in particular, but he does use the model of the computer that is reprogrammed as his model for learning more generally. In his discussion of experience, Rorty says that

computers are programmed to respond to certain causal transactions with input devices by entering certain program states. We humans program ourselves to respond to causal transactions between the higher brain centers and the sense organs with dispositions to make assertions. There is no epistemologically interesting difference between a machine's program state and our dispositions, and both may equally well be called "beliefs" or "judgments." There is no more or less intentionality, world-directedness, or rationality in the one case than in the other. (Rorty 1998, 141–42)

For this reason, Rorty argues, we should, following Wilfrid Sellars and Donald Davidson, reinterpret experience as "the ability to acquire beliefs noninferentially as a result of neurologically describable causal transactions with the world" (141). Experience is the noncognitive stuff that happens in the causal realm—the input that leads to the program states that we colloquially call "beliefs" or "judgments," which must be discursive if they are to be recognized as such.

Rorty urges us to "think of minds as webs of beliefs and desires, of sentential attitudes—webs which continually reweave themselves so as to accommodate new sentential attitudes. Do not ask where the new beliefs come from. Forget, for the moment, about the external world, as well as about that dubious interface between self and world called 'perceptual experience.' . . . All there is to the human self is just that web" (Rorty 1991a, 93). There is no "what it is like" to be that organism, there is no private inner space that constitutes a self, a space in which beliefs or perceptions reside. Thus, experience as the interface between the private realm of the mind and the public realm of the world is dispensable if we give up on the idea that the mind is a kind of thing—a mirroring device—and on the notion that knowledge involves privileged representations of objects in the external world.

The linguistic turn is part of overthrowing the commitment to a Cartesian model of mind as mirror, Rorty claims, and he credits Robert Brandom with carrying the linguistic turn through "by showing that if we understand how organisms came to use a logical and semantical vocabulary, we do not need to give any further explanation of how they came to have minds . . . to possess beliefs and desires, on Brandom's view, is simply to play a language game that deploys such a vocabulary" (Rorty 1998, 123). Thus the problem of how we come to have empirical knowledge, or how the mind can give us access to an external world of material things, is dissolved, since it only gets a grip on us if we have failed to take the redefinitions provided by the linguistic turn seriously.

Another redefinition that Rorty offers for beliefs is drawn from C. S. Peirce: beliefs should be understood as habits of action, and some beliefs "produce movements in the organism's muscles" (Rorty 1991a, 93). I am going to assume, for the sake of this exposition, that there is no deep problem in reconciling the redefinition of beliefs as habits of action with the idea that the linguistic turn shows us that to explain how organisms come to have minds, we need only account for how a vocabulary of beliefs and desires became the preferred vocabulary for accounting for human behavior. Rorty takes them to be consistent, so for the sake of the argument I will assume that there is no deep inconsistency here. The redefinitions raise a more fundamental question, however, about how well Rorty's account of the self as a web of beliefs and beliefs as "habits of action" that "produce movements in the organism's muscles" can work together. It is the slide from "action" to "movement" in this redefinition in which I am most interested. But before I address this, it is worth noting the absence of bodies and action in Kuhn's account and in Quine's. Notice that, of the three philosophers who talk about cognition as "reprogramming," only Rorty mentions the possibility that the entity being programmed can also move. Kuhn mentions that Johnny is "out for a walk" with his father, but this does not seem to be an essential ingredient in the story. This lack of activity should be our first clue that something is not right with this account of children, since most children come with bodies, and they move quite a lot, exploring their world by grasping, pointing, putting things in their mouths, and, yes, talking. Kuhn and Quine might argue, in response to this criticism of their child schemas, that bodies are not an essential part of the story of how children come to classify things. If this is the response they would make, then their accounts fit in with a long tradition of disembodied knowers in philosophy. However, the disembodied and stationary subject assumed by these model children does not seem to be consistent with the naturalistic model of human knowers—particularly in the case of children who are becoming knowers—embraced explicitly by Quine and implicitly by Kuhn, unless one thinks of knowers as simply brains. But understanding knowers as essentially brains is not really an adequately naturalistic account, unless one has a story to tell about naturalism that privileges certain subdisciplines of psychology or a story about why the natural activities of human knowers are not part of what we mean by "naturalism."

Presumably, however, we could expect that, as naturalists, Quine's and Kuhn's accounts of childhood language learning would draw on empirical studies of childhood learning. And yet, that does not seem to be true here: we have accounts that *sound* like naturalistic accounts. They sound vaguely scientific, as if they might have a body of empirical evidence behind them. But Quine's account, for instance, seems to have little or no support from child development studies.[6] Quine seems to assume that an account about neural input and how it issues in linguistic output is sufficient to account for childhood language learning, and that the claim that children learn to construct theories of the external world by linking up a range of stimuli with a particular utterance counts as an empirical claim. But in this respect we seem to have an a priori premise masked as an empirical claim. The story that Quine tells us about the holophrastic learning that children engage in, and the ways in which they come to use simple sentences that are only minimally theory-dependent, seems to be philosophical speculation, rather than empirically supported science.

Indeed, the evidence actually shows that childhood language learning is much more complicated than Quine's behavioristic story would lead us to believe it is. For instance, early childhood language learning requires that children be able to follow the gaze of a person who is trying to teach them the name of a particular object (e.g., "dog"). The experimental evidence implies that children do not just mechanically follow the head movements of an adult who is looking at a particular object; children follow the head movements more often, and gaze for longer, if the adult's eyes are open, rather than closed. Andrew Meltzoff argues that this gives us evidence that early language learning depends on the child's possession of the ability to attribute to the adult in this interaction the intention of looking at the object—that, in effect, the child must understand the adult as a cognitive agent and attribute intentions to her (e.g., intentions relevant to labeling an object "dog") (Meltzoff 2002, 15–16). Infants in their second year see head movements not simply as movements but as actions—that is, movements with an intention behind them, performed by an agent, not just a body. If this is so, then Quine's claim that children can learn the sentences he wants to call observational must be supported by a theory that attributes many innate capacities to young children if he is to account for their ability to learn these statements. The holophrastic account does not seem to answer many of the questions that researchers have raised about childhood language learning, and it in fact leaves much to be desired as a theory of that domain. It is not clear that Quine used any empirical evidence about childhood language learning in developing it.

Kuhn, it must be said, does at least make mention of the possibility that his account might have empirical data to support it—but the possible empirical evidence he mentions is just an experiment in computer programming at which he has almost succeeded. Note that this is not a proper experiment—Kuhn tells his readers that he has been trying to program a computer to sort data into groupings that could imitate the way in which he says that children learn to group entities—but he has no independent evidence that children do, in fact, learn in this way. Kuhn assumes that his success at programming a computer to sort data into groupings will support his claims that children learn to sort things into categories the same way.

What's more, the story that Kuhn tells about Johnny learning to categorize different kinds of birds is very different from the story he tells of scientific learning, which he characterizes as involving a good deal of practical activity. Learning to look through telescopes, constructing experimental settings, and the process by which students learn to replicate standard experiments in their disciplines exemplify bringing together material conditions and theory. In Kuhn's account in *The Structure of Scientific Revolutions*, theory is incarnated in activities that shape and reshape the material world—it is not just a matter of using language appropriately. Kuhn nevertheless thinks that the process that ends in Johnny learning to categorize assorted bird types is roughly the same process by which scientists become members of a particular scientific community. The "problem-solving" practices of the scientist are analogous to Johnny's attempts to classify different birds, Kuhn says. I shall be returning in chapter 6 to the aspect of practical activity that Kuhn seems to have left behind in his account of Johnny's learning. For now, however, I will focus on his account of childhood language learning in *The Essential Tension* (Kuhn 1977).

Unlike Kuhn and Quine, Rorty does not think that empirical science is a good resource for thinking about our thinking—at least for philosophical purposes. And yet, he seems to assume that Quine's version of experience is correct in its essentials—that what we get in "perceptual experience" is "thin input"; that it is essentially a physiological process; and that language learning happens on the other side of the natural/social divide. Language use and learning are essentially social processes, Rorty emphasizes, and while there is a linking-up of sensory states with words or verbal behavior in the process of learning language, the sensory states are really irrelevant to any story about human knowledge. Thus, the concept of experience is irrelevant to the story of human cognition, according to Rorty, because human cognitive practices are social practices, and the currency of those practices is language.

Quine's account of childhood language learning is thus insufficiently naturalistic, and Kuhn's account in *The Essential Tension* is based on an assumption about learning as a process replicable by a computer. Rorty's dismissal of the concept of experience—and the question of its role in knowledge—assumes Quine's theory about what we get in sensation from the world. According to this account, the input that human beings receive from the world is just that which would constitute the input to a computational device. The real action is only after that input arrives: at this point, it becomes the material that allows us to reprogram ourselves, or it becomes, in a different Rorty metaphor, the beliefs and desires that constitute the web that is our self.

As chapter 1 showed, part of this story is a story about what kinds of things perceptions are, and what kind of information we get from the world. In that discussion, as we saw, anti-foundationalists do not speak with one voice. Kuhn and Quine differ on whether we should focus on sensations or stimuli.[7] In chapter 3, I have argued that the question of the extent to which observation is theory-dependent cannot be answered in a straightforward way by appealing to empirical studies, since the question of which empirical approaches provide relevant data cannot be settled in advance, and the answer to the question about the penetrability of observation by theory at which one arrives will depend on what kinds of evidence one takes to be determinative, or even relevant. This methodological problem points to a more fundamental methodological issue: how ought we to think of the subjects whose cognitive lives we want to illuminate in philosophical and empirical studies? This methodological issue is just as important as the question of what kinds of information the world can give us through experience, and, as a matter of fact, the two methodological issues are connected.

The story about childhood language learning is marked by the absence of (a) a subject with a body; (b) a subject with intentional mental states; (c) a subject with a deep interaction with others; and (d) a subject with a point of view and agency. If we are thinking about real children and their learning, these absences are remarkable. Children's activity, whether it is their play or their physical manipulation of things in their surroundings, is essential to their development as knowers. It seems that in some versions of putative naturalism we find, in fact, just the opposite: rather than real children, we get child schemas. The larger point I hope to establish, and that I think is connected to these absences, is that the bifurcation of experience into "stimuli" and "discourse" seems, at least in part, to be a casualty of the retreat from the first-person perspective and the concepts of agency, intentionality, and the mental that are tied to it. This retreat, which Rorty and Quine explicitly champion, marks the methodologies of both behaviorism and computationalism.

A Flight from "the intentional"

I begin with the psychologist whose playing-card experiment Kuhn cites in his discussion of the extent to which paradigms (and the expectations they give rise to) influence perception. As a pioneer in what was called the "cognitive revolution," Jerome Bruner gives an account of the initial hope he had for that movement, and how the cognitive revolution lapsed back into what he characterizes as a new form of behaviorism. According to Bruner, the original impulse behind the cognitive revolution was the attempt to put meaning at the center of psychology, an undertaking that he and like-minded theorists believed required that psychology incorporate insights from philosophy, linguistics, and anthropology—in short, from a vast array of disciplines in the humanities and social sciences. A significant shift took place, however, when the emphasis of the research shifted from "meaning" to "information," "from the construction of meaning to the processing of information . . . the key factor in the shift was the introduction of computation as the ruling metaphor

and of computability as a necessary criterion of a good theoretical model"
(Bruner 1990, 4). As a result, "computing became the model of mind, and
in place of the concept of meaning there emerged the concept of computability. Cognitive processes were equated with the programs that could be
run on a computational device, and the success of one's efforts to 'understand,' say, memory or concept attainment, was one's ability realistically
to simulate such human conceptualizing or human memorizing with a
computer program" (6). This methodology, which Bruner calls "the new
reductionism" (6), could also accommodate the old stimulus-response
models of learning and associationist models of memory with some translation into the terms of information processing: "stimuli" became "input,"
"response" became "output," and "reinforcement" became the control element that fed information back into the system about the outcome of an
operation. The new version of information processing, like behaviorism,
made it possible to avoid talk about mental processes or meaning—terms
that behaviorism had made unacceptable, in an attempt to avoid subjectivism and mentalism.

Bruner's model of childhood learning departed from this approach,
and in important ways, from the "New Look" psychology—the approach
exemplified in the playing-card experiment—that he had inaugurated
with Leo Postman. Bruner's discussion of childhood language learning
begins with the child as a member of a family in which she learns not
just how to label entities (or identify playing cards), but how to construct
narratives. Narrative accounts in family settings are not neutral, Bruner
argues. They have rhetorical and illocutionary aims that are "partisan."
Children learn to use language while trying to do things with that language. Narrative accounts are not merely expository or descriptive, but are
designed to "put the case, if not adversarially, then at least convincingly
in behalf of a particular interpretation" (Bruner 1990, 85). The construction of these narratives starts from a narratorial point—to borrow an idea
from Daniel Dennett, we might call it "the narrative center of gravity."
Narrative accounts are structured by this narrative center of gravity, or
self. This self has a viewpoint and takes on different roles: victim, actor,
instigator, innocent bystander. The construction of a narrative points
back toward an "I" that is not simply a black box that transforms stimuli
into utterances. The fact that we have a "protolinguistic readiness for

narrative organization" (Bruner 1990, 80) explains the order of grammatical acquisition, and as we become competent cultural actors, we also learn new and different forms of narration. This is what Bruner calls the child's "entry into meaning"—meaning, not information processing. The entry into meaning involves the occupation of a narrative standpoint or perspective. In Heideggerian terms, we might understand this as the idea that the world is encountered as always already meaningful. The world is encountered as always already meaningful because we are born into a cultural and historical context (as well as a familial context, which Bruner points out), and because we are actively engaged with learning to get around (literally and figuratively) in the world. Meaning is already in the world; the subject of experience constructs narratives that can reconfigure those meanings, but the meaningfulness is not reducible to an account of computational brain processes.

Whether Bruner's approach is appropriately naturalistic—a question the epistemological naturalist might ask—depends, it seems, on what counts as "naturalistic." This brings us to the problem that Lorraine Code identifies in naturalized approaches to epistemology. Code argues that Quinean versions of naturalized epistemology are insufficiently naturalistic. Their conception of our epistemic nature is aprioristic. Quinean-inspired versions of naturalized epistemology assume, a priori, a version of individualism that is not true to the ways in which we carry out our epistemic tasks. In fact, the individualistic assumption is undermined by the empirical data that show that human beings carry out their epistemic tasks in social groups and communities. Individualism is at odds, or at least in tension, with naturalism, according to Code, since human life and the process of maturation—including human epistemic life and epistemic maturation—are marked by interdependence.

Given the variety of ways of understanding human beings and their epistemic tasks, why does the Quinean naturalist assume, without argument, that the individual information processor is the right model for human cognition? If Code is right, then not only is the assumption about what counts as a naturalistic approach undefended by the Quinean, but the theories dictated by that assumption are, in fact, empirically inadequate—they are not really naturalistic, if we understand naturalism as requiring that we take account of empirical evidence.[8] Code does not deny that the Quinean approach to naturalized epistemology might be one way of understanding human epistemic practices, but given its distance from our actual epistemic lives, the choice of this model would seem to require some justification. The extent to which it is undefended is the measure of its a priori status.

Quine's account of our epistemic lives begins with the idea that we are primates, and that the primary goal of our epistemic endeavors is brute survival. Our information-processing functions have allowed us to survive, he thinks, and this is the function in terms of which they are to be described. Accordingly, he ignores certain other phenomena in his characterization of cognition: the first-person perspective, for instance, and the deep and complex socialization that Bruner emphasizes, seem not to be very relevant from the perspective of survival. The Quinean naturalist might argue, too, that this is simply the philosophical expression of the model of human beings operative in the sciences: primates who have as their most fundamental epistemic task the interpretation of the stimuli captured by their sensory organs. Code does not dispute the claim that information processing is essential to human survival, but she does wonder about the extent to which it is an adequate model for framing epistemic problems: "although human beings could not survive were they unable to process information competently, were this all that they could do, the quality of their survival would at best be dubious" (1996, 8). As human beings, we are not just survival machines. We have concerns that go beyond survival, and we care enough about our epistemic practices to pursue questions about them by referring them to the empirical sciences, as Quine urges. That we wonder about such things is a sign that human life extends beyond a concern for simple survival. We are concerned about the quality of the life we seek to preserve, and, more to the point, we are even concerned that our evaluations of our epistemic practices (exemplified by epistemological theory) might be beside the point. Seeing us as simply aiming at survival is a reductive strategy, and one that can illuminate only a very narrow range of questions about our epistemic lives.

Furthermore, Code takes issue with the assumption that the dominant scientific model of human beings' epistemic practices is or should be information processing. While it might be the dominant scientific model in the branches of psychology that Quine privileges in his accounts, Code points out that we get a very different picture from the social sciences that study "cognition in the wild,"[9] rather than in the laboratory. Thus, the question of whether the account of childhood learning that Bruner offers has empirical support, the question I introduced at the beginning of this section, depends, to a certain extent, on the relative weight we are willing to give to the results of different methodologies for studying childhood cognitive development.

Even within the laboratory sciences, child-development studies make the picture of our epistemic lives and our epistemic trajectories more complicated than Quine's model would lead us to think it is. Infants' reactions to stimuli change rapidly over just a few short months as a result, for instance, of the development of sensorimotor abilities and shifting state organization (Vasta 1982, 19). The idea that the model of the human knower that is most "naturalistic" or "scientific" is the model of the human knower who takes in stimuli and turns it into theory is only supported if one focuses on a very narrow range of laboratory sciences, and even then it is not clear how much support it gets.

Infancy is a time of dramatic and rapid changes: changes in large and small motor skills, in memory, and in social skills. Studies of early childhood language acquisition show that many different abilities go into word learning. As Sandra Waxman puts it, word learning, even if we confine it to simple labeling, requires that a child solve a three-part puzzle. When an adult says, "Look at the dog," the infant must: (1) identify the relevant word from the ongoing stream of speech; (2) identify the relevant entity in the ongoing stream of activity in the world; and (3) establish a word-world correspondence (2002, 106). In order to solve these puzzles, children must be able to use morphologic, phonetic, and prosodic cues to distinguish the beginnings and endings of words and phrases and the functional grammar of particular words (e.g., noun, preposition). They must also, as I mentioned earlier, be able to read the adult as having the intention of labeling something; by ten months of age, they have developed this ability, which allows them to share the speaker's "line of regard" and engage in "joint attention" (106–7).

We are, then, presented with the following question: if any story that does justice to childhood language learning and development must be fairly complicated, why do Quine, Rorty, and Kuhn make it sound so simple? Rorty may be excused from setting out a simplistic story of learning as a process of "reprogramming," since he does not claim to be drawing on scientific studies to support this model, and his naturalism is just a rejection of supernaturalism. It does not extend to thinking that the empirical sciences have a better account of human beings than do poets or playwrights. Quine, on the other hand, has insisted that the empirical sciences give us our best examples of human knowledge, and he is eager to both recapture something like observation statements and redefine epistemology by appealing to psychology. Yet the empirical account he offers does not really seem to draw on empirical psychology, but only on a caricature of the human subject of psychological study. Kuhn, who cites the results of empirical studies in his accounts of paradigm formation and maintenance, does not do so in his account of early childhood categorization, but rather tells his audience that his account is supported by the fact that he has almost succeeded in programming a computer to perform this operation. What would make Kuhn's near-success in this effort seem like evidential support for the claim that human beings learn to shift their categorizations by having their "neural program" reconfigured? I think there's a hint of scientism here.

There are models of the human mind as computer that are used for particular kinds of problem solving in cognitive science. But what we have in the philosophical appropriations of the computational model by anti-foundationalists is the slide from the uncontroversial claim that "a computer model of cognition is useful for explaining some aspects of human cognition" to a fairly tendentious claim that "all aspects of human cognition can be explained by a computer model." From there, we move to the ontological assumption that (or, in Rorty's case, to the advocacy of a metaphor in which) human minds/brains just are computers, and that computation is at the heart of experience.

Given his antipathy to scientism and ontology, Rorty's assumption of this computational model requires special attention. Rorty merely suggests that we adopt this metaphor; he does not argue that the mind is a computational device. He seems to think that this metaphor is apt, however, because (1) it is not the metaphor of mind as mirror; (2) it is consistent with his claim that the only kind of information about the world that human beings get from the world is "the kind available to a computer";

and (3) it captures in material form the idea of the self as the self-reweaving web of beliefs and desires, which is, he says, to "see the self from outside" (Rorty 1991a, 93), that is, not to see it from the first-person perspective. Abandoning the first-person perspective on the self, where the idea of the privacy of the mental might be harbored, and with it the idea of the mind as mirror, is an essential aspect of the redefinition of mind, belief, and experience that Rorty is trying to carry out.

Rorty's advocacy of the metaphor of mind as computer is meant to highlight the extent to which experience, unlike discourse, is unimportant in our discussions of human understanding. "Experience" is a term that is still linked, Rorty thinks, to the Cartesian project, and the lessons we get from Wittgenstein about mind and language should lead us to abandon it. Experience is an aspect of sentience: it is that which we share with nonhuman animals and computers. Only sapience is really important when it comes to beliefs (which are inferentially related to other beliefs), thus only discourse is really important for understanding how we come to hold, and come to change, our beliefs. Rorty's advocacy of this new metaphor of the mind and the self is based on his idea that we need a new and different self-understanding, a new way to think about mind and language. The idea that experience is analogous to the input a computer receives is his attempt to move us beyond the Cartesian problems of epistemology, to get us to give up the idea of the eye of the mind that surveys private mental representations. And this requires that we give up the usual ways of understanding the connection between intentional behavior and the subjective perspective.

Action, Embodiedness, and Intention

Rorty introduces into his metaphor of the mind as a web of belief the suggestion that beliefs should be understood as "habits of action" that result in "movements in the organism's muscles—movements which kick the organism itself into action. These actions, by shoving items in the environment around, produce new beliefs to be woven in, which in turn produce new actions, and so on for as long as the organism survives" (Rorty 1991a, 93). With this modification, he introduces a form of embodiment into the story, although, as we will see, it is a rather odd form of embodiment. But he also, with the same move, reconnects his story to the pragmatists, and distances it from mentalistic language. Beliefs are "habits of action"—they translate into bodily movements, Rorty says, so they are not to be understood as items in a mind, hidden from view—they are connected to action.

Rorty moves from talking about how this self-reweaving mechanism produces movements in the organism's muscles to equating these movements with actions. Traditionally, however, philosophers have distinguished between "movements of muscles" and "actions." They might deny that the latter exist, but the distinction is usually recognized as reflecting a distinction between, for instance, reflexes, which are just unmotivated muscle movements, and actions, which we undertake for reasons. Rorty's strong commitment to the distinction between reasons and causes, which he gets from Sellars and Davidson (and which seems to be one of the few straightforwardly philosophical distinctions about which Rorty is not skeptical) means that he is not entitled to move so blithely from bodily movements to habits of action. Actions and movements are different things, and the idea of actions (rather than mere "movements" or "behaviors") is tied to the narrative and discursive function that Rorty thinks is central to an account of inquiry and justification as distinctively human activities.

Why does Rorty insist on telling a story about human action that sounds like the account of a robot in motion: robotic imagery of muscle movements that "kick the organism into action," resulting in items in the environment being shoved around? I think that Rorty's attempt to capture actions by discussing motions and behavior is connected to the "flight from the intentional," and with it the flight from the first-person perspective that I illustrated in the preceding section. Recall that the distrust of intentional terminology, and of first-person perspectives that constitute attributions of agency, is a distrust that Bruner argues characterizes both behaviorism and computationalism. Bruner's criticism of the shift to an information-processing model is that it gets something essentially wrong: meaning making is an activity, while information processing is a passive process. Rorty, of course, agrees that meaning making is not passive, and thinks that the foundationalist empiricist is wrong because she makes of it a passive process—the foundationalist invokes a "spectator theory of knowledge." Foundationalism is based on a representationalist model of mind, which is itself based on the assumption of an inner "I" that surveys these representations. But this concern about the passive nature of foundationalist theories of minds is what leads Rorty to argue that pragmatists should give up the term "experience," since he takes it to be a relic of that spectator theory.

Rorty's equation of experience with passive information processing is made possible, however, by the account of embodiment and activity that Rorty assumes. If an account of bodily activity is told only from the outside, then it is easy to see why bodily motion could be explained in robotic terms. From the first-person perspective on bodily activity, we get agency, but from an exclusively "outsider" perspective (the perspective that Rorty takes up in characterizing bodily movement in the robotic terms he uses above), we get only movement.

Thus, when Rorty describes the external perspective that gives us the self as nothing more than the self-reweaving web of beliefs, he is endorsing this outsider perspective as an antidote to the ruthlessly first-person perspective that enlivens the metaphor of the mind as mirror and the related metaphor of the mind's eye that inspects the images reflected in that mirror. But in his attempt to escape this model of the mind, Rorty has cut himself off from the concepts of agency and activity that would allow him to distinguish between habits of action and movements. By abandoning the model of mind as mirror for the model of a web of belief that is essentially a formal computer process, he has replaced one version of passivity with another and cut himself off from Dewey and James in the bargain. Agency and activity were core concepts for the early pragmatists—and, as I will show, are integral to redefining experience in a way that does not reduce it to stimuli that must "jump the gap" between sentience and sapience to become discourse. The image of childhood language learning that we get in Quine, Kuhn, and Rorty testifies to a difficulty in overcoming a dualism that animates their discussions of experience and perception: a dualism of the natural and the social. The dualism shows itself in the way in which the human body is understood in these accounts as simply a conduit for sensory information, an entirely passive, mechanistic, and biological thing, rather than being understood as a "lived body."

My discussion of the stories we get about language learning from Kuhn, Quine, and Rorty is meant to provide a window on the problem of naturalism-cum-scientism and to raise the issue of how best to understand the human subjects and their cognitive projects that I take to be the concern of epistemology. The assumptions about how children learn language that Kuhn and Quine invoke expose the assumptions about the nature of human learning that give rise to the bifurcation of experience into discourse and stimuli. Rorty's elaboration of these assumptions shows us that scientism can infect accounts of human beings offered by even one of scientism's most ardent enemies, and shows us that the body remains a sort of theoretical blind spot both for philosophers who reduce experience to stimuli and for those who eliminate it in favor of discourse. In the next chapter, I discuss the ways in which theories of the body, and feminist discussions of experience and epistemology that draw on those theories, show us different ways of understanding the embodiedness of the subjects of experience. Significant debates about agency arise yet again here.

CHAPTER 4

Feminist Discussions of Experience

IDENTITY, NATURALISMS, AND
DISCOURSE

Feminist theorists who have taken on the challenge of thinking about epistemological problems and their proposed solutions have generally assumed that philosophers and other theorists ignore issues of identity at their peril. Indeed, in some instances, ignorance about the epistemic aspects of identity has been characterized as the foundational condition for Enlightenment concepts of the knowing subject.[1] However, the concept of identity and categories of identity have themselves been subject to feminist critique. Feminist discussions of experience have been caught in this dilemma: how do we talk about identities and experience without assuming a naïve theory of identity that "essentializes" it, where to treat identity categories as "essences" is to treat them as natural kinds that are ahistorical and culturally invariable?[2]

The discussion about experience in feminist theory has been connected to this dilemma about identity because feminist theorists have also tried to use the idea of experience as a tool for exposing systematic bias, silencing techniques, and more generally problems grounded in epistemic inequality, whether that is manifested in the tendency to dismiss women's disgruntlement with aspects of their lives as an effect of premenstrual syndrome or menopause or in the attempts to discredit women's testimony about their lives or what has happened to them as crazy talk. The idea that women's experience—and the experiences of people who are relegated to other marginalized categories—could provide a view into the workings of political structures requires that there be some connection between those identity categories, the nature of those political structures, and the testimony offered in an attempt to make that nature known. For this to work, experience must be in some measure independent of ideological construction, while also being sensitive to, or affected by, ideology and political structures—a difficult balancing act.

Let me begin with some history, to show how the issue of identity arose as an important component of feminist critiques of epistemology proper and epistemological projects more generally. This field is vast, and I have had to make some choices about which theorists to focus on. My choices are mostly an effect of the narrative arc I am pursuing: the idea that the concept of experience went from being an essential component of what we call "Second Wave" feminist theory to being dismissed by theorists writing in the late twentieth century about identity categories. In later chapters, I take up more contemporary feminist discussions of identity and experience.

Another qualifier: The feminist positions I address in this chapter should not be taken to be a comprehensive history of accounts of experience. Furthermore, the group of feminists I've chosen to focus on is admittedly a "family resemblance" category—what connects Joan Scott, Donna Haraway, and Lorraine Code is not really a program in feminist epistemology as much as it is an engagement with the problems of identity and knowledge, and I think that focusing on them allows us to see the broad outlines of how the subject of experience comes to be problematized as a result of this theoretical skirmish.

Feminist Interventions in Epistemology: The Case for the Salience of Identity

In her 1991 book *What Can She Know? Feminist Theory and the Construction of Knowledge*, Lorraine Code asks a question the answer to which is of central concern to theorists concerned with identity and its epistemological subtexts: is the sex of the knower epistemologically significant? The idea that such a difference could have epistemological, and not just sociological, salience was, at the time the book came out, something akin to philosophical heresy in traditional philosophy departments. As one of my professors in graduate school said in the early 1990s: "Feminist epistemology would only make sense if it turns out that women do not reason according to modus ponens, or some other rule of logical inference." Susan Haack published an article as late as 1993 in which she argued that feminist epistemology could be understood as a viable approach only on the assumption that women have special ways of knowing.[3]

What both of these responses point to is the entrenched assumption that, in fact, identity categories are not epistemically relevant, unless one adopts the politically regressive view that women reason differently: that they do not use the logical rules that all rational beings use, or that they have some form of special "women's intuition" that either allows them to bypass the normal routes to knowledge or exempts them from the expectations we usually place on reasoning. Unless women's reasoning were different from men's, the very idea of feminist epistemology seemed to be incoherent. Such was the resistance to a story about the relevance of identity categories to knowledge claims—and the presumed model of a story that could support the idea of the relevance of identity categories— that operated in philosophy departments when Code wrote her book. The sentiment expressed by my graduate professor, and argued for in Haack's essay, was not hard to find in 1993.

Code's project—to raise the question of the extent to which the subject of traditional epistemological projects should be thought of as a fungible, abstract entity—was a challenge to the fundamental assumptions of epistemology in the Anglo-American tradition. The fungible and abstract subject of knowledge—represented by S in what Code terms "S-knows-that-p" epistemologies (Code 1993, 15)—was an essential component in the formulation of the problem of sensory experience and its relationship to knowledge, which for many philosophers was the synecdoche for all knowledge. The idea that knowledge is best represented by our empirical beliefs (e.g., that there is a computer screen in front of me, that there is a cat sitting on the floor beside me) gives a particular shape to the project of epistemology, because it assumes that the areas of knowledge that have least to do with the particularity of subjects are in fact our best models of knowledge. Traditional epistemology in the Anglo-American tradition took its charge to be the delineation of necessary and sufficient conditions for knowledge claims, assuming that in this project, the question was simply the question of how and when any subject (S) could be said to know a particular proposition p. The assumption behind this model of epistemological inquiry was that any subject should be able to stand in for S—that questions about race, gender, sex, and so forth, were irrelevant to epistemology properly so called.

Code argues that, while delineation of necessary and sufficient conditions for knowledge claims that could insulate those claims from skeptical challenges would indeed be a major breakthrough, it seems likely that only very trivial or thin claims would ever achieve such a status. Traditional epistemological projects, aimed at necessary and sufficient conditions for knowledge, might well succeed by those standards, only to be left holding a booby prize. Signaling that the shift to a more complicated account of subjects of knowledge would lead to a different approach to epistemology, Code says, "once one seriously entertains the hypothesis that knowledge is a construct produced by cognitive agents within social practices and acknowledges the variability of agents and practices across social groups, the possible scope even of 'definitive' justificatory strategies for S-knows-that-p claims . . . could conceivably be discovered only for a narrow range of artificially isolated and purified empirical knowledge claims, which are paradigmatic by fiat but are unlikely to be so 'in fact'" (1993, 15). While the traditional epistemological project might succeed in virtue of its narrow focus on thin empirical claims, it's not clear that these are the kinds of knowledge claims that people actually care about. More important, in my view, however, is the fact that Code tells us very clearly and explicitly that the story about subjects—what they are, what their lives are like—is essential to defining the epistemological project that she thinks worth undertaking. This is actually an orientation she shares with Quinean naturalists, but whereas for Quinean naturalism, the subject is to be understood simply as a primate, for Code, the subject is to be understood as enmeshed in a larger context of social and political life, in which epistemic concerns are a part. Thus, Code's argument makes salient the ways in which our conception of the subject of knowledge is relevant to the conception of epistemology—its goals, its methodologies, and its paradigms of knowledge.

Compare, for instance, Quine's framing of the problem of epistemology (how does a primate, with just the information provided by his sensory receptors, get from the thin input of stimuli to the torrential output of scientific theory) to Code's. In Code's account, we have cognitive agents who carry out their epistemic tasks in social groups and are embedded in social practices. The project of making sense of the world, and of themselves, is carried out in a dialogue between individuals and within groups of people who are sometimes like-minded but who also disagree. Their epistemic tasks are not best characterized as the process of linking up stimuli and theory, and the resources available to them are not limited to the resources inside their heads, those provided by their sensory organs, or to the resources provided by a language that they have been taught and left with. Here we have another aspect of feminist approaches to epistemology: the critical attitude toward the assumptions of individualism that underpin traditional epistemological projects.

In addition, Code's account specifically invokes the idea of cognitive agents, which, while not excluding Quine's recognition of our primate nature, includes more than that nature. One of the major problems with Quinean versions of naturalized epistemology, according to Code, is that advocates of this model too often take on Quine's assumption that our epistemic tasks are essentially information-processing tasks. Cognitive agents have both more resources at hand for pursuing their epistemic goals and larger issues to deal with than just how they get from the sensory input they receive to theoretical physics. They are also responsive to, and critical of, norms that govern their epistemic lives and their political lives.

Code's argument for the importance of a properly naturalistic account of knowing subjects and their epistemic practices also pointed toward the importance of theoretical accounts of subjects and their social and historical horizons. Thus, the project of revitalizing epistemology was also linked to discussions in the disciplines in which theories of identity and identity construction are worked out. This included not only the social sciences and cultural studies, but also literary approaches. While the former could draw on empirical data, the latter could draw on the analysis of narrative, a way of making sense not confined to texts. The appropriate background for the naturalistically minded epistemologist was not limited to neuroscience, then, but could draw on sociology, history, anthropology, and literary theory to try to make sense of the full range of human epistemic endeavors, as well as the changes in and challenges to identity constructions in different cultures or different traditions. For the feminist critique of epistemology, identity—including, but not limited to, gender identity and racial identity—is an important axis of analysis in the repertoire of the naturalistically minded epistemologist.

But although they embraced identity (and, for some, the alignment of characteristic types of experiences with those identity categories), many feminist theorists were also leery of mainstream empiricism and of epistemological individualism, meaning that the concept of experience had to be disentangled from its moorings in those methodologies.[4] But skepticism about whether experience, even if redefined or critically evaluated, could serve the purposes of feminist theory persisted.

Joan Scott concludes her essay "The Evidence of Experience" by saying: "Experience is not a word we can do without, although, given its usage to essentialize identity and reify the subject, it is tempting to abandon it altogether. But experience is so much a part of everyday language, so imbricated in our narratives that it seems futile to argue for its expulsion" (Scott 1991, 797). Given that she cannot, by fiat, expel the term, and that it serves a variety of purposes in everyday modes of discourse, Scott argues that historians and others interested in the lives of marginalized groups should aim rather at redefinition and interrogation.

The term "experience" is implicated in essentialism about identity and in the process of reifying subjects, Scott claims, because its use in discussions of identity politics, and its invocation as the quarry sought by historians trying to recreate and recapture the past, is premised on the idea that there are subjects that exist independently of discourse and whose identities and experiences are "natural" (or given), rather than constructed. Behind the concept of experience lurks a particular theory of subjects of experience that Scott believes is itself responsible for the kinds of marginalization that historians seek to document. In other words, the idea of subjects who have gender (or class, race, or sexuality)-specific experiences assumes that subjects have such experiences because they are members of a particular identity category, and this assumption leaves in place the assumption that the categories themselves are immune to interrogation and criticism; that they are ahistorical categories that can be picked up and moved from culture to culture, time period to time period. The attempt to delineate and describe women's experience, or gay male experience, assumes that who counts as a woman, or as a gay man, and, by the same token, who does not, is settled—that is, these categories are "natural,"[5] rather than socially negotiated and discursively constructed.[6] The subject of experience is thus "reified:" identity categories are treated as entities like rocks or stars, rather than as the products of social construction. This reinforces the idea that there is something that is essential to, and that links, those who are grouped under the same category. In philosopher's terms, Scott is arguing that identity categories are treated as natural kind terms, their proper referents discovered, their essences defining their rightful membership in particular identity categories. According to Scott, the term "experience" is tied to both a troublesome epistemological tradition and a troublesome theory of the subject.

Compare Scott's reluctant inclusion of the term "experience" in feminist political theory to the following invocation of experience from Patricia Hill Collins:

Black women's work and family experiences and grounding in traditional African-American culture suggest that African-American women as a group experience a world different from that of those who are not Black and female. Moreover, these concrete experiences can stimulate a distinctive Black feminist consciousness concerning that material reality. (Collins in Nicholson 1997, 246).

Or this from Catherine MacKinnon:

What is it about women's experience that produces a distinctive perspective on social reality? How is an angle of vision and an interpretive hermeneutics of social life created in the group, women? What happens to women to give them a particular interest in social arrangements, something to have a consciousness of? How are the qualities we know as male and female socially created and enforced on an everyday level? Sexual objectification of women—first in the world, then in the head, first in visual appropriation, then in forced sex, finally in sexual murder—provides answers. (MacKinnon in Nicholson 1997, 158)

In the accounts that Collins and MacKinnon offer, we find the premise that identities and experiences are tied together in ways that give particular subjects, with particular racial and gender identities, access to both objective conditions in the world (e.g., racial and gender stratification and oppression; the ubiquity of the sexual objectification of women) and classificatory schemes for the types of people who are subject to those conditions. In the case of the Collins quotation, the claim is even stronger: theorizing about these experiences can be the basis for political action and for a new way of understanding oneself and the world. The ground for this form of appeal to experience appears to be called into question by critiques like Scott's.

The idea that some identities give privileged access to certain kinds of knowledge in virtue of the experiences that unify or mark those identities is most clearly expressed in versions of standpoint epistemology, and the quotations from Collins and McKinnon incorporate some of the assumptions of standpoint theory. The idea that the identity category of "woman," for instance, can be understood as having some "unifying themes"—that living in a society that is organized by gender and sexual hierarchies means that those who are marked as members of a particular gender or sex category will have common experiences—is part of the theoretical background for MacKinnon's political analysis. Collins argues that in virtue of membership in the categories of "Black" and "woman," Black women live in a different world than do people who are not both Black and women. We might think that this claim is hyperbolic: do Black women really live in a different world than do white men, we might ask? Yet Collins thinks that the hyperbole is warranted—that material conditions of work and life, mediated by culture, do in fact give rise to different "worlds" because the world and its cultural expression are continuous. According to Collins and like-minded theorists, identity categories give rise to characteristic or stereotypical life paths or pursuits, and since one's identity is partly an effect of how others treat one, the idea of identity categories giving rise to different worlds is part of what it is to live as particular, embodied human subjects.

In the approaches to feminist theory that we find in Collins and MacKinnon and in allied approaches, the concept of experience is an essential theoretical pole, and this concept of experience is used both to articulate identity categories and to motivate political and epistemological projects. As with the early American pragmatists, for these feminist theorists, the term has been useful, because it points both outward, to the world, and inward, to the subject—it is the point at which subjects and the world come together. And as with the American pragmatists, feminist theorists invoke experience as a way of connecting the everyday and prosaic elements of life with larger theoretical themes.

But just as it presents a challenge to the centrality of the concept of experience in nonfeminist philosophy of science and epistemology, the linguistic turn challenges the relevance of appeals to experience in feminist discussions of epistemology and identity. From the vantage point of discourse theorists, appeals to experience seem suspect at best, politically retrograde at worst. This development has been a challenge to the very viability of feminist epistemology in important ways.

Feminist discussions of epistemology and experience have generally been concerned with showing how the conception of the subject of knowledge that is assumed in traditional epistemologies is too abstract. An analysis of the subject for whom knowledge is claimed—as well as the relevance of social and political structures that give rise to identity categories—is a central focus of the feminist critique of traditional epistemology. Advancing this project requires that these identity categories be treated as "real," but the extent to which gender categories are interwoven with biological categories, combined with feminist suspicions about the natural/ social distinction, presents a challenge to so treating them. While feminist epistemologists are critical of the extent to which the universal subject of epistemology is assumed to be neutral and fungible, and to the extent that such fungibility is at least partly an effect of the ways in which that subject is taken to be independent of its body, feminist discussions lean toward taking embodiment seriously, in a nod to naturalistic approaches. But feminist theorists, unlike philosophers like Quine and Kuhn, have been suspicious of attempts to appeal to "the natural," so naturalism is, to some extent, seen as a repository of ideology about bodiliness, reinforcing the idea that bodies and their qualities are analogous to brute nature: that which is what it is regardless of what we believe about it. Naturalism is not without its risks, then, because of its neighborly relations with crude forms of biological determinism and with a strong distinction between nature and culture. To the extent that feminists understand bodiliness to be a minefield for women, feminists resist reductive approaches to bodies. So feminist theories that take identity to be relevant to epistemological issues walk a fine line between taking bodies and identity to be important axes of analysis, and thus treating them as real, and challenging the ways in which the reality of those categories has been used and interpreted as evidence for claims about the unchanging "essence" of womanhood or race. So feminist epistemologists have tried to emphasize the extent to which identity is connected to the body, but cannot be reduced to the body. And insofar as identities and experience go together, they, too, share this uneasy relationship with naturalistic approaches. So the concept of experience, as a concept that is tied to realism, to identity categories, to the attempts to critique and subvert ideology, and to a theory of the subject, has had its highs and lows as each of these issues was critiqued or embraced, and its place in feminist discourse continues to be contested.

In the previous chapter, I have argued that the way that anti-foundationalists like Kuhn, Quine, and Rorty link language to experience is based on a troublesome understanding of the body. Those approaches see the body as a conduit for sensory information. Rorty assumes that the concept of experience is entirely captured by this bodily interception of noise from the world, in which these causal events give rise to discursive events. Hence, the concept of experience can and should be jettisoned. Quine draws an analogy between human bodiliness and the bodiliness of other animals, and focuses on the extent to which the body is a conduit, via the brain and sensory organs, for information. Kuhn, in attempting to give an empirically based account of how our experience of the world can be understood in terms of the gestalt switches that characterize paradigm shifts, draws the analogy between programming a computer to categorize things and teaching a child to categorize things. In the process of learning to categorize, Kuhn claims, human beings are programmed. Rorty, too, makes use of this metaphor. Bodies and brains are entirely natural entities, and on one side of the language learning process, we have a natural information processing chain (stimuli or nondiscursive causal events), while on the other side—the social side—we have meanings and language. The natural and the social are separate realms in these accounts.

Feminist understandings of bodies and bodiliness are more complicated than the accounts we find in Rorty, Quine, and Kuhn, since feminists see bodies as socio-natural entities—they are not just natural, since they are marked by social meanings, and are even regulated and literally shaped by those social meanings. Feminists try to navigate between the Charybdis of too much abstraction, in which bodies are irrelevant, and the Scylla of reductionism, in which the category of "woman" is understood to be a natural, biological category. Yet the debate about the role of appeals to experience in feminist discussions of identity and knowledge presents this dilemma: does navigating between these require that we give up the term "experience"? And is "experience" too tied to a version of empiricism to be a viable axis of feminist discussions of identity?

Joan Scott's Critique of Experience: The Linguistic Turn and Anti-foundationalism in Feminist Theory

The argument that Scott presents, in a variety of related essays,[7] is complicated, and some of the arguments are aimed specifically at particular debates among historians about historiography. Leaving the particulars of those debates aside, I want to focus on the larger epistemological issues that Scott's critique raises for feminist theorizing, and on the issues about the nature of subjects of experience that arise from this strand of theorizing.

Scott's critique can be usefully understood as drawing on some of the theoretical resources of the linguistic turn, as well as on critiques of foundationalism. For instance, in her criticisms of the tendency of historians (and, by extension, feminist theorists of identity) to treat experience as raw data for historical or interpretive narratives, she invokes the claim, common to anti-foundationalists, that experience does not give us unmediated access to the world, and that any putative piece of evidence counts as such only against the background of a going narrative or theory. Similarly, she argues, as do linguistic-turn theorists like Rorty, that experience is not prior to language. It is not waiting outside language as the original data that then gets expressed through language. As we learn from Rorty's analysis, experience happens on one side of a natural/social divide, and has only causal, rather than meaningful, connections to language. Rather, the experience that is the putative referent or prompt of such narratives is in fact "produced" by such narratives, since the experience that makes it into discourse is already inside discourse; there is no "outside" discourse, according to this analysis. Experience is itself constructed by the discursive resources available at the time, and it has no essential nature independent of its capture by those discourses.

Furthermore, like Rorty, Scott argues that the assumption that there is something like "women's experience" is itself a function of dominant discourses of exclusion and discursive practices that mark differences that are then reproduced through such narratives. The coherence of the concept of "women's experience" depends on a practice in which some narratives count as authentic and others as inauthentic. The regulation of the borders of authentic women's experience requires the exclusion of competing accounts of the nature of women's experience through charges of inauthenticity, delusion, or false consciousness, thus reinforcing an account of what it is to be a woman—to belong properly to that category—that assumes that the category is not contested.[8] The commonality of the experiences of members of the group is created by these narrative strategies, rather than existing prior to those narratives.[9]

In his discussion of this debate in the field of history (2005), Martin Jay points out that appeals to experience in historical narratives seem to support two seemingly inconsistent approaches to experience: the first is a view of experience in which past experiences can be detached from their historical contexts and subjects and relived in the present by the appropriately trained historian; the second is a view that leads to a balkanization of history, in which women are the best writers about women, African Americans are the best authorities to write about African American history, workers are the best writers about the working class, and so on. The first approach to experience assumes that there is some "transcendental subject" of experience (like the epistemological subject Code singles out as the replicable, abstract subject of "S-knows-that-p" epistemologies) who can faithfully reconstruct past experience in the present—a subject whose universality guarantees that such experiences are not left behind as a casualty of incommensurability. Although the second approach claims to reject the idea of the universal transcendental subject who could transmit the experience of the past to the present faithfully, Jay argues, it actually draws on that concept of the subject in a new guise. While there is no universal (and abstract) subject in this latter account, women historians, in virtue of being women, have privileged access to the experience of women in the past; the category of "woman" playing the role that the abstract subject plays in the first, universalist, approach (Jay 2005, 253).

Scott's argument, then, can be read as an extended discussion, not just of epistemology, but also of the concept of the subject. Carrying Scott's argument a bit further than she has, we can put the issue this way:

appeals to experience seem to carry with them, like a shadow, the idea of the transcendental subject. And this very subject—taken to be an entity that exists "naturally" or as a given, and whose experiences are its possessions or events that happen to it—is the subject that feminist theory has been trying, in its discussions of identity, to exorcise. But the assumption of identity categories, and their use in discussions of experience, reintroduces precisely this concept of the subject that feminist theorists were trying to purge.

The critique that Scott levels at appeals to experience in cultural studies and the field of women's history emphasizes the extent to which the identities of the subjects of putative experience are not prior to their epistemological projects. Rather, the experiences they use as evidence for these projects are themselves at stake in, and constructed by, those very projects. This is the force of the claim that subjects are "constituted through discourse" and that experiences are produced by discourse (Scott 1991, 779); identities do not precede the accounts of experiences and the epistemological and political projects that draw on them and attempt to represent them. Rather, the processes of authorization, which involve the negotiation of claims of authenticity and veridicality, are the processes by which such identities are constituted, rather than represented. Furthermore, this story about subjects means that their first-person accounts are not necessarily reliable accounts of what is really happening—these accounts cannot be accepted at face value, but themselves call for interrogation.[10]

Scott's argument shares many affinities with Rorty's critique of experience, as I've said. But she combines this critique with a Foucauldian analysis of the nature of the subject of experience and Foucault's critique of visibility, which he sees as another way in which people are controlled through disciplinary knowledge practices. Scott's conclusion is that feminist politics cannot do without experience, but she warns of the dangers inherent in naïve appeals to experience.

What kinds of appeals to experience does Scott have in mind here? The term "experience" is so ambiguous that we might reasonably wonder if she has in mind what other philosophically minded critics and advocates do in their discussions of the problem of experience. I think that she has in mind something that is very like the concept of experience that Rorty critiques, and that is, to some extent, the legacy of the marriage of anti-foundationalism and the linguistic turn. I think, furthermore, that Scott's embrace of the linguistic turn and suspicion about the concept of the subject, though having their provenance in different theoretical concerns and commitments, share with the Quine/Kuhn/Rorty model discussed in the previous chapter a distrust of the first-person perspective and the intentional vocabulary licensed by that perspective. Detached from the first-person perspective of an agent/subject, experience becomes only "experience."

Scott begins her essay with an analysis of Samuel Delany's narrative of his political epiphany in a gay bathhouse in 1963. This narrative motivates her discussion of appeals to experience. In this narrative, Delany identifies his experience as central to the process of coming to understand himself, not just as a gay man, but as part of a potentially powerful political movement. And Delany tells us that he is committed to writing about his experience in the bathhouse in order to break the public silence about sexual practices that has kept the institutions, and potentially massed power, of male homosexuality invisible. In Scott's words, "[t]he point of Delany's description, indeed of his entire [autobiographical account] is to document the existence of those institutions in all their variety and multiplicity, to write about and thus to render historical what has hitherto been hidden from history" (Scott 1992, 23). Scott's gloss of Delany's project, which is subsequently the target of her critique, is that it depends on the assumption that "knowledge is gained through vision; vision is a direct, unmediated apprehension of a world of transparent objects. In this conceptualization of it, the visible is privileged; writing is then put at its service. Seeing is the origin of knowing. Writing is reproduction, transmission—the communication of knowledge gained through (visual, visceral) experience" (23–24).

Rorty and Scott, like Code, share a distrust of the philosophical tendency to understand experience as modeled on visual perception, a tendency that Rorty attributes to a model of mind in which the mind is understood as a mirror that reflects (or fails to reflect) accurately the objects outside of it.

To understand Scott's critique better, a detour into Rorty's discussion of feminism and philosophical argument is helpful. Rorty sounds themes similar to Scott's in his critique of the use of experience by Dewey and in his discussion of feminist appeals to experience. In both, Rorty's attempts to replace the term "experience" with "discourse" go back to his fundamental distrust of language that seems to rely on a realist commitment to objectivity. In his discussion of feminist politics and epistemology, Rorty urges feminists to give up on overt and covert appeals to "the facts" of women's oppression and to "the truth" of women's experience in favor of a prophetic voice that seeks to project a vision of the future, not to describe the world as it is. The key to bringing about social change, Rorty argues, is the narrative reframing of current practices and the projection of a vision of the future with which present practices compare unfavorably. Feminists need strong poets, prophets, and artists to bring about social change, not strong epistemologists and metaphysicians. And attempts to focus on what is true now, rather than what kinds of vision for the future we might enact, will not do the work needed (Rorty 1991b).

But discussions of experience are not only tied up with a discourse of realism and fact in feminist politics—they are also connected to discussions of identity, as I have argued. So, for instance, the grounding for a category of "woman" is not merely in biology or culture—the class of people we characterize as women are also said to share certain kinds of experiences that can be used to articulate a collective identity. But Rorty objects to this use of experience as well. Identities are forged, not found, and the grounds for the kind of solidarity of interests that animate feminist and other progressive social movements need not be common experiences.

Scott's critique of appeals to experience in historical narratives draws on the critique of occularcentrism and has many affinities with Rorty's attempt to replace "experience" with "discourse," but Scott is more worried than Rorty by the politics of appeals to experience. Scott does worry that the concept of experience that we find in discussions of identity—"women's experience," for instance, or "queer experience"—is saddled with the objectionable metaphysics and epistemology that Rorty singles out. But she worries, in addition, that appeals to experience "naturalize" (in her terms) difference and identities, treating them as unanalyzable givens, and treating experience as the evidence for the existence of these natural groupings of types of people: "History is a chronology that makes experience visible, but in which categories appear as nonetheless ahistorical: desire, homosexuality, heterosexuality, femininity, masculinity, sex and even sexual practices become so many fixed entities being played out over time, but not themselves historicized" (Scott 1991, 778). Thus, historical narrative is at odds with the project of critically evaluating these categories, since the narratives depend on treating the categories as given, and on not critically evaluating them.

This approach to historical evidence further ignores the fact that experiences only count as evidence with respect to a particular narrative, according to Scott. Experience does not carry its evidential status on its sleeve, but can only count for (or against) a going narrative. Scott offers this analysis of the interplay of experience and theory (or narrative) as an alternative to what she sees as an objectionable turn toward foundationalism in history, exemplified by the treatment of experience as an unanalyzable given to which historical accounts must be accountable. According to Scott, historians have replaced appeals to "brute fact" or "simple reality"—terms put off limits by a rejection of foundationalism and naïve empiricism— with appeals to experience. But as with appeals to "brute fact" or "simple reality," Scott argues, appeals to "experience" function to block poststructuralist moves toward greater interpretive license (Scott 1991, 780). In this disguised return to foundationalist methods, experience is the evidence to which all interpretations must be accountable, and it serves as the bedrock upon which interpretations are constructed. It thus serves as the "foundation" that, like unmediated sense perceptions in foundationalist and positivist empiricism, can constitute the uninterpreted or unmediated "given." Thus Scott's argument aims to highlight the way that the logical structure of historical explanation (with its appeals to experience) mimics the logical structure of foundationalist empiricism. Like Rorty, Scott is committed to a version of anti-foundationalism in which the lines between experience and theory dissolve. And though Rorty will happily pitch the concept of "experience" into the theoretical dustbin because of its baggage of realism and the model of the mind as mirror, Scott claims that we cannot just do this. But her reason for claiming that we cannot just discard the term "experience" seems to be the uselessness of such a gesture: "people will continue to use the term," Scott implies. This is a surrender, not a justification.

Situated Knowledge: Visibility, Occularism, and Experience

Although she does not explicitly address the issue of the evidential status of experience, Donna Haraway's discussion of the need for a new approach to the problem of objectivity touches on themes related to Scott's concerns. Whereas Scott warns against using the metaphor of vision and visibility, however, Haraway thinks that this need not imply a transparent apprehension of the real, or invoke the image of a passive spectator. In fact, Haraway argues, we can, and should, develop an account of embodied vision that can underwrite an alternative account of objectivity. We can use the metaphor of vision to understand objectivity as something other than a view from nowhere, she argues.

Haraway sees the objectivity debates in science studies and feminist theory as based on a false dichotomy between what she calls the "god trick"—seeing everything, but being nowhere—and a relativist stance that treats all knowledge claims as equally "constructed" and on a par with one another. Both are unacceptable, Haraway argues, and neither takes seriously the partiality of perspective that is constitutive of seeing.

The "god trick" is "a leap out of the marked body into a conquering gaze from nowhere" (Haraway 1988, 581), the attempt to see everything from nowhere, as in the proverbial "view from nowhere" that is taken to be the hallmark of traditional conceptions of objectivity. However, vision is always from real eyes (whether organic or technological, Haraway reminds us), and since real vision must be embodied, it is always situated in space, and so always partial. But more than that, different kinds of eyes and different kinds of brains process visual information differently. The "view from nowhere" is thus at odds with itself—there cannot be anything like what we think of as a "view" that is not embodied, not "somewhere." And relativism—which Haraway characterizes as an attempt to occupy every place, to be everywhere at once, likewise severing vision from perspective—is equally untenable if we take the actual process of vision seriously. In each case, the knower is able to deny responsibility for what she has "learned to see."

Neither the relativist nor the viewer from nowhere need take responsibility for any particular knowledge claims about the world, the former because she has refused to commit to the truth or plausibility of such claims; the latter because her claims simply represent the way things are. Connecting knowledge to the exercise of power, Haraway argues that the metaphor of vision as a disembodied, disinterested, and passive apprehension of the way the world is has allowed people who claim to have a "god's eye view" to exercise power over others without being accountable for doing so, and has allowed relativists the freedom to abstain from action because no particular perspective can lay claim to their allegiance.

Scott's analysis and critique of experience and the project of documenting what she calls the "history of difference" invokes this dilemma as well. Although the project of making the experience of marginalized others visible through historical narrative has been successful, Scott argues, that success is due in large part to its use of traditional canons of historical research in which the experiences of women, people of color, gay men, and lesbians are treated as overlooked evidence, based on a "referential notion of evidence which denies that it is anything but a reflection of the real" (Scott 1991, 776). Appeals to experience both rely on a concept of experience as a foundation to which historical narratives must be accountable and invoke the passivity of visual experience as a privileged form of knowledge. The enshrinement of visual experience and related notions of the passivity of the subject of such experience as the paradigm of knowledge contribute to eliminating interpretive possibilities. The passivity of visual experience means that the theorist can evade taking responsibility for the analytical tools and frames she chooses to use to construct her narrative.

While Haraway recognizes that the metaphor of vision for the process of knowing has fallen into disrepute, she sees that metaphor as offering a promising prospect for understanding the situatedness of all knowing, if vision is properly understood. Haraway wants to reclaim the metaphor of vision for feminist purposes:

I would like to suggest how our insisting metaphorically on the particularity and embodiment of all vision (although not necessarily organic embodiment and including technological mediation), and not giving in to the tempting myths of vision as a route to disembodiment and second-birthing allows us to construct a usable [because it allows us to sort knowledge claims and projects], but not an innocent [because it is accountable for its particularity and situatedness], doctrine of objectivity . . .

. . . Feminist objectivity is about limited location and situated knowledge, not about transcendence and splitting of subject and object. It allows us to become answerable for what we learn how to see. (Haraway 1988, 582–83)

Haraway's discussion of how she came to think that the metaphor of vision could be redeemed is instructive. She writes that she came to this insight while walking with her dogs and wondering what the world looked like for creatures, like her dogs, whose eyes lack a fovea and have very few retinal cells for color vision, but who have huge neural processing and sensory areas for smells (583). The fovea is responsible for the level of detail in human vision, which allows us to read. It is also responsible for most of our ability to see colors. The part of the human brain committed to processing visual stimuli is largely committed to processing foveal vision—allowing us to see fine print, or small details—while the anatomy and processing of canine vision is most useful for hunting prey in low light. Dogs have less visual acuity but better night vision than humans as a result of the structure of their eyes. Thinking about the ways in which the anatomy and needs of her dogs affect the way they see the world leads Haraway to reject the assumption that vision is a passive, disembodied faculty that creates distance between the knowing subject and the object of knowledge:

the "eyes" made available in modern technological sciences shatter any idea of passive vision: these prosthetic devices show us that all eyes, including our own organic ones, are active perceptual systems, building on translations and specific ways of seeing, that is ways of life. There is no unmediated photograph or passive camera obscura in scientific accounts of bodies and machines; there are only highly specific visual possibilities, each with a wonderfully detailed, active, partial way of organizing worlds. (Haraway 1988, 583)

Haraway's point is that a more naturalistic approach to vision is the remedy for the tendency to think of vision as not perspectival. She also shows that vision can be used as a route into thinking of the ways in which vision exemplifies the mingling of the "natural" and the "artifactual." Thus, she argues that naturalism—real naturalism, not a mythologized version of scientific knowledge—is a friend to feminist projects. Understood appropriately, scientific knowledge need not constitute the other of feminist theory.

For Scott, the metaphor of knowledge as visibility involves us in a representationalist model of mind even if we reject the idea that vision is a passive faculty. While it may be true that embodied vision—the way we actually see things—involves "specific ways of seeing, that is ways of life," Scott nevertheless believes that our appeals to experience "naturalize" these ways of seeing (Haraway 1988, 583). For Scott, what is objectionable about this naturalizing move is that it makes the categories of difference seem to be ahistorical givens. Naturalizing identity categories makes it seem that they are just there to be observed, the way we see rocks and stars. Thus, to draw out Haraway's metaphor of ways of seeing as ways of life, the appeal to experience and to the identity categories of race, gender, sexuality, and so on, reifies our way of life. The ways of seeing that characterize that way of life are taken to be natural and given, rather than historically negotiated.

Both Haraway and Scott are taking aim at a conception of knowledge that allows the knower to excuse herself from the scene of knowledge. That is, both Haraway and Scott are critical of models of knowledge in which knowers are allowed to ignore responsibility for the organizing frames or narratives they choose to use, and for Scott, the representationalist model involved in the understanding of knowing as seeing is irredeemable if our goal is to understand the ways in which knowledge involves choices and, as a result, responsibility. Haraway thinks that an analysis of the real processes of vision are an appropriate antidote here, because such an analysis will make more salient the ways in which all knowing is embodied and, as a result, particular and perspectival. Scott, however, worries that any emphasis on the connection between bodies and experience is a way of trying to save something of experience from "the linguistic turn"—that is, to try to isolate a nondiscursive authenticity for "lived experience" in order to prevent it from being subsumed under language and discourse and to allow it to act as the foundation upon which to build an ahistorical category of "woman" (Scott 1991, 787).

It is hard to see how Haraway's attempt to reorient the metaphor of seeing can be a way of adequately addressing problems about responsibility. The appeal to a scientific understanding of visual processes and the embodied nature of visual experience and knowledge does not lead to an understanding of knowledge as something for which we are responsible, since the biological and anatomical aspects of vision are not something over which a knower would have control. Haraway's equation of ways of seeing with ways of life, and her emphasis on visual systems as active and interpretive, pushes the boundary between the nondiscursive, merely causal processes of vision and the discursive realm of interpretation and meaning. In this account, however, the boundary between that for which we have responsibility (what we have "learned to see") and that for which we are absolved of responsibility is moved backward, so that the knower is now responsible for the interpretive systems that make up the visual. But now it is not clear that there is anything for which the knower is not responsible, and this is particularly troublesome when it comes to the role that embodiment plays in Haraway's account. How are we to understand the analogy between "technological" eyes (the prosthetic devices that Haraway mentions) and our organic eyes that, according to Haraway, show us the extent to which vision is theoretically informed? While we can understand how artifacts like telescopes and microscopes are manufactured with theoretical considerations in mind, it is difficult to see how organic eyes, which are not artifacts, can be so understood.[11]

Perhaps, according to Haraway, my eyes are artifacts? How ought we to understand this suggestion? Who is to be regarded as the creator of these artifacts? I myself? My culture? The family that raised me? Do my eyes "encode" theory the way that computers are encoded? And if we do think that theories or narratives are the hardwiring or software of our vision (as Popper and Kuhn seem to say), it is difficult to see, again, how we can be said to be responsible for the theories, narratives, and frames we "choose" to use in our interpretations of the world, since such choice would seem to be merely a logical possibility, not a real possibility.

Haraway's metaphor of situatedness might invite the extension of the concept of physical positioning to the elaboration of a story about responsibility for what we see, but there are clearly limits to this. I might physically move to a different spot in a room to see the bird at my bird feeder better, for instance, but in what sense can I "move" metaphorically to be a better interpreter, or to "see" differently and better? Would such "movement" just amount to adopting the appropriately naturalized approach to epistemology that Code advocates—an approach that would emphasize the importance of theories of identity to an understanding of epistemic communities and epistemic practices? If so, then we are responsible, essentially, for good epistemic hygiene. However, if this is where we end up, then it is not clear how useful the metaphor of vision is for a discussion of knowledge. If it is, in fact, my eyes—technological and biological—that are interpreting systems, then the most I can do is move them around with me, not really change them substantively; and if my interpretive frame is analogous to my eyes, then it, too, might be "moved around," but it is not clear that this metaphor of bodily movement can capture the ways in which I should be held responsible for my interpretive choices in a way that preserves the normative force of that requirement.

This would appear to be the crux of Scott's worry about the ways in which appeals to experience "naturalize" categories and knowledge claims. If categories of identity are naturalized, they are treated ahistorically; if appeals to experience "naturalize" knowledge claims, they invoke the transparent access we are taken to have to the natural world via our sense perception, modeling historical knowledge on our knowledge of the natural world, ignoring the interpretive choices we make in constructing historical narratives, and the ways in which we choose to count some experiences as authentic and constitutive of identity categories.

I think that the attempt by feminists to use the idea of vision as theoretically informed to try to talk about the extent to which we learn to see race, gender, and so on, and the attempt to try to marry vision and responsibility in these accounts, is a dead end. This, though, has more to do with the models of vision and theoretical frameworks that most of these accounts assume, and it is a version of the story that we get from Kuhn.

Kuhn and the Camera

The Kuhnian analysis has provided feminist politics with a particular model of activism: a model in which recognizing the ways in which our experience of the world is shaped by our identities is an essential part of the political process. In a recent workshop I attended on teaching about race, class, and gender issues, the moderator emphasized the value of trying to get students to adopt a different "perspective" or "mind-set" that would allow them to see the ways in which privilege operates to structure their experience of the world. Helping students to recognize the effects of class, race, or gender privilege is a process that must begin with getting them to take up a different perspective, according to the moderator, which will allow them to have different experiences of the world. Quoting from the Scott (1991) essay on experience, the moderator reminded us that "experience is always political."

The claim that experience is always political is as close to a cornerstone of twentieth- and twenty-first-century feminist theory and politics as we are likely to come. Postmodernists, analytic feminists, pragmatist feminists, standpoint theorists, feminist phenomenologists—I think it is fair to say that none would object to the claim that experience is always political. But what does this claim amount to? To say that experience is always political is often taken to mean that we learn to see the world in certain kinds of ways that support certain kinds of political agendas, and that our experience of the world is an effect of the theories we already—consciously or unconsciously—accept. Such theories make us take notice of certain things and ignore others. According to this account of experience, our experiences of the world are interpretations of the world, not simply data we receive from "brute" reality, and are structured by—indeed, perhaps determined by—our "perspectives" on that world. These "perspectives" are themselves understood as the conceptual schemes that yield these interpretations of the world, which we often mistake for direct, unmediated apprehensions of reality. Perspectives are, in essence, theories that we learn, and that we mobilize in our attempts to know the world. They might also be called "worldviews." In this sense, the claim that experience is political amounts to a reiteration of the Kuhnian model of experience.[12] The problem with this model is that the ways in which theories, "frameworks," or "perspectives" are treated in these accounts encourage us to think of them as things we carry around in our head (or in our eyeballs), organizing schemes for the raw material we get from the world.

Let us look again, however, at Haraway's attempt to elide the distinction between organic vision and technologically enhanced vision. We can think of this move as inviting a different approach to the issue of realism. When we think about Haraway's story of her dogs' vision, we can see that we have a story of different forms of access to the world. Dogs' vision is framed by dog needs and goals, understood as being dictated by the characteristic goals of canine life. There is a bit of a stretch involved here, of course, since few of the dogs I know still need to hunt to eat—or if they hunt it is mostly for their dog food, or the sandwich that some careless family member left lying around. Nevertheless, thinking about the extent to which organic vision and technologically enhanced vision can be structured by purposes or goals can help us think about a different form of realism. The world encountered by me, a dog, and someone looking through a microscope is, in a trivial sense, one and the same world, but each form of vision presents different aspects of that world, and so the "worlds under a description" are different. They each emphasize different elements of the one world, while ignoring others. But note that we are now really thinking of vision as purpose-informed, not theory-informed. In her take on Haraway's cyborgian model of vision, Karen Barad (1999, 2007) argues that the goal of what she calls "agencies of observation" cannot be captured by representationalist models of mind. The goal of agencies of observation is to bring forth phenomena; the agencies of observation show us that the distinction between observer and observed is not a metaphysical given, since the observer brings about the phenomena to be observed by the use of apparatuses through her intervention. In any given scientific observational setting, the legitimate observation must be negotiated, as the observer considers how much of the phenomena observed is an effect of interference with the apparatus in use, or of misuse of the apparatus. Barad thus emphasizes that metaphors of vision, if they are appropriately naturalistic, actually show the extent to which the observer/observed line is negotiated, and that observation is tied up with agency. I will have more to say about this later; for now, let us turn to Scott's attempt to deal with the ways in which experience is political.

The Literary, the Representational, and the Question of Realism

The literary model of historical studies that Scott advocates is meant to be an alternative to the representationalism and realism that she thinks is tied up with claims based on experience. Scott's literary model, like Rorty's hermeneutic model, substitutes "discourse" for "experience" as the central concept, and replaces the goal of recovering the experiences of heretofore invisible others with the goal of analyzing the way in which different interpretations of personal experience and historical narratives come to take particular shapes. Scott implies that part of this goal will also be the abandonment of discourses of realism—analyses that claim to be correcting the historical record—in favor of a description of how one interpretation comes to displace other interpretations. The latter model does not require that we think of one interpretation as better than another, and allows us to avoid reifying categories of identity and treating experience as a bodily-based, private, and authentic "given" that is prior to discourse.

In this I think we see one of the major concerns that Scott and Rorty share: it is a distrust of anything that is even remotely related to "truth-talk," and the term 'experience' is tied up with truth-talk and realism through its claim to be a form of contact with the world—something that Rorty explicitly rejects as essential or even desirable in discussions of politics and identity. For Scott and Rorty, it is fair to say that the meanings associated with the term "experience"—its immediacy, its bridging of the subject/object divide, its connection to the world—are too troublesome, and the term itself should be kept at arms' length. And while Scott's position is, in the end, a reluctant acknowledgement of the necessity of using the term, it seems that she and Rorty will not go along with this quietly. Even if the meanings associated with "experience" are there to stay, Scott hopes that a new methodological approach might make the connections between experience and what she thinks are less attractive concepts (truth, contact with the world) more tenuous.

Haraway's goal of reclaiming the metaphor of vision in an attempt to articulate an ideal of objectivity is sensitive to the cautionary lesson that Scott wants to teach. Haraway, unlike Scott, is willing—eager, in fact—to hold on to the "contact with the world" constraint, but her attempt to elaborate an ideal of objectivity in which the knower is responsible for her knowledge and the choices she makes is not captured well by the appeal to eyes as interpretive systems; the "interpretation" that goes on at the level of the physiology of visual systems does not admit of the strong evaluation and attributions of responsibility that Haraway hopes will come out of this more naturalistic account of vision, even if we try to extend the metaphor by attending to body positioning as essential to perspective. The language of epistemic virtue does not felicitously map onto the metaphor of the bodily positioning and partial perspective that Haraway says constitute the actual body-based processes of vision. The voluntarism that would be required for us to think of knowers as responsible for their beliefs, and that would allow us to criticize or praise them on those grounds, cannot be incorporated into Haraway's new metaphor of partial perspective and body-based vision. What is missing here is an account of agency to which one can pin a concept of responsibility.

In contrast, Scott's emphasis on discourse and theoretical constructions removes from consideration the question of how our narratives can be said to be accountable, or responsive, to a world of events and occasions, and, indeed, undermines the motivation one might normally have to criticize accounts that play fast and loose with facts, one of the things for which we hold historians responsible. Without some conception of "fact," then, the distinction between history and fiction is a casualty. This outcome might seem either desirable or deplorable, however, depending on whether one thinks that there is any value to be had in any forms of realism—whether one takes the good faith effort to describe what happened truly as a worthy epistemic goal, which, even if not achieved, is enough to distinguish historical discourse from fictional discourses. And yet, if Rorty and Scott are right, this interest in "getting things right" is a step on the road to realism and representationalism. And if we agree with their evaluation of realism and representationalism, it is not a step we ought to want to take. Both Scott and Haraway emphasize the importance of responsible approaches to narrative construction and knowledge claims, and both want to emphasize that interpreters, historians, and other theorists have choices to make about the way in which they approach their topics, and the way they describe events, subjects, or occasions. Yet, as I have argued, the place of agency in these accounts is unclear. It is not clear that Scott is entitled to a concept of agency, and thus to a concept of responsibility, given her claims about the discursive construction of the subject of experience, and it is not clear that Haraway's metaphor of situated knowledge can make sense of the idea of choice. Scott rejects realism, while Haraway thinks that some form of it is legitimate, and even necessary.

Talk of experience is a way of denying that we have unlimited choices about how to describe the world, but it is also a way of invoking a form of responsibility: our responsibility to be true to the way the world is. That there is no single way the world is does not absolve us of the responsibility for trying to say truthfully how the world is. Our interpretive choices are constrained by the responsibility of truthfulness in our nonfictional narratives.

The move to abandon the term "experience," and the connections it has with the world, is also a move toward eliding the distinction between knowledge we get from inference and knowledge that we get from experience. And while some philosophers might agree with Rorty that this distinction does not matter very much, this seems to me to miss the point, for while we might grant the critic of experience the claim that the justificatory status of a belief is not importantly affected by whether the belief is one we arrive at through experience rather than by means of inference, nevertheless, the durability of a belief and its relative resistance to revision might be better accounted for in terms of this distinction. We might say that beliefs that we arrive at on the basis of experience are (contrary to what Quine says) more durable than those we have arrived at via a process of inference.

It is this very durability that Scott seems to object to: appeals to experience in justifications seem to imply that the claim in question has a certain sort of authority. Whether particular claims ought to be granted that authority, however, is debatable. For instance, if I tell you that I know from experience that a particular student is going to be trouble, or that the resolution being discussed at the faculty meeting will probably not go anywhere, or that I know from experience that there are sometimes huge blizzards in upstate New York in March, I am giving a shorthand notation of my credentials. I am saying in the case of the faculty meeting that I have been around this place long enough to have a pretty good sense of what's going to happen. In the case of the blizzards, I am citing my personal experience of upstate New York winters. In the case of the student, I am indicating that I know enough about this student—or about student behavior in general—to be able to predict how things will turn out. Now these particular claims might not deserve the authority that I am claiming for them. The concern that seems to motivate critiques of appeals to experience is that such appeals can serve to shield particular claims from criticism; rhetorically, the appeal to experience is a way of closing down discussion. But denying the whole class of claims based on experience such authority on the basis of this concern legislates a priori about the epistemic status of appeals to experience.

First-Person and Third-Person Perspectives and the Place of Avowals

Moreover, Scott's attempt to abandon the first-person perspective that is invoked in appeals to experience because of its privacy is an over-reaction. Scott seems to see experience as tied up with a concept of liberal individualism or the transcendental subject that she thinks is itself tied up with an objectionable theory of agency and subjectivity. Her concern seems to be that appeals to experience, and the subjective, private sense of "what it is like" that such appeals trail behind them, assume that there is an agent "inside"—an agent who exists as a metaphysical given, unified and transparent to itself—that has experience that is independent of, and a possible corrective for, language and discourse. As I hope to show, this concern about the metaphysical overtones of "agency" can be addressed by taking a naturalistic approach to experience, and this approach should also show both the promise and the defects of Haraway's attempt to reclaim the metaphor of vision for knowledge. Haraway and Scott are both right to emphasize the ways in which vision and experience are not passive apprehensions of a "given," and while Haraway's naturalistic move is the right kind of move, her account of the ways in which vision and experience are embodied does not adequately capture the active nature of experience and perception. Scott's linguistic turn abandons naturalism entirely, and Haraway's naturalistic account of vision is not naturalistic enough. And while both Scott and Haraway express a desire to introduce the concept of responsibility into discussions of knowledge, the appeal to experience is meant to draw attention to the fact that, in some cases, we do not have control over our beliefs, since sometimes "the world" or facts force our acceptance of certain beliefs. It seems that underlying Scott's critique of appeals to experience is discomfort with this idea that sometimes the world makes our mind up for us, and that we do not have complete interpretive freedom; yet, at the same time, she revolts against Enlightenment concepts of freedom and agency.

In his criticism of Scott's critique of experience—and the linguistic turn in history in general—John Zammito dubs such approaches "stipulative pantextualism" (Zammito 2000, 299); it might also be called "linguistic idealism." John McDowell, making a similar criticism of Rorty and Davidson, argues that this amounts to "frictionless spinning in the void"—or, in other words, a language game that makes reference only to itself. Such a system of beliefs (or texts) constitutes a self-contained system lacking "contact with the world," according to McDowell (1996). If we are to have knowledge that is knowledge of the world, and not just this frictionless spinning, then, McDowell argues, experience must be able to play a role in our knowledge of the world that isn't simply causal. Human spontaneity—the freedom that characterizes the exercise of our rational capacities—must be balanced by receptivity to the world if we are to have knowledge of that world. Experience must, in some sense, constitute a rational constraint on our knowledge, and this entails that it cannot enter as a mere cause of belief. It must have some cognitive content, and it must, if any kind of empiricism is to be saved from the fires, serve as a possible corrective to theory. So it cannot be simply an effect of those theories, but must at least to some extent retain its independence from a particular theory.

But the dialectical nature of experience played out in these debates about history and identity highlights the need to retain something of experience's connection to a first-person perspective without thereby becoming something that is taken ipso facto to be the touchstone of unquestionable epistemic claims. And while some first-person claims do lay claim to truth prima facie on the basis of their "feltness" (e.g., "I seem to be in pain"), or in virtue of their status as "sense data reports" (e.g., "I seem to see red here now"), to assume that all appeals to experience must be granted this critical pass would seem to confuse claims about the evidence I have for my beliefs about the world with announcements about my internal states. And while the concept of "experience" does invoke the first-person subjective position, it also, when used in discussions of empirical knowledge, or empiricism more generally, is meant to invoke the bridge between the private, subjective realm and the public, objective realm—the world, that is. Since as evidence experience must participate in both the private and the public realms, it is both subjective and objective. The meaningfulness of experience is made possible through language, narrative, and theory, but it is also ineluctably personal—and sometimes it forces us to change our theories, create new terms, revise our narrative dramatically, as William James and John Dewey noted. In James's words: "Nature sometimes, and indeed not very infrequently, produces instantaneous conversions for us. She suddenly puts us in an active connection with objects of which she had till then left us cold. 'I realize for the first time,' we then say, 'what that means!' This happens often with moral propositions. We have often heard them; but now they shoot into our lives; they move us; we feel their living force" (James 1950, 2: 321).

Sometimes the world compels a particular belief from us. And while the discourse theorist may want to insist that this is a mere psychological fact about us, the psychological fact is an essential element of what it is that we mean by experience. Any account of experience that denies the ability of experience to bring about such changes in virtue of our sense of its reliability and the window onto the world it provides us as subjects abandons its claims to be about experience at all.

Similarly, any appropriate account of experience must recognize both the "natural" aspect of experience—as expressed in Haraway's attempt to reconstruct a viable metaphor of knowledge as vision on the basis of real vision—and its social and practical mediation. It must also, however, recognize the extent to which experience compels judgments or beliefs from us, and must balance that against the extent to which we can be said to be "responsible" for our beliefs. Theorists who think that experience is an important element in our accounts of our epistemic lives are both resisting the idea that we have complete interpretive freedom and also staking a claim to the concept of the agent and subject who has experiences to which her epistemic narratives are accountable.

CHAPTER 5

Naturalism and Agency

I began with an account of how the concept of experience fell out of favor in philosophy over the course of the twentieth century, a victim to, on one side, a scientific naturalism that sought to ground experience in an account of stimuli, thereby sidestepping issues about "the given" and the constituents of the world; this was complemented by a turn to the cognitive sciences as the best theoretical home for an account of human knowers. On the other side, critics of appeals to experience who embraced the "linguistic turn" emphasized its theory-dependence, and the incoherence of something that is prior to, or evades, the realm of discourse. Feminist theorists, for whom experience was a way of connecting epistemology with identity, initially used the concept happily, but they nevertheless became more critical of the term as the twentieth century closed, and the ascendancy of anti-foundationalism here, as in "mainstream" or "straight" philosophy, meant that the concept of experience needed to be rethought, or abandoned.

Sonia Kruks argues that the "linguistic turn" in feminist theory, exemplified in Scott's critique of experience, is useful to a certain extent, but that it leaves us with this paradoxical position: while claiming that subjects are merely "discursive effects," theories like Scott's that emphasize discursivity undermine the concept of individual agency; yet such theories rely on a fairly robust notion of interpretive freedom, which seems to undermine, in turn, the claim that subjects are merely discursive effects

(Kruks 2001, 143). That is, the interpretive freedom that is captured by jettisoning "experience" and its related sense of being accountable to a world is lost again if we think that interpreting subjects are nothing but the discourses that construct them. To put this into the terms of "responsibility," it is difficult to see how we can hold people responsible for their interpretive choices if they are not really making any choices. According to Kruks, this paradox seems to demand a space for something like experience that is not wholly constituted by discourse, and for a subject of experience that exists independently of discursive effects. Kruks argues that to make sense of the concept of agency, we require the nondiscursive—experience and the subject of experience—that is defined out of existence by the linguistic turn, and that phenomenological approaches, with their emphases on "lived experience" and "the sentient subject," offer feminist theory a different theoretical ground upon which to construct a viable theory of experience.

The main virtue of phenomenological perspectives, according to Kruks, is that the phenomenological tradition actually takes our embodied nature to be an important element in an account of experience. The "lived" aspect of experience is ignored or eliminated by a theoretical approach like Scott's that substitutes the term "discourse" for "experience."

Scott, in a criticism of a similar argument she finds in Christine Stansell (1987), remarks that "this kind of invocation of experience leads back to the biological or physical 'experience' of the body" (Scott 1991, 787n26). Scott does not tell us what might be objectionable about that connection between embodiment and the invocation of experience, other than that it assumes a "prediscursive reality directly felt, seen, and known" (786). Yet, Kruks's point seems to be that invocations of the bodily basis of experience need not take the body as a primitive, and that phenomenological models of experience offer a more nuanced approach to the incorporation of the body into a theory of experience by using the concept of the body-subject. By replacing the traditional subject with the body-subject, Kruks says,

"their [i.e., subjects'] knowledge will be situated and perspectival, and their forms of cognition and motivations to act will be in some measure sentient and affective. We must acknowledge, in short, that there are ways in which we come to know, think, and act with our bodies. The body is not merely the medium through which discursive effects flow (though it may sometimes be this). Nor is it, as an alternative reductionism would hold, the site of a biological determinism, even though biology is not wholly irrelevant to human knowing and acting. (Kruks 2001, 144)

Like Haraway, Kruks thinks that a more naturalistic approach to experience is possible without the risk of biological reductionism.

Linda Martín Alcoff argues that the question of the viability of a phenomenological approach for feminist theory tends to divide social scientists from humanists, with social scientists being more willing to adopt phenomenological approaches and insights and humanists being more suspicious of that tradition. According to Alcoff, poststructuralist humanists are suspicious of what they see as phenomenology's treatment of subjectivity and subjective experience "as cause and foundation," whereas for poststructuralists, subjectivity and subjective experience are "epiphenomenon and effect" (Alcoff 2000, 42). Alcoff argues that poststructuralist criticisms of experience were right to be suspicious of the assumed incorrigibility of experience, since even in subjective experience, ideology could find a home. But she also argues that the appeal to discourse leaves no place for the prediscursive or the inarticulable. This poses a problem for our attempts to entertain the very concept of an experience that does not match up with the dominant discourses of the domain. What do we say, for instance, about the experiences of a child subjected to what we now call molestation, but who had these encounters before the modern juridical and medical discourse of pedophilia? That the molestation did not exist? That it must have been created by, and as an effect of, the dominant discourse of harmless bucolic pleasures, and so could not have been experienced as trauma or harm? The turn to discourse here leaves us with a subject whose resources for description and self-description are limited by those made available to her by the dominant discourses. The idea of experiences that are somehow "out of step" with their time is hard to make sense of in this account (Alcoff 2000, 55).

Chapter 6 will take up Kruks's and Alcoff's suggestion that phenomenological models of perception can open up a more nuanced approach to experience by recognizing the ways in which knowing subjects come to know the world as lived through the body. For now, it suffices to note that Kruks's argument is aimed primarily at addressing the issues that Scott raises about the constitution of the subject of experience. Like Haraway, Kruks wants to emphasize the perspectival nature of vision and its essentially embodied nature, but while Haraway uses this to try to reconstruct a better model of realism and objectivity, Kruks uses it to try to develop an account of the subject of experience for purposes of working out a viable conception of agency, and capturing the nondiscursive, "affective" aspect of experience. Kruks's argument against the linguistic turn in feminist theory is that it cannot make sense of agency in any way that does not trade on the Enlightenment model of "a disembodied, positionless, meta-subject that hovers above and contemplates its subject position(s)" (143). And while she recognizes that the discursive realm is not irrelevant to experience, she argues that the emphasis on discursivity to the exclusion of the bodily and affective aspects of experience simply fails to deliver even on its own terms. A phenomenological model allows us to think of experiences as "an interconstituency of the physical, the cognitive, and the cultural/discursive," which have "the lived body" as their site (149).

This approach to the incorporation of the natural and the physical into a story about experience differs from those of Rorty, Quine, and Kuhn, for whom the only aspects of the body relevant to experience are the brain and the sensory receptors of the body. Notice, too, that the phenomenological approach does not assume that the proper analog for human cognition is computation, the assumption common to those theorists, nor does this approach attempt to sideline the first-person perspective and agency, as the computational approach and the linguistic turn do. However, the extent to which a discussion of experience can avoid a troublesome invocation of the naturalness of the body might still bother linguistic-turn theorists. It is thus time to consider the place of "the natural" in these discussions, and the extent to which it can be used as a resource for reconstructing the concept of experience.

The Natural, the Social, the Discursive

As Kruks and Scott both recognize, the concept of experience has connections with the ideas of "the natural" and the "bodily." This is a virtue in Kruks's view; in Scott's view, it is unwanted baggage, carrying in its hidden compartments the objectionable cargo of realism, representational theories of knowledge that model knowing on seeing, and the Enlightenment abstract subject. Haraway argues that even if appeals to experience seem to invoke the idea of vision in the formulation of their epistemic authority, the appeal to vision can be understood in a way that does not involve characterizing vision as a passive faculty and can accommodate a story about the responsibility of the knower in the formation of knowledge claims. I have argued, however, that Haraway's conception of the visual processes of interpretation does not do the work she wants it to do: that the metaphor of eyes as visual-processing systems does not provide the necessary resources for this story about the centrality of responsibility as a primary epistemic virtue in the new version of objectivity she proposes.

Let me begin by making some distinctions that will help us see what is at stake in this debate. Rebecca Kukla points out that the natural has been defined in opposition to a number of different categories of the unnatural: (1) the supernatural (that which is immune to, or outside of, the realm of causal laws); (2) the artificial or artifactual; and (3) the deformed or the abnormal (Kukla 2009). "Natural" and "naturalism" are thus multivalent terms.

For John Dewey, the adoption of a naturalistic approach implied rejecting the idea that human beings had two different and distinct natures. Dewey's insistence on understanding human beings as organisms was meant as an insistence on the unification of their supposed bifurcation into physical objects and self-conscious, reasoning beings. According to Dewey, our physical nature is permeated by our willing, striving, and reasoning, and our willing, striving, and reasoning are fulfilled in our physical activity in the world. Yet the investigation of nature has been inextricably connected to the discourses of the sciences, and a significant issue for naturalism is the question of what it is to give a sufficiently naturalistic account of phenomena. The attempt to be a naturalist thus has a strongly normative component: which disciplines count as legitimate sciences? Which subfields of which sciences are the ones the naturalist ought to consult on a given question? This process is essentially an evaluative one, going back to the inquirer's picture of human beings and her ideas about what constitutes scientificity. A short review of our three representative naturalist anti-foundationalists shows us how little agreement there is on the proper form of naturalistic inquiry.

Quine, for whom naturalism amounts to the redefinition, whenever possible, of philosophical problems into the terms of empirical science, appeals to a narrow range of scientific models. Quine's account of childhood language learning is a model in which the entirely natural, causal processes of vision are linked up with the social performances of language without any initial idea on the part of the child that these utterances have meanings.[1] The process is achieved through simple conditioning. In Quine's account, we share with other primates the ability to receive information from our environment (stimuli) by way of our sensory receptors, and these pathways of stimuli (which occur in the individual) are correlated with our version of primate noises: words and phrases. Thus, on one side of the divide, we have an entirely causal, mechanistic process; on the other, we have a connection to other human beings via language. Individualistic processes of perception are, through training, coordinated with public performances of language, and thus with concepts. From there, we move from simple utterances to extended chains of reasoning. The proper model for understanding human beings is the individual primate, who comes to connect a particular range of stimuli to certain utterances through conditioning. Thus, our commonsense theory of the world, and eventually theoretical physics, is born.

Rorty's version of naturalism is a rejection of supernaturalism, but not necessarily an embrace of empirical science. Although he accepts the Quinean story about the entirely causal chain of events that constitute sensory experience, Rorty concludes on the basis of that story that experience cannot be interesting in an account of our sapience—our cultural practices of giving and asking for justifications— but is instead the province of natural science. Our connection to the world via stimuli is a completely causal and essentially private affair. It is only on the public/social side that we find reasons, and these are necessarily discursive. From one perspective we are merely computing machines; but this aspect of our nature is of interest only to natural scientists. Rorty denies that the natural scientific account of us is a more fundamental account of our nature than the one that emphasizes our sapience; it is merely a different account. Furthermore, the natural scientific account is still irrelevant to a story about justifications, because justification is discursive, and it concerns the practices we make use of in understanding each other. Our narratives are essential to understanding, and these are linguistic and discursive practices.

Kuhn's naturalism encompasses a larger array of scientific pursuits, including history, which he uses as the data to be explained in his theory of scientific revolutions and gestalt switches. Kuhn's account of the ways in which our experience of the world is "trained" shares some of Quine's and Rorty's assumptions about the role of the brain and the sensory receptors in sense experience, and his story about the ways in which brains are "rewired" owes much to the naturalistic understanding of human cognition that underwrites computational models and to a story about human psychological functioning that connects it fundamentally to brain activity. Kuhn, unlike Quine, does not think that the subject of experience receives stimuli—"stimuli" are theoretical posits, and so they have no privileged role to play in an account of how we come to organize the world, unless we assume that a particular branch of psychology is not just a model, but an account of the way the world really is. Thus, Kuhn is fairly ecumenical in his approach to the sciences, and he, like Quine, thinks that they can tell us something about how we construct theories and how we get on in the world. Yet, unlike Quine, he is willing to draw from sociology, from social psychology, from computational theories of cognition—in essence, from anywhere he can find support for his theories.

Nevertheless, for all of these theorists, a psychological explanation is an explanation in terms of brains or brain states, and the bodily vehicle that carries around the brain is mostly irrelevant. Furthermore, brains—and the subjects of experience that are co-located with them—are essentially individualistic and self-contained causal systems. We get "hooked up" to others through language, and language use is the overlay of sociality that makes these private, physiological states communicable.

Discourse and Identity

The feminist discussion of the ways in which identities are epistemically salient pushes us toward the question of how to understand those identities. In feminist theory, appeals to naturalism depend to some extent on our willingness to treat the analytic categories of the social sciences (like race, class, and gender) as real entities. Yet Joan Scott warns us that this risks treating them as ahistorical and natural givens—to extend this critique, it might mean that we end up treating them as on a par with categories like "rock" or "star." If we do that, we ignore the extent to which human beings' self-interpretations actually influence how they act, how they are in the world. Trying to connect experience to bodiliness only reinforces the tendency to treat identity categories as ahistorical "natural" entities, and the tendency to see experience as "given" or transparent, in Scott's analysis. Naturalistic approaches seem to run the following risks: the body, if understood in the terms of the natural sciences, is contrasted with the realm of the social, and treated as an acultural, ahistorical entity. Furthermore, the categories of the social, if treated naturalistically, are then in danger of being treated as just such naturalized—that is, unchangeable, ahistoric, "given" entities—as rocks and stars.

Feminist theorists who take the linguistic turn seriously worry that appeals to experience are in fact regressive, since they lead us to treat identity categories ahistorically, as natural entities. And yet, as Linda Martín Alcoff argues, identity categories do, in some sense, mirror natural entities—they are, in important ways, "given" the way that natural entities like rocks and stars are "given."[2] We are born into a world in which certain kinds of identities are thrust upon us and connect us to a history: "the identity 'Chicano' for example, signifies a colonial history with present-day reach into the political economy of the labor market. . . . Individuals have agency over interpretations of their history, but they cannot 'choose' to live outside history any more than they can 'overcome' their horizon. The praxis of the past has formed the practico-inert of their environment" (Alcoff 2006,114–15). Thus, we are born into a world that includes natural entities like rocks, stars, tables, and other people. We are also born into a world in which history has been "sedimented" in traditions and in the ways in which we are placed—and place ourselves—in social structures that themselves are both real and artifacts of history. Insofar as identity categories are part of what it is to be born into a particular culture at a particular time, with a particular kind of body or particular ways of speaking and acting, they are just as real as are the trees and grass that make up our physical environment.

This is the move that Scott resists. The claim that identities are discursively constructed is, in her analysis, a way of challenging their concreteness, their givenness. In this respect, it seems that Scott has perhaps underemphasized the materiality of discursive practices. In Karen Barad's words,

realists do not deny that subjects are materially situated, constructivists insist upon the socially or discursively constructed nature of objects. Neither recognizes their mutually constitutive "intra-action." . . . Efforts to incorporate material factors in social constructivist accounts have been debilitated by the reductive choice between repositioning the material world outside of discourse or anthropomorphizing nature. On the other hand, the incorporation of discursive factors in realist accounts hinges on a reconsideration of the representational status of language and a foregrounding of the productive dimensions of discourse. (Barad 1999, 2)

This dilemma arises out of a subject/object dichotomy that disguises the ways in which subjects and objects are co-constituting, Barad argues. Identity categories exemplify this material/discursive dual aspect: physical and biological characteristics are partly "there," but partly picked out or highlighted in social interactions. Their meanings are not purely biological or physical, but they are constituted by the entanglement of the physical, the historical, the cultural, and the economic, to name a few elements of their discursive context. The idea that we could just refuse identity categories is like saying we can refuse to recognize oncoming traffic, or the social and environmental degradations involved in environmental racism. It is of course true that the physical and morphological aspects of identity categorization are constructed, but they are also material. They constitute the environment into which we are all born. For organisms like us, they are matter with meaning, and the matter and the meaning cannot be easily disentangled. And while identity categories might have their history in colonialism or racist categorization or patriarchy, they also have their productive aspects: they produce affiliative relationships, comfort, solidarity, or home. Their meanings are multiple, and the value of keeping them in play cannot be settled by one yardstick. Scott's resistance to treating identity categories as real in the way that rocks and stars are real seems to be a remnant of a story about the discursive that is overly linguistic. In the next section, I propose a way to do justice to the extent to which experience is both natural and socially mediated and molded. This discussion should go some way toward showing us how to reunite our biological and sociocultural, meaning-making sides, the two aspects into which contemporary anti-foundationalism has cleaved human beings.

John McDowell and Second Nature: Biological, Intentional, and Discursive

John McDowell sees the problem of experience as a symptom of the presumed dualism of nature and reason: we can understand experience in naturalistic ways, as the entirely causal sequence of events in which the world "impinges" on one's body, brain, and sensory receptors, but if we do so, we must abandon the attempt to understand the process of arriving at beliefs as a normative activity. We see this in the dilemma that plagued Popper, for instance, in his attempt to articulate what "empirical content" might amount to. According to McDowell, the presumed dilemma arises as a result of an unnecessarily narrow construal of "nature" and "the natural," in which "nature" is identified as "a description of things that subsumes them under nomothetic descriptions that are acceptable to the disciplines we call the natural sciences" (McDowell 1998, 122).[3] Examples of this approach to nature would be the accounts of information processing that we find in Quine, Kuhn, and Rorty.

McDowell wants to reclaim the terms "natural" and "nature" from the natural sciences, arguing that philosophers have too readily ceded those terms to the "nomothetic" sciences. The argument he is concerned with is one that takes as its starting point the claim that sensory experience is a natural phenomenon—the premise common to Popper, the logical positivists Popper opposed, and Quine, Rorty, Scott, and Haraway—and concludes from that that the attempt to justify claims or beliefs by appealing to experience is to commit a "naturalistic fallacy," since there is no way to bridge the normative natural gap opened up by the difference between what is justified versus what merely happens. The assumption here is that sensory experience happens to us—it is simply the "stimulation of sensory receptors" (Quine 1969, 84)—while knowledge is something for which we are responsible; our epistemic practices admit of evaluation. Our beliefs call for justification, not merely for description or for an account of how we ended up with them. Our beliefs call for an account of why we are justified in holding them, not just how we ended up with them. Causal accounts are descriptive accounts, while justificatory accounts involve norms and a background of reasonableness. Compare two different answers to the question, "Why are you standing here?" In the causal account, I might say that I was pushed, but in the justificatory account, I might say that I wanted to be able to get a glimpse of the moon. In the first, I provide what McDowell characterizes as an account rising only to the level of "exculpation" (a denial of responsibility and choice), whereas in the second, I have provided a reason for my choice to occupy that spot, putting that action into a broader context of my motivations and intentions. The problem of experience seems to be that an appeal to experience is supposed to do both: give a causal account of how I came to have a certain belief, and provide my justification for holding that belief. Thus, experience occurs at the crossroads of my existence as a biological entity and as a rational entity. But if the "logical space of causes" and the "logical space of reasons" are thought to represent dichotomous, mutually exclusive "spaces," then experience cannot be both a cause and a reason, just as, under the operative assumptions of mind/body dualism, something cannot be both mind and body, but must be one or the other.

The assumption that the "logical space of reasons" is distinct from "the logical space of nature," and that this logical space of nature is exhausted by that which can be subsumed under natural law, lurks in the concern that appeals to experience constitute a form of the naturalistic fallacy. McDowell wants to remind us that we need not adopt the latter assumption. He agrees that the "logical space of reasons" cannot be reduced to or subsumed under the realm of the natural, inasmuch as it is sui generis, but he thinks that it can nonetheless be understood as arising out of our "animal natures" (McDowell 1996). When we find meaning in things, we place them in the logical space of reasons, and thus outside the logical space of nature, but the way in which we come to be creatures that can find meaning in experience is itself a natural event, in the broader sense of "natural" that McDowell is recommending. Our "second nature" allows us to place experience in the logical space of reasons and McDowell argues that our human nature is mostly second nature (McDowell 1996, 87). Second nature, while molded by and arising out of our first (i.e., biological) nature, is also shaped by our upbringing (*Bildung* is McDowell's term for this):

Our *Bildung* actualizes some of the potentialities we are born with; we do not have to suppose it introduces a non-animal ingredient into our constitution. And although the structure of the space of reasons cannot be reconstructed out of facts about our involvement in the realm of [natural] law, it can be the framework within which meaning comes into view only because our eyes can be opened to it by *Bildung*, which is an element in the normal coming to maturity of the kind of animals we are. Meaning is not a mysterious gift from outside nature. (McDowell 1996, 88)

The invocation of *Bildung* as the process through which we come to maturity, and that helps us develop as creatures for whom meaning can "come into view," is meant both to block charges of supernaturalism and Platonism and to explain how something like human responsiveness to reasons and meaningfulness can arise out of the purely biological creature of first nature. The idea that meaning "comes into view" is interesting here for its implication that meaning is there to be discovered, but can only be discovered as a result of a particular process of education and training.

Some of McDowell's readers, however, are dismayed by what they see as a suggestion, rather than a positive theory about second nature and *Bildung*.[4] McDowell responds that the concept of second nature is meant merely as a corrective: it is meant to correct our tendency to suppose that our responsiveness to reasons is something that cannot belong to the realm of the natural (McDowell 1998, 124).

It is the creep of scientism—or, put in less tendentious terms, the displacement of hermeneutic approaches by natural scientific approaches—that McDowell wants to halt. McDowell explains his effort in his 1996 book *Mind and World* as an attempt, "not to bring hermeneutic understanding and scientific explanation together, but rather to keep them out of each other's way, with a view to our not seeming to face a threat that the aspirations of scientific understanding to completeness in its own terms, which are surely fine aspirations, leave no room for hermeneutic understanding" (McDowell 1998, 125). Thus, McDowell wants to emphasize that his primary goal is therapeutic, rather than constructive. In essence, McDowell wants to remind us that the terms "nature" and "natural" can be construed as encompassing more than the domain of inquiry of the natural sciences, where rule-governedness and mechanistic causal accounts are the definitive characteristics of the realm of nature. A more capacious understanding of "nature" and "naturalism" can accommodate our sense that human beings are natural entities, without assuming that all our activities need to be accounted for in terms of the natural sciences: "Consider how easily we can be led to accept the label 'natural sciences' or 'Naturwissenschaften' as if any other mode of conceiving things than that which is characteristic of that kind of intellectual discipline necessarily involves conceiving things otherwise than as elements in nature" (McDowell 1998, 122). But McDowell does not want to revert to Platonism or supernaturalism in that attempt, and indeed he thinks that we need not assume that we must either be naturalists or Platonists.

McDowell argues that this "relaxed naturalism" allows us to bring together the ways in which our engagement with the world is both passive (i.e., dictated by the world) and active (i.e., part of our capacity for spontaneity or our capacity for rational agency). He says that this is important, not just for understanding sense perception, but also for understanding bodily movement. As an example, he asks us to consider something analogous to sense perception,

the capacity to move one of one's limbs, as it appears in the framework of a naturalism that leaves nature disenchanted [the approach characteristic of "bald naturalism" or "scientism," which uncritically adopts the model of nature offered by the natural sciences]. . . . such a naturalism distances a sui generis spontaneity from a subject's enjoyment of sensibility, given that sensibility is a natural capacity. In a parallel way, it distances a sui generis spontaneity from exercises of the power to move one's limbs, given that that power is natural. The result is a similar difficulty in our reflection on bodily action.

Kant says, "Thoughts without content are empty, intuitions without concepts are blind." Similarly, intentions without overt activity are idle, and movements of limbs without concepts are mere happenings, not expressions of agency. I have urged that we can accommodate the point of Kant's remark if we accept this claim: experiences are actualizations of our sentient nature in which conceptual capacities are inextricably implicated. The parallel is this: intentional bodily actions are actualizations of our active nature in which conceptual capacities are inextricably implicated. (McDowell 1996, 89–90)

McDowell's point here is that it seems that the movements of our limbs brought about by exercises of will can be understood as mere happenings, rather than as "actions," and bald naturalism privileges this account. But we can also understand these movements naturalistically as our capacity to act, as our ability to express our intentions as the motivated movement of our limbs. This is the distinction that Rorty tries to push out the door in his attempt to define the self as a reweaving web of beliefs. I argue in chapter 3 that he needs this distinction if he is to make sense of beliefs as "habits of action." The robotic account of bodily movement that Rorty invokes in telling his story about how the body is involved in belief acquisition must be transformed into a body that acts, and that has habits of action—not mere regularities of movement. And this he cannot do with his pinched concept of nature and the body.

But is the yoking together of bodily movement with intentional activity a violation of a commitment to a naturalistic account of human behavior? McDowell thinks it is not, since it is just as natural for human beings to act out their intentions, if we accept this more capacious concept of "natural," as it is for our muscles to move our arms. The latter account only displaces the former if we are committed to a model of nature that assumes that the only legitimate model of the realm of the natural is that offered by the nomothetic sciences, or as I argue in chapter 3, if one is committed to a form of behaviorism or latter-day behavioristic methodology in which the first-person perspective of agency is ruled out of the bounds of the natural.

At this point, we can return to the concerns raised by feminist theorists about appeals to the body and to identity categories. Such appeals, the critics claim, run the risk of treating identity categories as ahistorical, and bodies as "natural" rather than "constructed" entities. The problem with treating identity categories and bodies as ahistorical and "natural" is that this amounts to treating them the way we treat rocks and stars: as entities that possess their qualities independently of human attempts to understand them. And the notion that bodies and identity categories are "natural"[5] and fixed is often the first step in arguments for the naturalness of hierarchically arranged social structures and roles. But note that feminist theorists are not saying that it is always wrong to treat bodies as having ahistorical qualities. For instance, some research programs may operate with an assumption of ahistoricity: medical research or basic biological or chemical research might be examples. But the slide from treating bodies as having ahistorical qualities (for certain purposes) to the justification of particular arrangements of gendered labor, or of particular ways of understanding human functions (sexuality as aimed at reproduction, for instance) happens much too easily,[6] even if the arguments that go from description to normative conclusions are unsound.

The idea that the body can provide experiences of the world that are intelligible would seem to depend on an idea of the human body as something other than analogous to a rock or a star. This points toward an understanding of human bodies that recognizes that they are different in important ways from rocks and stars. And it is here that McDowell offers the possibility for understanding the human body, and the processes by which we turn our experiences into knowledge claims or justifications, in a way that does not assume that the body is just a natural entity whose experiences are simply causal events that happen on the "natural" side of the natural/social divide. Rather, the idea that we become agents, and that we become capable of knowledge as we are educated—not simply trained, as the children in the examples of childhood language learning in chapter 3 are trained—should silence any concerns about the natural-ness of experience. Experience is "natural"—connected to a body—but it is also socially shaped and developed without being entirely constructed by or reducible to language. The process of Bildung can be understood as partly a linguistic exercise, and partly a form of know-how, connected to our ways of judging and interpreting that take the material provided by experience to construct narratives. In this, McDowell's account tries to pull back together, and intertwine, the natural and the social: the realm of causes and the realm of reasons. Human bodies are different from other bodies in being the site of this exchange and entanglement.

McDowell wants to draw a distinction between the attempt to reduce the realm of nature and the natural to the way the world is framed conceptually and methodologically by the natural sciences and his relaxed naturalism. Relaxed naturalism tries to recapture the terms "nature" and "natural" for uses that are not beholden to the natural sciences. The attempt to reduce the realm of nature to the natural and physical sci-ences is an impulse that McDowell attributes to scientism—or, in my less tendentious phrasing, to the assumption that hermeneutic understanding should, whenever possible, give way to natural scientific explanation. One can be a naturalist without becoming scientistic, McDowell thinks, and his invocation of second nature is meant to remind us that a broader con-ception of nature is available.

Yet, as his critics have urged, McDowell would seem to owe us a more detailed account of the processes by which we acquire second natures if we are to seriously entertain the suggestion that this constitutes an improvement, rather than a trivialization, of our understanding of naturalism. McDowell resists giving such a positive account, saying that the invocation of second nature is meant to be a mere "reminder" and that no positive account is necessary.

The problem, however, is that the process to which McDowell refers as *Bildung* does not seem to belong in any self-professing naturalist's list of naturalistic endeavors. When Penelope Maddy lists the disciplines that the naturalist's understanding of human beings and the world draws upon, the list is conspicuously weighted toward the natural sciences. While Maddy argues that naturalism is more an "approach" than a "doctrine," and that naturalism involves "a resolute skepticism in the face of any 'higher level' of inquiry that purports to stand above the level of ordinary science," we are still left wondering what would count as "ordinary science" (Maddy 2001, 37, 39). Maddy rejects the imputation that the naturalist must be operating, at least implicitly, with some kind of demarcation principle that puts astrology and theology on the non-science side of the line, while including as sciences physics, physiology, psychology, and linguistics.[7] According to Maddy, the naturalist applies no necessary and sufficient conditions in her use of the term "science": "as a native of the contemporary scientific worldview, she simply proceeds by the methods that strike her as justified . . . the naturalist can proceed naturalistically without any demarcation criterion" (Maddy 2001, 48). What marks off the naturalistic approach is, not an attempt to explain the world or human beings through the disciplines we appropriately call "sciences," according to Maddy, but a sense that the "scientific method" is the best approach to understanding the world. However, "scientific method" does not refer to a method of falsification; there is no special criterion that would demarcate scientific reasoning from other kinds of reasoning. Maddy says that the term is an informal term of ordinary language "used in familiar, rough-and-ready fashion" (48–49), and that "what carries the weight here is not these general terms [like "science" or "scientific method"] but the individual behaviors: e.g. the faith in 'ordinary evidence' like the Einstein-Perrin case for [the reality of] atoms" (49). Maddy sums up the naturalistic attitude this way:

The naturalist begins her inquiry from a perspective inside our scientific practice, which is, in turn, an extension of common sense. She approaches philosophical questions as broadly scientific questions, insofar as this is possible . . . she undertakes a scientific study of science, understood as an undertaking of human beings—as described by her theories of psychology, physiology, linguistics, etc.—who inquire into the structure of the world as described by her theories of physics, chemistry, biology, botany, astronomy, etc. In the process, she aims to understand how and why particular principles and practices either help or hinder her efforts to determine how the world is, and she attempts to fine-tune her overall methodology in light of this understanding. (Maddy 2001, 50)

The naturalist need not commit herself to metaphysical materialism, since presumably such a question does not admit of an answer by appeal to the standards of science. It is, in Carnap's terminology, an "external question," so the naturalist can either ignore it (as an external question) or take it to be an internal question, at which point it becomes not a metaphysical issue, but a methodological one (Maddy 2001, 51–56).

Is this naturalism in conflict with McDowell's version? It seems that in some respects it excludes McDowell's relaxed naturalism and in some respects it could include it. Maddy's claim that the naturalist's reliance on science or the scientific method is best understood as an extension of common sense, as a faith in "ordinary evidence" (49) in which the naturalist begins from within the ongoing and revisable web of scientific practice and then uses those commonsense methods of asking for, and providing evidence, in coming up with her beliefs about the world, seems to share common ground with McDowell's sense of the ways in which mature human beings would come to be responsive to reasons. But there is other evidence that these two naturalisms would not fit together so well. Maddy lists those disciplines that would delimit the naturalist's understanding of human beings as "psychology, physiology, linguistics, *etc.* . . . " (50 [emphasis added]); the extent to which Maddy's version of naturalism is compatible with McDowell's "relaxed naturalism" would seem to depend on how she fills in that "etc.," as well as whether she is willing to count as psychology and linguistics the subfields or theories that draw more on social scientific or humanistic approaches. If by "psychology" she means "computational neuroscience," for instance, and if by "linguistics," she has in mind "psycholinguistics" or "neurolinguistics," then it is not clear that she and McDowell share any common ground; if, on the other hand, she has in mind, in addition to these, developmental and child psychology, social psychology, theories of language acquisition and sociolinguistics, discourse analysis, pragmatics, and semiotics, then there might be some common ground here.

Yet while Maddy, like Quine, emphasizes the continuity between science and common sense, her example of "ordinary evidence" in which the naturalist has faith seems far from ordinary: the Einstein-Perrin case for the existence of atoms would seem to constitute fairly specialized knowledge, rather than what we normally think of as ordinary evidence of the experiential variety. So, on what grounds would we say that the Einstein-Perrin case for the existence of atoms would count as an extrapolation of our garden variety reasoning about everyday experiences? It would seem that either Maddy needs a demarcation criterion of some sort, or the Einstein-Perrin case for atoms would end up bearing family resemblances to a wide array of commonsense examples of reasoning. The scientific method that Maddy cites seems to have rather vague boundary conditions. So I think we can set aside the idea that what distinguishes the naturalist from the non-naturalist is that the naturalist is committed to something called "the scientific method." Given the broad sense of "scientific method" that Maddy wants to use, it would seem that everyone is a naturalist, even, presumably, McDowell. But this doesn't get us very far.

The crux of the matter about what counts as an adequately naturalistic approach is, I think, the issue of how best to understand the human beings who grapple with these epistemic practices. Here much depends on what Maddy will allow in with that "etc." According to McDowell, human beings are natural entities—here he agrees with Quine and Maddy—but they are the kind of natural entities that, given the right upbringing, can come to recognize certain kinds of demands—the demands of reason—as holding for them and as being "there anyway," even if one has not been taught to recognize them. It is interesting to note that McDowell draws on Aristotle's ethics to elaborate this theory of second nature. It is in Aristotle's account of the virtues, he thinks, that we find an appropriate corrective to the tendency to cede the definition of "nature" to the nomothetic sciences.

For Aristotle, the acquisition by human beings of an ethical character is the paradigmatic example of the acquisition of a second nature. And while McDowell uses this to talk about the ways in which human capacities are actualized through proper upbringing, these capacities and upbringing are not limited to moral virtues. They extend, we might say, to a type of "epistemic virtue"—the development of the possibility for being responsive to reasons, for being "accountable to the world," for having meaningful experience of that world. In addition, this developmental process is the grounding for agency and responsibility. Norms come into view only for the kind of animals we are, but they are recognized as holding even if one's "eyes" have not been opened to them—they are "there anyway."

In this story, our status as truth seekers and evaluators is not part of our first nature; we become truth seekers and evaluators as a result of the kind of upbringing that develops our natural capacities and opens our eyes to the realm of the normative. That process of education allows us to take up our places in the space of reasons. The dichotomy between the natural mechanistic system of sensory organs and the language user that Rorty and Quine presuppose in their stories about experience, which leads to the bifurcation of experience into stimuli and discourse, is thus undermined. In recognizing the epistemic demands made on us by experience, we act as both a natural entity and a reason-giver. We understand that our experiences demand certain responses: acquiescence, explanation, query, revision of our beliefs. This is because our experiences present the world to us in a certain way, McDowell argues. Experiences are biologically based, but they also carry with them prima facie veridicality. So while they are biological events with psychological effects, they have veridicality built into them, as presentations of a world that is independent of us and to which we must be accountable.[8]

Simon Blackburn has taken issue with McDowell's metaphorical appeal to the "space of reasons," as well as with his characterization of the project of *Mind and World* as a defense of a relaxed naturalism. Blackburn praises McDowell for his identification of a problem with Quinean approaches to naturalized epistemology and attributes that identification in part to McDowell's use of the metaphors of the "space of reason" and the "space of causes": "Quine, for instance, makes the same mistake that . . . Locke and

Hume made, of conflating data in the sense of brute causal impingements from without, and data in the sense of basic reasons for beliefs. . . . This can be put by saying that he confuses the denizens in the space of reasons with those in the space of causes" (Blackburn 2006, 1, 203). Yet Blackburn is critical of a particular use to which McDowell puts this metaphor in his attempt to account for the epistemic value of sensory experience, arguing that the metaphor invites a particular kind of metaphysical inflationism to get out of hand in McDowell's accounts of the conceptual realm. Consider Mary, Blackburn says, who believes that there is butter in the fridge. She arrives at that belief by going to the fridge and looking to see if there is butter there, and the fact that she saw it there is how she came to have that belief. "So when we say that Mary is justified [in believing that there is butter in the fridge] because the butter was there and she saw it, are we taking justificatory relations 'outside the conceptual sphere'? We are taking them as far as the butter and the fridge. Mary is certainly justified, and by that plenipotent way of earning the title, namely that she got the right result, and did so by exercising an activity exactly adapted to getting the right result, and that she knew to be so adapted" (207). McDowell's attempt to recast this story about epistemic warrant as an exercise of conceptual capacities, with the attendant issue of the realms within which such capacities are exercised, unduly muddies the waters, Blackburn thinks: "That the butter is in the fridge is a potential exercise of conceptual capacities? Surely not. That the butter is in the fridge might be, for instance, a reasonable matter for gratitude or source of amazement, but it is not a potential exercise of a conceptual capacity for which one is then grateful or at which one is amazed" (207). Blackburn implies that the activities of a bodily subject, located, like the butter and the fridge, in the causal realm, are being ignored in McDowell's story about the exercise of conceptual capacities.

Compare, for instance, McDowell's invocation of second nature and Blackburn's discussion of Mary. McDowell says that we make a mistake when we think that the description of nature that we find in the nomothetic sciences captures nature tout court, and that this is what makes it difficult to understand how perceptual events, which are natural (causal) events, could constitute reasons or justifications for beliefs:

The mistake here is to forget that nature includes second nature. Human beings acquire a second nature in part by being initiated into conceptual capacities, whose interrelations belong in the logical space of reasons. Once we remember second nature, we see that operations of nature can include circumstances whose descriptions place them in the logical space of reasons, sui generis though that logical space is. This makes it possible to accommodate impressions in nature without posing a threat to empiricism. (McDowell 1996, xx)

Now Blackburn:

if we were to adopt McDowell's spatial imagery, we might say that Mary's receptivity is within the sphere of her spontaneity, meaning that the way she makes observations is something over which she exercises rational control. But then we might equally find ourselves saying that her spontaneity is within the sphere of her receptivity, meaning that the way she thinks about things is responsive to what she observes. Perhaps we want to say both these things, but the metaphor of spaces and spheres then gets in the way. . . . The problem here is that McDowell does not succeed in cementing the idea of an observation firmly into the idea of activities within the world, techniques of discovery and manipulation which are possible to us only as situated within the same spatial and causal world as the things which concern us, the realm of law. (Blackburn 2006, 208)

Blackburn insists that what it is for Mary to observe the butter is for there to be "impingements" from "outside" her, caused by the butter "reflecting light and doing other buttery things" (208), that the butter's chemical composition is part of what makes it observable, and that Mary's activities of "going and looking" to see if there is butter in the fridge are a way of exploiting these facts. By describing Mary's activities, observations, and subsequent justificatory status in terms of her exercise of conceptual capacities, Blackburn seems to be saying, McDowell makes this into something that sounds like what goes on in a mind (albeit perhaps an extended mind), allowing "the world" to be absorbed into the justificatory and rational framework of the mind. Blackburn argues that "the world" is exiled from McDowell's account by the attempt to exile the realm of causation and law from our accounts of justification and our explanations of our epistemic practices. Putting these activities back at the center of the account will give us the naturalism that McDowell is after, Blackburn says, since it explains how the "initiation into the sphere of the conceptual" or "the space of reasons" takes place in particular, concrete situations. Our "second nature" is acquired, not just through the discourses of rationality, but in the interactions with the world—the realm of causation.

Let me begin by saying that I am not sure that there is a lot of difference between McDowell's claims and Blackburn's counterargument. Blackburn is right, however, to try to give activity and practical engagement in the world a more prominent role to play in a naturalistic account of mind and knowledge. In McDowell's defense, we should note that what Blackburn says about the importance of "going and looking" is compatible with McDowell's understanding of what it is to be in the space of reasons. Consider what McDowell says in "Knowledge and the Internal Revisited": "Like most adults, I know that I can tell a green thing when I see one (in the right conditions of illumination)—that is, . . . I recognize my own authority as a reporter of greenness" (McDowell 2002, 101). I recognize this reliability not as a result of a chain of inference, McDowell says, but rather "my reliability about that kind of thing . . . is held firm for me by my whole conception of the world with myself in touch with it, and not as a conclusion of an inference from some of that conception" (101). Blackburn's criticism of McDowell, and McDowell's argument about the extent to which one's sense of the authority of one's experience is based not on inferences but on a prediscursive framework within which I engage in discursive practices, shows us the extent to which an account of experience that is overly intellectualized or that sees it as essentially input to a computational device fails to capture an important element in our understanding of experience. Experience is an encounter between a subject and the world, but this subject also has a prior commitment to an understanding of herself as part of, and accountable to, the world. Her activities in the world both support this self-understanding and provide the background against which she pursues her epistemic goals.

And while McDowell's discussions of practices and *Bildung* usually mention social practices and language as paradigmatic forms of practice, Blackburn's criticism points to the realm of bodily activity as an essential part of this background of practices. To be in the world is to be a body in the world, but it is also to "know one's way around" in the world—to know what one needs to do in order to find out if there is butter in the fridge.

Rorty's criticism of representationalist models of mind is headed in the right direction in this respect. He wants us to give up on the idea of the mind as a mirror that accurately (or less accurately) represents the world. But Rorty's embrace of an account of experience in which it is either meaningless noise or discourse, which he thinks follows from the rejection of a representationalist model of mind, only does so if we accept a particular story about the human body and sense perception that takes the realm of law to be the only adequate account of the body. But accepting this account of the body means that the activities of the body are sealed off from the process by which the "web of belief" reweaves itself. If the web inhabits a body, it does so the way a ghost might inhabit a robot. The body in this account is not the lived body, through which intentions are acted out; it is simply brute matter. And while seeing the human body as brute matter might work for some purposes, the assumption that the ontology of the body is just the ontology of brute matter seems to be the kind of a priori theorizing that Rorty should abjure. McDowell argues that we can hold on to both naturalism and agency if we give up the assumption that the human sensory system is to be understood exclusively in the terms of brute nature.

McDowell's main concern is that we may make the mistake of assuming that the only way to understand ourselves and our epistemic practices naturalistically is by understanding ourselves as essentially complicated computing machines. Thus, he argues that the question of getting things right is only part of the question about knowledge; Mary's being able to answer the question of whether there is butter in the fridge is only a part of the puzzle of what it means for her to be in the space of reasons. Experience is not just reporting on what is out in the world—it is also a way of relating ourselves to the world, a way of understanding ourselves and our capabilities.

Blackburn thinks that McDowell's attempt to make room for a more hermeneutic methodology introduces a number of different, unpalatable problems. First, Blackburn thinks that the causal account of how we come to have our beliefs gets mislaid in McDowell's analysis: Mary can be justified in her belief that the butter is in the fridge because she went and looked, and it was there to be seen. Trying to recast this process in terms of the exercise of spontaneity tied up with receptivity, we might say, rephrasing Blackburn's criticism, is to give an overly intellectualized account of what it is we do when we try to know things.

Blackburn's criticism can be addressed, I think, if we do not interpret *Bildung* as a kind of "encoding" of theory as rules for drawing inferences, but rather as a kind of practical activity. And our story about what kind of subjects we are—and what kinds of things we can come to know or understand—is entangled with our account of what the world is, and what and how we can come to know it. I think what is at the heart of Blackburn's unhappiness with McDowell's use of the terms "space of reasons" and "space of causes," however, is Blackburn's sense that McDowell has made this process of knowing into an essentially mentalistic one. We are bodily subjects, located in the world with those things that we want to know about, and it is this that allows us to engage in activities designed to help us know that world, Blackburn argues. This is what he thinks is missing from McDowell's account. Yet Blackburn also sees that the Quinean approach to naturalized epistemology is inadequate.

Naturalism, Psychology, and Philosophy

To link up with the discussion in chapters 1 and 2, let us look briefly here at the methodologies of cognitive psychology, further elaborated on in chapter 6. In his critique of contemporary psychology's approach to meaningfulness, Edward Reed says that most branches of modern psychology share the assumption that "whereas sensations can and should be explained physiologically, more complex subjective states require some psychological—or even computational or quasi-logical—explanation" (Reed 1996, 15). Because of this assumption, different kinds of psychological machinery are thought to be necessary to account for meaning, such as unconscious inferences or "processing." Psychological processes are then whatever constructive activity occurs in the gaps between the physical processes.

Reed says that this assumption is what dictates the experimental designs for cases like the investigations of "filling in," the optical illusion known as the phi phenomenon, or of Rorschach tests: the design of these experiments involves unstructured or ambiguous situations (visual illusions), which the subject in the experiment is asked to describe. The goal of these experimental designs is to isolate whatever the subject "adds" through inference or processing. According to Reed, this captures the assumption that "meaning is a construction of psychological processing, never a fact of the world" (14). And it is this assumption that he thinks shows what is wrong with psychology.

This critique can shed some light on the McDowell/Blackburn disagreement, and, more important, it offers us the possibility of reframing the problem of experience and meaningfulness. Blackburn's objection to McDowell's metaphors is that they underemphasize (or make invisible) the extent to which we are bodies in a world of things. McDowell's use of the language of mental states or minds, which Blackburn thinks the terms "conceptual capacities," "receptivity," and "spontaneity" are, disguises the extent to which our epistemic practices are connected to our bodiliness and the physical characteristics of the things we want to know about.

Now, of course, McDowell wants to avoid the idea that sensations are physiological events that must be processed in order to be meaningful as much as Reed does (I do not think that Blackburn shares this concern, just to be clear; I think he is perfectly happy to say that the world— including human animals— is a world of brute objects). To show that we do not have to choose between the "Myth of the Given" and the "frictionless spinning in the void" of coherentism, because both of these assume that sensation is just unstructured, nonconceptualized "data," is, after all, the goal of McDowell's book *Mind and World*. The Myth of the Given assumes that this unstructured, unconceptualized stuff can provide justification for our beliefs because it comes from the world; the coherentist rejects that claim because sensation is merely the consequence of a series of causes. We can get off the seesaw between these, McDowell argues, by giving up the model of sense experience that they share, which relies on an overly reductive model of nature and the natural.

But McDowell's choice of strategies for extricating experience from this is to use the Kantian language of conceptualization and receptivity, both of which still have strongly mentalistic overtones, according to (my version of) Blackburn's objection. Blackburn argues for an account in which bodily activities play a more central role in our accounts of knowing. Here we can insert Reed's claim that meaning is cemented to activities in the world, not an output of brain (or mind) processes. Unlike the unstructured visual presentations of the Rorschach test, which try to isolate what the subject fills in to give the unstructured stimuli meaning, Reed argues that "the normal situation of an animal in its structured environment" (Reed 1996, 14) does not require a story about mental representations or about how ambiguous stimuli are processed. Meanings are tied to the practical activity of an organism in its environment; they are embodied in the physical environment itself, not represented in a mind or produced as a result of the central instructions encoded in a brain or other computational device.

Bildung is not only the way we learn language and the models for reason-giving—as McDowell says, it is the process by which we learn to recognize meanings that are already there. But Reed emphasizes the fact that this process involves active, embodied exploration of an environment: "That we are embodied, made up of cycling hormones and intricate networks of nerves, is a fact. But it is also a fact that we exist in a different way, at a different level: as explorers of our surroundings, as actors who strive to make a difference in the world, and as interactors who enter into both conflict and cooperation with our fellows" (5). We are both biological systems and agents who actively engage with a three-dimensional world. The mechanistic model that Reed sees at the heart of the computationalist paradigm of cognition supports the idea that it is the task of the brain/mind to construct representations of the world that are adequate to the task of guiding action. Reed says that the approach to psychology he champions—the ecological approach first introduced by James Gibson—does not see psychological processes as taking place in a brain or mind; it sees its challenge as understanding "how organisms make their way in the world, not how a world is made [i.e., constructed or represented] inside of organisms" (11). The meaningfulness of experience is not a brain or mental function (understood as something happening "in my head"); rather, it is the way we discover the world and our relationship to it through our active engagement with it.

To Be a Language User Is to Be an Agent

The idea of agency is required to understand the difference between moving my limbs and acting (in McDowell's example); we see how this also works in the conception of "the agencies of exploration" that Reed puts at the center of his account of ecological psychology. McDowell's account of *Bildung* also shows us that the process of developing a second nature is a one of becoming a member of a particular community in which we take responsibility for, and are held responsible for, our epistemic practices.

In this respect, we are both constrained by experience and can be held responsible for our judgments. To connect this to the feminist discussion of experience, this allows us to see both the ways in which we are responsible, to some extent, for our narratives, and the ways in which we are constrained by the idea of being truthful. We are not entirely interpretively free, because we are accountable to our experiences of the world, but we are also responsible for the kinds of epistemic practices we come to use. Rather than understanding ourselves as input-output machines, or brains with photoreceptors attached, or as disembodied discursive effects, we can see ourselves as agents. And seeing ourselves as agents does not mean seeing ourselves as supernaturally endowed or as transcendental subjects. "Agents just make things happen, they make their way in the world or, in the present jargon, they encounter their environment. These agents encountering the world are flesh and blood. . . . Hormones can change these agents' states of readiness and so can external stimulation. But the actions of these agents are not the effects of just these, or any such causes. Their actions are part of a stream of regulatory activities that are typically self-initiated, and modified and regulated by both internal and external factors" (Reed 1996, 19). Actions are part of a cycle of regulation in which all organisms engage. That cycle involves an exchange in which the actor responds to, and modifies, the world. Actions and the agents who perform them cannot be understood apart from that world, since actions (and not simply motions) are the material embodiment of the meaning of that world.

Agency also differentiates language use from mere utterance or noise making. Richard Heck distinguishes speaking (and writing) from the mechanical aspects of speaking (simply moving my mouth, tongue, and jaw is not necessarily rational action). So, for instance, if I tell my daughter that I'm proud of her, or suggest that she bring her umbrella, I am doing so purposefully; my language use is the primary rational action. My speaking to her involves the mechanical movements of my mouth, tongue, and jaw, but these are different actions, achievable without the intentional activity of using language (Heck 2006, 23–24).[9] Thus, the very concept of language use and discourse is embedded in an assumption of agency and intention.

Daniel Dennett (1978) argues that we attribute agency to entities in order to explain and predict their behavior, and that these attributions are to be evaluated pragmatically. But the position I have outlined above would imply that we attribute intentions (and agency) not so much in the attempt to explain behavior, but, in human affairs, as a way of understanding—as part of a relationship that develops or that we take on as part of our *Bildung* or "initiation into the space of reasons." Understanding goes beyond interpreting a speaker as having intentions. It also involves taking them seriously. To take someone seriously is to take them to be making avowals at least sometimes: telling us what they take to be true, or how it is with them, both of which are essential to the persuasive force of their claims.[10] In these circumstances, we take them to be performing actions of avowal, and part of taking them seriously as agents is taking them to be capable of avowals, including avowals about their experiences.

Viewed from the third-person perspectives of the anthropologist, the historian, or the sociologist, the analysis of experience is an opportunity to learn about how a subject understands her world: what she takes to be important, how she organizes that world, and how those understandings are deployed in explanation.[11] But from these perspectives, such "experiences" are merely data points, or phenomena in need of explanation. The ironizing scare quotes here and in Scott (1992)'s title imply that they are to be taken as revealing the world, not as it is, but as a given subject interprets it. They are not taken to be standard avowals.

The challenge that arises for the historian, the anthropologist, or the sociologist in understanding how personal (first-person) and impersonal (third-person) perspectives on a given experience or experiences relate to each other is the challenge of grappling with an irreducibly personal phenomenon (experience) from an impersonal perspective ("experience"). Yet, when viewed from the impersonal perspective, the grounds of experience's epistemic and rhetorical authority threaten to slip away—its veridicality can be called into question, its theoretical grounds or constitutive practical frameworks viewed and criticized.[12] The impersonal perspective is, essentially, a critical or ironic position. This is not true, however, in our ordinary conversational episodes, in which we take the speech performances or declaratives to be something more than data points. In taking the speaker or writer seriously, we understand that we are asked not just to report on whether it seems to the speaker that her experience shows her thus-and-so. We are asked to do more than simply report on her beliefs—we are asked to think of them as being worthy of recognition as truth claims.

Taking up a critical position with respect to our own experiences is sometimes an achievement, however. It is, in essence, the stance of objectivity and critical distance. But this stance also seems to threaten to make the very phenomena it seeks to critique disappear: in taking up a third-person perspective toward our own experiences (and those of others), we do not necessarily commit ourselves to the world-disclosing nature of those experiences—we hold them at a distance, so to speak, without avowing the truth of their deliverances. Experience then becomes "experience"—no longer carrying with it the presupposition of veridicality or the assumption of a revelation from an objective world, and shorn of its subjective bases.[13] From the impersonal perspective we have only "experience"; it is only by recognizing the occupation of the first-person perspective that we can get nonironic, no-scare-quotes experience. So it is not that the critical perspective is never appropriate. However, when we take this critical stance we essentially give up our appreciation of the subject as an agent and legitimate self-interpreter and interpreter of the world. Scott does not perhaps fully realize this.

This asymmetry between third-person and first-person perspectives manifests itself in the analyses of agency as well; while the critical, impersonal perspective views the subject's "experience" as data points— as providing us with information about how the subject interprets the world—the output of that interpretation, when viewed from this perspective, can only be behavior, rather than agency. Attributions of agency are ways of understanding what people are doing that necessarily invokes the trappings and presupposition of subjecthood.[14] Viewed from the third-person perspective, agency can be inferred or imputed, but in taking up a third-person perspective toward some being, I am at the same time viewing that being as an object—that is, as a non-subject. The sideways-on view of a person and her claims is then different from the first-person or participant perspective that has agency as its essential ingredient, and that avows certain beliefs or commitments. In the case of both experience and agency, the idea of a first-person perspective is essential to the constitution of these concepts. The third-person perspective that Scott's account privileges—the perspective of critical distance and objectivity—threatens the concepts of experience and agency with dissolution, since the first-person perspective from which experiences are avowed nonironically is itself taken to be a discursive effect. To claim that the first-person perspective is a discursive effect is to take the impersonal stance, the critical stance that is structurally similar to Dennett's "intentional stance." The claim that the first-person perspective is a discursive effect amounts to the claim that there is no fact of the matter about what does and does not have intentions, and what should or should not be entitled to being taken seriously. This move might be appropriately called "the textual stance." Texts may be produced by a variety of entities, and the meanings of texts are not tied to intentions and authorship. However, if we take up the textual stance, we thus cease to commit ourselves to the idea that there is some fact of the matter about what kinds of texts are produced by entities that have intentions. And if we do this, it is difficult to cross the bridge back over to taking seriously the claims that the text producer makes.

The bifurcation of experience into "discourse" and "stimuli" that I have been tracking leads to this particular conflict between the third-person "objective" or critical stance and the first-person stance of avowal. The objective stance that Scott and Rorty (as well as Quinean naturalized epistemology) privilege is inconsistent with attributions of agency, since taking up the impersonal perspective is just that perspective that is constituted by exiling agency. To see oneself or others from the impersonal (or third-person) perspective is just to interpret them as behaving, rather than as acting, since the intentions that would make something an action rather than mere behavior are ruled out of order in these accounts.[15] The anti-foundationalist premises from which Rorty and Scott derive their claims about experience, and to which they appeal in arguing that agency is conferred, would be expected to deliver these verdicts on experience and agency, because we can get only "experience" and behavior when we take up this critical position. Looking at these instances of speaking and writing, not as an anthropologist, but as someone who is part of the practice, means taking the speaker or writer seriously. But, in the attempt to avoid the model of mind as mirror, Rorty and Scott replace it with a model of mind as interpreting machine that "outputs" behavior, and so the first-person perspective is vacated.

The literary approach to narratives of experience that Scott advocates is related to this anthropological approach because it involves taking such narratives, not as truth claims, but as artifacts that can reveal to us how identities are constructed. Treating them literarily, however, even if we do not take them at face value as avowals, still involves seeing speaking and writing as actions—as having authorial intentional activity behind them, even if that is only so that we can distinguish these artifacts from mere noise or visual conceptual art. The concept of linguistic performance and the concept of agency are intertwined. To talk about discourse is to recognize, at least implicitly, the role of an agent.

CHAPTER 6

Experience Recaptured

Human beings are the part of the natural world that produces culture.
—EDWARD REED, *Encountering the World: Toward
an Ecological Psychology*

McDowell emphasizes the concept of "rational freedom" by emphasizing our ability to take responsibility for actions as a result of their basis
in intentions.[1] I have argued that action and agency are premised on the
idea of a first-person perspective. In contrast, behavior is described from
the impersonal perspective. Agents, as a result, can have a story about
what it is like for them from the inside, which may or may not fit with
the story an observer would tell. Furthermore, the idea of experience as a
disclosure of the world is grounded in a first-person perspective, and it is
this perspective that is undermined by both appeals to computer models
of cognition and attempts to reduce experience to discourse.

I have argued that the very concept of discourse and linguistic performance (as opposed to meaningless noises) depends upon a recognition
of agency, and that the attempt to explain agency and the first-person
perspective as discursive effects—and the attempt to treat experience as
discursive effect—leads to an inability to take these narratives as truth
claims, or as attempts at truthful description. The attempt to reduce experience to discourse is thus to a certain extent unstable: the claim that the
first-person perspective is a discursive effect, and that agency is a discursive construction, depends on assuming that there is something called

"discourse" that is different from mere vocal noises. But the distinction between discourse and vocal noise depends on a distinction between the intentional activities involved in communicating and unintentional noise-making (or a randomly generated text). To understand an entity as using language rather than just making noises is to understand that entity as trying to communicate. The attempt to escape the first-person perspective, which characterizes the attempt to reduce experience to discourse, is thus caught in a conundrum—without agency, there is no language and thus no discourse. Furthermore, the attempt to undermine the authority of appeals to experience that is characteristic of discourse theorists' criticism of feminist uses of the term risks treating avowals as mere reports and not taking the speaker who appeals to her experience seriously. So there are both conceptual problems with this attempt to replace "experience" with "discourse" and ethico-political objections to doing so.

I have also argued that the dominant approaches to reducing experience to stimuli are not necessarily the most naturalistic approaches, and that the question of naturalism and experience goes back to our understanding both of what human beings are and of how our sentience and sapience work together. But an adequate understanding of how our sentience and our sapience work together, I have argued, depends on a more complicated understanding of bodies, epistemic practices, and epistemic norms like accountability to the world than we find in methodological approaches to experience that assume that it can be redefined as either stimuli or discourse. So, treating experience as stimuli, which is another manifestation of the desire to purge the intentional from the concept of experience, misses the aspect of experience that ties it to epistemic virtues like accountability to the world. Treating experience as discourse misses the bodily aspect of experience, and, like the attempt to treat experience as stimuli, seems motivated by a distrust of the first-person perspective and the intentional.

The attempts by twentieth-century anti-foundationalists to redefine experience as either stimuli or discourse are symptomatic of a tendency to assume that human beings and their cognitive and interpretive functions are split between our biological nature (sentience) and our meaning-making activities (sapience). The concept of agency is essential, however, to a concept of discourse and sapience, and the bifurcation of our sapience and our sentience is tied both to skepticism about agency and the status of the first-person perspective and to an overly narrow construal of the realm of the natural. In this chapter, to show that a naturalistic story about ourselves does not require that we leave our meaning-making activities out of the picture, I investigate an alternative to the models of cognition and perception that have dominated Anglo-American versions of naturalism in discussions of experience.

This alternative model is variously captured by what Robbins and Aydede (2009) call "situated cognition" and what Susan Hurley and Alva Noë call an "enactivist" approach to perception. These approaches to mind, perception, and cognition are really a loose collection of approaches, shared by a number of like-minded theorists, including not just Robbins, Aydede, Hurley, and Noë, but also Andy Clark, Shaun Gallagher, Evan Thompson, and Edward Reed, among others. My aim here is mainly to introduce this model as an alternative to the understanding of the subject of experience that we find in the linguistic turn, the anti-foundationalist reduction of experience to sensory stimuli, and the naturalistic approach to epistemology to which that reduction leads. Advocates of naturalizing epistemology are, of course, explicitly drawing on psychological theory, but, as I have argued, those in the Quinean tradition seem to draw on a fairly narrow range of subfields of psychology. Linguistic-turn theorists, on the other hand, do not see themselves as drawing on psychology, and if the term is understood to mean the scientific discipline of psychology, that claim is true. But my discussion of the assumptions that ground Joan Scott's and Richard Rorty's critiques of appeals to experience show that they still implicitly draw on a model of psychological subjects. In essence, I have argued by way of analyzing these trends in twentieth-century anti-foundationalism that the discussion of experience is, sometimes explicitly, sometimes only implicitly, a discussion of the relationship between philosophy and psychology. So it would seem that having a better understanding of the different permutations of psychological accounts is useful for thinking about what a naturalistic approach to experience might involve.

Situated Cognition and Ecological Psychology

Although particular aspects of situated cognition and enactivism have been debated,[2] their theorists share a commitment to ecological psychology and its central concepts of "ambient and ambulatory vision" (as opposed to "snapshot vision"), "environment," and "affordances."

Ambient and Ambulatory Vision

Ambient vision arises from the natural movement of the head; ambulatory vision is enabled by movement of the whole body. Whereas the standard experimental design models for vision perception in the 1970s treated the eye and the brain as the essential elements, "natural vision depends on the eyes in the head on a body supported by the ground, the brain being only the central organ of a complete visual system," James Gibson writes (1979, 1). Gibson argues that attempts to study perception in experimental contexts impose certain constraints on visual experience that limit the extent to which the results of those experiments can apply to natural vision. Gibson criticized attempts to study vision experimentally that focused on "snapshot" or "aperture" vision, and then drew conclusions about visual experience tout court on the basis of those attempts. The design of these experiments dictated that the subject's head be immobilized and a stimulus provided for the eye-brain system to "take a snapshot" of it, so to speak. This prevented the subject from turning her head and did not allow, let alone invite, her to get up and walk around. Gibson conceded that the research programs dedicated to aperture vision had been very successful, but he argued that this development led to the assumption that all vision is aperture vision. Ambient and ambulatory vision are different kinds of vision, according to Gibson, and they had not been adequately studied because of the assumption that these natural forms of vision could not be controlled experimentally. Gibson's book *The Ecological Approach to Visual Perception* tries to correct that mistaken assumption, and he includes a number of examples of experimental design that do not require that the subject be immobilized and in which the subject's interactions are more natural. To understand perception better, Gibson argues, the standard experimental design is inadequate.

Environments

The aspects of ambient and ambulatory vision overlooked by the standard experimental design are not just the aspects that have to do with the subject's bodily movement. These experimental designs also neglect the extent to which the environment in which a subject (Gibson uses the word "animal" to designate the subject of perception) finds herself is itself essential to the process of ambient and ambulatory vision and thus essential to our ordinary, every day perception. Gibson defines the environment of an animal as its surroundings, but he warns that an animal's surroundings are not limited to the physical objects in its environment: "the words animal and environment make an inseparable pair. Each term implies the other. No animal could exist without an environment surrounding it. Equally, though not so obvious, an environment implies an animal (or at least an organism) to be surrounded. . . . The mutuality of animal and environment is not implied by physics and the physical sciences" (Gibson 1979, 8).[3] Environments are the surroundings of animals, which are defined as perceivers of an environment and actors in that environment. Thus, environments are constituted by the presence of an organism or animal—they are not just a collection of brute physical objects. Animal environments also include other animals, plants, and, in the case of human beings, cultural and social influences. Environments provide both resources for, and obstacles to, action. The environment and the animal constitute an interactive dyad.[4]

Affordances

The environment-animal dyad gives rise to affordances, which are "opportunities for action, not causes or stimuli; they can be used and they can motivate an organism to act, but they do not and cannot cause even the behavior that utilizes them" (Reed 1996, 18). Affordances are always there for the subject to perceive them, but they are not, according to Gibson, to be understood as "perceiver dependent"—the affordances of an object are there whether a particular observer perceives them or not. Thus, Gibson talks about objects "offering" things to a perceiver, and this is not driven by the perceiver's needs; rather, "the object offers what it does because it is what it is" (Gibson 1979, 138). Gibson sees the virtue of this approach in the fact that the theory of affordances (and ecological psychology more generally) offers a new definition of meaning and value: "the perceiving of an affordance is not a process of perceiving a value-free

physical object to which meaning is somehow added in a way that no one
has been able to agree upon; it is a process of perceiving a value-rich ecological object" (140). Here Gibson challenges the stimulus-response model
of perception, as well as the idea that sense perception is an entirely physical, causal sequence in which the brain/mind processes the raw, meaningless material provided by the sense organs. Gibson also redefines what
objects are, and how a perceiver relates to those objects. The subject of
experience encounters a world as a world of affordances because the subject of experience is not a simple reactive biological system, but rather an
actor and protagonist making her way through the world, and actively
engaging with it. The meanings of objects are connected to those activities and evoked by them.

Note that this model changes the contours of the debate about the
causal efficacy of physical objects and the lack of such causal efficacy for
moral values. According to the analysis of physical objects provided by
ecological psychology, the causal efficacy of the physical objects in the
case of scientific observation, which Gilbert Harman thinks distinguishes
scientific observations from putative cases of ethical observation, cannot be understood without an understanding of the object's affordances.
Harman recognizes that observation is theory-dependent in both these
cases, but insists that the causal chain present in the case of scientific
observation is essential to the observation in a way that the causal chain
involved in seeing the cat being tortured is not. For the ecological psychologist, this is a distinction that makes no difference. In both cases, the
objects or events in question can motivate, but not cause, the observer to
do something. The efficacy of the object goes back to its inclusion in a
feedback loop between actor/animal and world that cannot be reduced to
the internal states of the observer. The observation of the electron is made
possible through the arrangement of the physical world in a particular
way, and it is this practice-based aspect of observation (about which I'll
say more later) that constitutes the affordances provided by the electron's
presence. The difference between the causal efficacy of the electron and
the causal efficacy of the cat-burning that Harman cites is simply a matter of different affordances, not a difference between a causal chain that
fully explains an observation and one that does not. The observations in
both cases depend on environments that make possible particular kinds

of perception, and those environments are not constituted exclusively out of brute physical objects.

Gibson distinguishes his position from gestaltists like Kurt Koffka on the basis of what he takes to be the troublesome version of "two world" metaphysics that plagued gestaltist attempts to explain perception. Gibson is eager to distinguish his account from that of theorists who assume that there are two different objects in any interaction between a perceiver and the world: the physical object (or geographical object) and the behavioral object (or phenomenal object). In the "two world" accounts that Gibson criticizes, only the latter exhibits demand character on the basis of a perceiver's needs and past experience. In Gibson's words: "it was the phenomenal postbox that invited letter-mailing, not the physical postbox [for gestaltists like Koffka]. . . . I prefer to say that the real postbox (the only one) affords letter-mailing to a letter-writing human in a community with a postal system. This fact is perceived when the postbox is identified as such, and it is apprehended whether the postbox is in sight or out of sight" (1979, 139).

Postboxes are both cultural and natural items; recognizing them as such depends upon living in a particular kind of society, and upon certain kinds of technology (e.g., writing) and communication practices. But they reach beyond even this, to governmental systems and interstate/intrastate boundaries. When I visited Botswana in December 2010, I was reminded of the extent to which the humble mailbox also intersects with colonialism. Prior to colonial rule by the Boers and the British, and even in the early years of that rule, the Batswana[5] didn't have mailboxes, but mail trees: particular trees near the towns of Molepolole and Palapye were used by the locals as spots to deposit mail destined for other parts of southern Africa. The trees had notches or holes that allowed people to put mail there, and the expectation was that anyone who was traveling to the next town would carry the mail with them if they found any there. Similarly, travelers would deposit mail in the tree when returning to the village after visiting neighboring villages. The mail tree was, essentially—as we interpret it now, in retrospect—an early post office, except that service was irregular and free.

The Boers, vying for control of what would become Botswana, took over part of what is now southern Botswana and named it "Stellaland."

They established a colonial mail service, but the borders of delivery were dictated by the Boer-imposed borders, over which there was dispute with the British. Stellaland stamps, which were purchased, were only good within the country's borders, borders that were dictated by the Boers' attempt to take over this part of Botswana.[6] In the meantime, the London Missionary Society established a series of settlements in southern Africa, as well as a rudimentary mail runner service. The London Missionary Society settlements were connected by a road that Cecil Rhodes came to call "the Suez Canal" because of its essential role in connecting the British colonies of central and southern Africa. When the British became the colonial administrators of what was then called Bechuanaland, they created an official postal service, as well as a railroad service. The railroad service helped the British and the natives of Bechuanaland transport mail; it also helped develop the gold and diamond mines that made Cecil Rhodes rich.[7] The mailboxes in an exhibit about the history of the Botswana Postal Service that I saw in the National Museum showed this series: pictures of early mail trees, Bechuanaland mailboxes (red metal boxes with a curved top, marked with the Royal Mail symbols one sees in England), and finally the mailboxes labeled "Botswana," still red and still shaped like the Royal Mail letter boxes familiar to anyone who has visited England. Thus, the colonial history of Botswana's mailboxes is "written into" their material expression. Had the Boers won their battle to control modern-day Botswana, or if the native tribes had retained control of the area, mailboxes would look different, and the early mail trees show the extent to which affordances can be found for objects that are not "really" mailboxes. Mailboxes afford letter mailing to a letter-writing human, as Gibson says, but they are also material symbols tied to history, and the affordances they provide are integrated into and dictated by historical forces and political institutions.

What is interesting about the collection of approaches to experimental psychology that trace their lineage back to Gibson's ecological psychology, and makes them promising as approaches to rethinking the nature of experience, is that, like the early American pragmatists, the model of human beings that these approaches embrace is of "an organism" that makes its way around and through an environment. The environment is not just a collection of inert objects, but a field of opportunities and obstacles—that is, the elements of the environment are understood in terms of the kind of activity they can make possible.

Many empirical studies support the ecological psychologists' claims about perception.[8] My primary interest here is in using this model as a jumping-off point for a story about experience that does not invite us to reduce it to discourse or to the merely causal prompts that lead to non-inferential utterances (stimuli). Furthermore, the feminist discussion of the social meanings of bodies and the ways in which history constructs certain environments—as offering, for instance, the possibility of identifying oneself (or the inevitability of others identifying one) as a woman, or as Latino—shows that this talk of "organisms" and "environments" must not be understood in a reductive way. Our environments include trees and grass, but they also include more complicated examples of social/natural boundary crossings, such as mailboxes, telescopes, racial and gender hierarchy, and institutions that are anchored in or exploit the social-natural world, such as economic systems.

The Content of Sensory Experience

Naturalistic accounts of the theory dependence of perception depend to a great extent on the assumption that sensory experience is "thin," an assumption found typically in the account of the information available for constructing theories about the world offered by Quine, who adopted it from received mid-twentieth-century psychological theorizing. According to Irving Rock's (1984) summary of theories of perception, gestaltist and empiricist theories of perception, which draw, respectively, on rationalist and empiricist philosophical models of mind, similarly characterize the stimulus that the eye receives, called the "optical array." The gestaltist explains our ability to move from this thin sensory stimulus to rich mental representations in terms of spontaneous interactions in the brain that are activated by the proximal stimulus, while the empiricist explains our ability to move from this thin input to rich output by appealing to unconscious interpretations of that input (Rock 1984, 12). But neither model questions the assumption that the input is "thin," and we see from Gibson's account how experimental design can encourage (and make real) this assumption. The assumption that sensory input is thin is paired with the assumption that aperture vision is the only kind of vision to produce what Alva Noë (2004) calls the "brain-photoreceptor" model of mind, in which the input available to the experiencing subject is analogous to that available to a camera, and the brain then "processes" that thin input to produce, from two-dimensional images, a world of three-dimensional objects.

The brain-photoreceptor model of mind, and the account of vision it encourages, gives rise to a number of problems in epistemology and the theory of perception. However, the interesting issue for my purposes at the moment is the fact that this model seems to be a return to the "spectator theory of knowledge" that Rorty and Dewey both reject: in fact, Dewey also calls this the "photograph idea" of knowledge. It is the assumption that the knower and the world are cut off from each other, and the goal of the knower is passively to reflect what is happening in this world from which she is separated. Dewey's objection to this approach is that knowledge comes about through a process of inquiry and experimentation, and that if we shift our model of human knowers, recognizing human inquirers as organisms, we can see that knowledge comes about as a result of the interaction of world and knower. The process of inquiry is a process of intervening, not a passive reception of images. The model of cognition and perception that is operationalized in the standard, non-Gibsonian approach to studying perception is the spectator model, and according to Dewey, it is objectionable, not only because it gives rise to certain epistemological problems, but also because it is insufficiently naturalistic.

Although most perception and cognition researchers who implicitly embrace the stimulus-response model or its expression as the brain-photoreceptor model would surely have strong objections to being called Cartesian dualists, an element of Cartesian dualism continues to survive in this approach to the theory of perception. The brain-photoreceptor model shares with traditional Cartesian dualism the idea that the knower is operationalized as an abstract and disembodied subject. The advocate of this model might object that there is, in fact, a body, and that the charge of Cartesianism is unwarranted. I think the charge is warranted because the body that is taken to be the repository of the brain-photoreceptor system is still a fairly abstract entity; it has none of the life and purposive activity that characterize animate creatures. The knower has a body, in this story, but is not really embodied. The body in this model is the lumbering robot that Rorty invokes in his account of the proper understanding of the self "from outside" (see chapter 3).

The absence of a subject who is meaningfully embodied might have a number of sources. One might be the worry voiced by Rorty and Scott about the very concept of agency; another might be the worry that many feminists have about naturalizing the body. But more than this, I suspect that the idea that we are our "worldviews" is too tantalizing a metaphor, and we have not noticed that the metaphor of the worldview has been cashed out in highly theoretical (and intellectualized) terms—in terms of theories of language or webs of belief. The translation of subjects into "worldviews" or webs of belief is a move away from understanding subjects as embodied.

What is wrong with the idea of worldviews? The problem is that it is often used the way Rorty invokes the idea of the self as a "self-reweaving web": in essence, it assumes that theories are carried around in subjects— either as information in brains or as self-enclosed inferential webs that dwell in subjects. But the idea that there is some natural division between the world and a subject who perceives or interprets it, which animates this model, is itself a problem.

Karen Barad's (1999, 2007) discussion of "agential realism" emphasizes the extent to which the technologies of observation in the sciences expose the pragmatic nature of the observer/world distinction, since what counts as "the observed" is phenomena, produced technologically by subjects who manipulate and intervene in the world. Joseph Rouse puts it well in his discussion of the problem of using the term "perspective": "Perspectival locations are often conceived as subject positions, external to the situations upon which they provide a perspective. The notion of perspectival differences may then seem to require some aperspectival grounds that differentiate them" (Rouse 2002, 235). In essence, the idea of worldviews or perspectival locations depends on a standing and given subject/object dichotomy—a dichotomy that, according to the ecological psychologist, looks much fuzzier. Where the subject ends and the object begins is not settled a priori, but is constantly negotiated.[9] Talk of worldviews keeps alive the assumption that theories are "in the head" (or, as in the case of the computational models of cognitive science, "in the brain"); theories are taken, in the first, non-physicalist story, as mental items—as essentially the arrangement of concepts in a web of belief that is carried around by a body/subject. A physicalist version of this will interpret theories as software. By passing through the theories in the head of a subject (the software), sensation becomes meaningful discourse.

Some cognitive scientists have bemoaned the absence of a body in philosophical theories of mind,[10] but the body that is usually incorporated in cognitive science models is usually only a brain, or perhaps a brain in a body that is essentially an object like other objects. Gibson's alternative account of the embodied mind is the starting point for situated and enactivist approaches to cognition and perception. In place of the assumption of the thin optical array, Gibson suggests that "to see things is to see how to get about among them and what to do or not do with them. If this is true, visual perception serves behavior, and behavior is controlled by perception. The observer who does not move but only stands and looks is not behaving at the moment, it is true, but he cannot help seeing the affordances for behavior in whatever he looks at" (Gibson 1979, 223). According to Gibson, our perception of objects always involves something more than mere sensation—it always draws objects into a web of possibilities for action (rather than a web of beliefs), and thereby understands them as meaningful. The meaningfulness of objects is not inferred, arrived at through abduction, or projected onto a thin skeleton of sensation—it is part and parcel of the presentation of the object itself.

While some might object that this is still essentially a psychological account of knowledge, I urge its adoption as an alternative to the psychological accounts that philosophers tend to favor, and as a more nuanced bridge between philosophy and scientific psychology. Even though the model of empirical knowledge that I'm advocating owes much to empirical psychology, it offers a naturalistic account of human beings without indulging in reductivist tendencies, while holding out the promise of helping us understand ourselves and our cognitive lives in new ways. In addition, and more important, however, it also supports the idea that practical activity is essential to cognition, connecting this particular branch of philosophy of the mind-body to theories of practices—and to the practical activity of inquiry that James and especially Dewey put at the center of their accounts of knowledge.

Practices and Epistemic Virtue

McDowell's claim that in perception cognition is drawn on in receptivity can be reframed in terms of the way that objects are drawn into a web of possibilities in practices. Blackburn's example of Mary, who wants to know if there is butter in the fridge, can be understood in this way: thinking about the dinner she is going to make (or about tomorrow's breakfast needs), Mary wonders if there is butter in the fridge. As Gibson would say, even if she just stands and looks into the refrigerator, she sees either that there is or is not butter, and this presents other possibilities for her: does she go to the grocery store to buy butter? Make something different? Ah, here is heavy cream. Maybe that will work in place of the butter. Mary's epistemic activities are part of a larger project, and the discovery that there isn't any butter in the fridge is part of a revised plan of action. The reorientation of epistemology in terms of activities allows us to let go of some of the problems of the theory-dependence of perception, as well as the problems about how we can understand our knowledge to be accountable to a world. Our knowledge activities are always already in a world; they take place against the background of an environment in which objects, events, and other people structure and support our projects of "getting around" in it.

Philosophers concerned about the dangers of relativism will balk, however, at the claim that the disenchanted world of the objects of the natural sciences is not more objective and ontologically fundamental than the ordinary world of affordances that ecological psychology puts at the center of accounts of cognition and perception. Many philosophers have a sense that physics tells us what is really in the world, and the rest of it is just anthropocentric construction or projection. This is often linked to the idea that what we get in experience is really only stimuli, not objects or situations.

Blackburn's example of Mary is meant to establish the importance of the causal realm for understanding knowledge and to confute the idea that we can judge ourselves to see "more or less what we like" (Blackburn 2006, 210). It may seem that I have opened the door to the possibility of a promiscuous and unconstrained "seeing" and distorted Blackburn's account by turning it to my own purposes to boot.

Let me address the problem of unconstrained seeing first. Blackburn is right that the extent to which affordances are invested with cultural meanings will mean that there might end up being many things that people see in an environment that we do not at present see. But this is just an empirical fact, and not a particularly interesting one. Trained musicians can perceive things in music that I cannot; wine connoisseurs can separate out different aspects of a sip of wine that I cannot; people who are handy with cars can look under the hood of a car or listen to the noises it makes and see or identify many problems that I cannot see or hear. The question to be asked here is not "Are the things that the musician, the wine specialist, and the mechanic say are there really there?" but rather "Do I trust [so-and-so's] judgment in this case?" A track record in getting things right will help us answer this, but the pure question of whether the phenomena the musician, the wine specialist, and the mechanic claim are there to be perceived really are there is orthogonal to that issue, since I cannot really judge their track records for correctness on this score. That is, I cannot judge independently whether they have actually seen in the past what they claim to have seen, since I cannot, in these cases, see the phenomena they see (or hear). I might know that my daughter's harp tuning in response to her hearing that a string is out of tune makes the harp sound better; I might know that the wine specialist tends to recommend wines to me that I turn out to enjoy; I might know that my auto mechanic has a knack for fixing whatever is wrong with my ten-year-old car. But the knowledge I have of the results of the judgments made by the specialists in these cases is not the same as being able to verify for myself that what they claim to see or hear is really there.

Concern about relativism is concern, in the end, about whose account I should trust, and for this we have only our judgments of epistemic character and virtue to go on. Truthfulness is one element of this; another is our confidence in the know-how we think these authorities possess. So I think that Blackburn's worry about relativism cannot be allayed by appeal to a more basic scientific description of atoms and the void, even if we grant him that definition. Some society might well come along in which Picasso's intentions and the meaning of the U.S. Constitution are said to be perceptible, and presumably they would have a story to tell about how to go about seeing these things, or they would have practices constructed around the evocation of these phenomena.

To be fair, Blackburn is willing to entertain the possibility that some forms of perception might best be understood as the refinement of sensitivity, but he worries that without the resources for delimiting legitimate instances of seeing provided by an account of causation in perception, we end up without the grounds for querying the purported expert observer or connoisseur. The question of whether an observer has really perceived something or is just seeing what he wants to see—projecting, that is—can only be entertained from the "sideways-on" perspective, Blackburn argues, and the process of querying our own and others' confidence in what we or they take to be simply given in perception is an essential part of good epistemic hygiene. Sometimes the connoisseur or the trained musician will not be able to give us much explanation of what he or she saw or heard, but Blackburn's real point here, I think, is just to raise the issue of justification practices and the value of narratives in these instances.

Again, though, this does not seem to be at all controversial, and, in fact, if we accept Gibson's way of drawing the line between more and less basic descriptions, the trained musician and the trained scientist come out pretty much on the same side—their refined sensibilities are just that; their descriptions are not more basic because they are not there for everyone to see. What Gibson will not entertain, and I take Blackburn to be hankering after, is a story about the objects we perceive that entitles us to think that "the physical objects of physics" are somehow more basic than the physical objects of ecological psychology: this is the first possible objection I raised about my use of Blackburn's argument. And here is the conundrum, it seems to me, that confronts any naturalist: which naturalistic account do we embrace? Do we take only or primarily the naturalistic story we think is the one that a physicist would give, or the naturalistic account that we get from an ecological approach to psychology? Both of these accounts give us a story about causation, but the causal entities that are part of that story differ. Understanding epistemological projects as practices provides us with ways of making distinctions.

In response to what I take to be Blackburn's more fundamental concern that, without a story about a more stripped-down ontology, we risk the possibility of relativism, I can say that the ecological psychologist does lay claim to a more fundamental ontology, but it is the ontology of everyday objects and our ways of taking them as meaning-rich. If Blackburn wants to argue that the physicist's ontology is more fundamental (and note that the Mackie-ish argument from queerness will not work here against the ecological psychologist—see my discussion in this chapter), then he will need a story of demarcation for the sciences that can do that work. In the absence of such an account, we can only decide on the basis of what it is we want our naturalized epistemology and our theory of experience to do. The rationale for accepting the ecological account is, to my mind, based on the fact that at least when it comes to naturalized epistemology, we want to be accountable to a wide array of real-world knowledge practices, and Blackburn's deployment of the Mary example is evidence of that. An account of the physics of the butter-in-the-refrigerator situation might be useful to her in some other way, but if we are trying to understand not how she arrives at a theory of the physics of butter and refrigerators, but how she moves through the ordinary, everyday world of objects and people, then the level of resolution we need is not subatomic particles in motion but rather people, places, things, and the activities we engage in as we try to come to know them and ourselves. If our concern about experience is that it be a way of being accountable to the world, then it is not clear that we need to do battle over whether the world of physics is more real than the world of everyday objects and activities. Both, it seems to me, have a claim to being world enough for our purposes.

Situations, Activities, and Epistemic Agency

Blackburn's emphasis on the activities of investigation in this case offers an opportunity to see the extent to which, in our everyday cognitive activities, and perhaps even in experimental science (Kuhn 1996 [1962]; Hanson 1958), it is situations, rather than objects, that are the primary "input" of experience. The butter is either in or not in the fridge; it is an important ingredient in the evening's dinner plans. Mary's recognition of its presence is not just about it being in the fridge, "doing buttery things." If Mary had been looking for orange juice instead, the butter would of course present itself to her as it reflected light of a certain wavelength, and so on, but it would present itself to her only as much as the light in the fridge does—that is, as background to her search for orange juice. Thus, the epistemic issues of relevance and importance come to the fore when we think in terms of epistemic practices and activities, and they are captured better by the model of situated cognition than they are in more orthodox versions of cognition that focus on objects (or simple perceptual states, like color sensations) rather than on objects in situations.

We should note here that the issues of relevance and importance are not inconsequential in classical epistemology either. As any graduate student in an epistemology class could tell you, numerous true beliefs do not necessarily improve one's epistemic situation: one can know many truths without necessarily knowing any important ones. The fact that our epistemic lives are organized around the ideal of not just having true beliefs, but having true beliefs that are important or useful, further supports the move to a model of situated cognition.

The enactive approach to perception allows us to dissolve some of the problems of the theory-dependence of perception. By adopting this approach, we can see that the impasse between the Churchlands and the Fodors of the cognitive science world—or between the realists about identity and the skeptics of identity of the feminist political world—can be avoided by understanding perception as a kind of "skillful activity," emphasizing the ways in which action is actually constitutive of perception and experience of the world. That is, we can come to see that the conundrum at the heart of claims that experience is always political, or that it is always theory-dependent, is an artifact of a model of mind that ought to be rejected. To put it in the words of the (unfashionable, but sometimes perspicacious) logical positivists: the theory-dependence of observation is a pseudo-problem.

For the standard model of perception that takes the mind/brain to be an information-processing machine, which I have been attributing to Rorty, Quine, and, on his bad days, Kuhn, perceptual experience is merely the input that guides action, or that is to be explained. Borrowing from Gibsonian approaches to the study of vision, enactive theories emphasize the ways in which we directly perceive certain aspects of the world through the learning that accompanies active exploration of the world. Drawing on work on the development of perceptual capacities, theorists committed to the enactivist model argue that active engagement with the world through self-initiated activity is essential to the development of those capacities, and that self-initiated activity is also essential to the process of adapting sensation to the world. Learning to see in simple cases of sensory perception is not really a matter of interpreting sensory input; it is a form of know-how (Noë 2004).[11]

The Fodor-Churchland debate (and the related issues in feminist politics) are, according to the enactive approach, "debts incurred by a failure to make room in an account of perception, for the role of action" (Noë 2004, 18). The problem with drawing conclusions about perception and experience generally on the basis of responses to the Müller-Lyer illusion, for instance (as in the case of the Fodor-Churchland debate), is that this experiment is an isolated perceptual test that is two-dimensional—it does not present us with the challenge or opportunity for exploring, and it misrepresents the know-how that is constitutive of perception by assuming that the issue can be settled by appeal to the relationship between stimulus and response.[12] The stimulus is taken to be the thin visual input that characterizes the information available to what Noë calls a "brain-photoreceptor," and the problem of visual experience when we assume the brain-photoreceptor model of the perceiver becomes the problem of understanding how the brain could "use" a two-dimensional retinal image to infer the existence of a three-dimensional object. The problem of visual experience becomes the problem of how the brain interprets this thin input.

Similarly, the empirical evidence that Kuhn takes to support his claims that visual perception is dictated by a paradigm is drawn from a test in which a subject is shown a series of cards and fails to notice that some of the colors of the cards are mismatched with their suits. In fact, Kuhn says, the subjects actually fail to see the cards that have such mismatches. We can compare this to the example of change-blindness, in which, when we are asked to watch a video of people passing a basketball around and to count how many passes are made, we fail to notice a person in a gorilla suit who walks right through the scene. In the case of the cards, Kuhn argues, we literally cannot see something that violates our expectations—a moral that he then applies to the case of paradigms and experience. Scientists literally cannot see counterexamples or falsifying evidence. In the case of the video clip of the basketball game, we are so intent on counting the number of times the basketball is passed (in a rather rapidly changing and visually challenging scene) that we fail to notice the unexpected: the gorilla standing in the middle of the scene. The gorilla in the basketball game, like the red spades and black hearts, are not part of our theory of the world. Rather, they violate our expectations—they are anomalies, in Kuhn's way of putting the issue.

But why think that attention is dictated by theories rather than by tasks, in these cases? The enactivist argues that the issue is not so much a question of the theories we entertain in our heads as it is the extent to which our construction of the situation is aimed at a particular activity—counting the number of passes in the basketball game, or reporting the cards we see. The Gibsonian approach to perception rejects the assumption that we can learn something important about natural, lived sensory perception from the card experiment or the Müller-Lyer illusion, and helps us see, as in the case of the video of the basketball game, that perception is action-based because it is informed by tasks. In addition, the Gibsonian approach rejects the central dogma of classical empiricism that continues to animate both computational models of mind (on which Fodor's approach to cognitive science depends) and the Rortian-Quinean thesis of the theory-dependence of perception: the premise that sensory input is "thin."

Ecological psychology and the enactivist approach to perception that draws on it do not only challenge the traditional empiricist characterization of the world and the information we can get from it; these approaches also challenge the account of the subject of experience that traditional empiricism embraces. The meaningfulness of experience is not conferred by theories, language, or neural programming; rather, it is to be found in the activities of getting around in the world. Experience is meaningful to agents who encounter the world as a field of possibilities for and obstacles to action. And one element of that field is the accretion of cultural artifacts and cultural expectations, which are as important in the determination of opportunities and obstacles as floors, tables, and chairs.

It is important that we not think of "possibilities and opportunities" crudely, either. We might think, "What kinds of possibilities for action are afforded to me by the horizon? Or the stars in the sky?" If we think of the possibilities and opportunities in crude ways, we might think that our perception of these elements of our environment cannot be tied up with our agency. But there do seem to be aspects of our perception of limit points like these that constitute opportunities or obstacles, if only fanciful ones. The horizon might be understood as an invitation to go beyond our present locale, as an invitation to a voyage, or the suggestion of possibilities beyond our immediate perceptions; the stars can have a similar effect, as well as providing us with opportunities for the appreciation of beauty and wonder. If nothing else, as Gibson points out, they always specify one's own locatedness: "information about the self accompanies information about the environment, and the two are inseparable. Egoreception accompanies exteroception, like the other side of a coin. Perception has two poles, the subjective and the objective, and information is available to specify both" (Gibson 1979, 126). Furthermore, Gibson argues, some parts of a subject's field of view are understood as the "stationary and permanent" environment, as a result of her turning her head and looking around, and of her movement in and through an environment. These elements of her background give her a sense of her range of activity. The horizon or the stars can be specified as beyond reach, as the background that specifies her range of possible activity. Minimally, however, this approach shows us that self-understanding and perception are mutually implicated, and this applies not only to physical objects but also to our interactions with others. The seeing of others and their reactions to us are part of the process by which the self is understood and specified. Insofar as I move through the world, I encounter events and people who help specify my own way of being in the world. Egoreception accompanies exteroperception.

Kuhn's Mistake

Up to this point, I have been taking Kuhn to task for his attempt to explain gestalt switches as successful reprogramming. As chapter 3 argues, his story about Johnny and the classification of birds encourages us to think of learning as a kind of programming and reinforces the brain-photoreceptor model of perception and cognition. But as any careful reader of Kuhn will have noted, his attempt to explain the gestalt switches that characterize changes in paradigm by way of computer programming really does not fit with his rather extensive discussion of paradigms as embodied in practices. According to Joseph Rouse, Kuhn's attempts to challenge models of science in which theory, rather than activity, plays a central role have not been fully appreciated. The emphasis on activity that Kuhn advocates connects as well to his attempts to challenge the representationalist epistemology dominant in philosophy of science. According to Rouse, Kuhn's emphasis on intervention rather than representation in the epistemology of science has been overlooked in discussions of his philosophy of science by both his critics and his champions. In attacking what they see as a troublesome irrationalism (captured by the claims that scientists who accept different paradigms live in different worlds, and that paradigms are incommensurable), Kuhn's critics have assumed that his position can only be understood as making claims about beliefs that scientists hold. In this model, theories are a set of beliefs linked together by inferential relations. Thus, this subset of Kuhn's critics assume that scientific theories are essentially captured by ideas. Kuhn enthusiasts often make the same mistake in their arguments about the relativity of 'worldviews," treating theories as essentially entities that are "in the head" and projected onto the world.

Rouse does not say that Kuhn's critics have misread Kuhn, and as we have seen, Kuhn himself seems to encourage and partly accept the representationalist way of reading him. But the Kuhn who has been left in the shadows, Rouse argues, is the Kuhn who presents us with a truly novel way of understanding science as a set of practices. According to this reading of Kuhn, "Paradigms are not primarily agreed-upon theoretical commitments but exemplary ways of conceptualizing and intervening in particular empirical contexts. Accepting a paradigm is more like acquiring and applying a skill than like understanding and believing a statement" (Rouse 1990, 30). "Conceptualizing" here is not a mental activity, as we can see from Kuhn's claims about what it is for a student to learn what force is: "If . . . the student of Newtonian dynamics ever discovers the meaning of terms like 'force,' 'mass,' 'space,' and 'time,' he does so less from the incomplete though sometimes helpful definitions in his text than by observing and participating in the application of these concepts to problem-solutions" (Kuhn 1996 [1962], 37). Concepts are not ideas or beliefs—they are applications: ways of arranging and intervening in the material world. To share a paradigm is to share a practical orientation, to be facile with the recognition of problems and to recognize analogies between problems one has already encountered and solved and new problems.

Rouse argues that this reading of Kuhn shows us that observation is not that important for science. If, however, we understand observation as the kind of "skillful activity" that Noë urges we do, and not as a passive reception of information from the visual world, then we can agree with Rouse but also recognize the role of observation and sensory experience as part of the practical cognitive activity in which human beings engage. Experience, for both this version of Kuhn and for enactivists and practice theorists like Rouse, is a cornerstone of our cognitive activities, and its "theory-ladenness" is to be understood, not as a worldview captured by a set of implicitly or explicitly held beliefs, but as ways of acting in the world. In Rouse's words (glossing a point from Kuhn): "Changing from one paradigm to another is not like a conversion to new beliefs but is like a conversion to a new form of life. Such conversions in science are usually accompanied by extensive reasoning and argument. But this cannot be conclusive . . . because the force of these arguments is fully apparent only to those already at home in the new disciplinary field" (1990, 34). Paradigms are ways of acting and intervening; as such, they are grounded in a good deal of nondiscursive know-how. The acceptance of a new paradigm is a new way of getting around in the world, and it too will have a fund of nondiscursive know-how that helps run it. The world is organized in new ways, not in the head, but literally, materially. This might, Rouse suggests, be a way of understanding Kuhn's claim that scientists who use different paradigms are living in different worlds: the world is a set of situations; it is not primarily a world of objects. Scientists who live in "different worlds" do so because of the material configuration of the world that is part of their experimental interventions. Situations are aspects of the world that encapsulate relationships among objects, relationships between subjects and their surroundings, and know-how about getting around in the world so understood. They are not projections, but are rather contexts for action, funded by our past experience and our future plans. And since human beings are active beings, the world shows itself to us in meaningful ways, arranged as situations.

Feminist Theory, Situated Cognition, and Enactivism

Feminist theory contributes to this way of reframing epistemological problems and the philosophy of mind-body by reminding us that social and cultural phenomena are real things—they constitute the surroundings of human beings. Furthermore, feminist theory and other theoretical approaches that take identity seriously provide more sophisticated understandings of bodies. Feminist theorists emphasize the ways in which bodies are lived as having certain kinds of gendered/racialized/sexualized meanings. Not all bodies are the same, and yet some bodies have characteristics in common. Social hierarchies and cultural expectations play out in the ways that others understand us, and then echo in the way others' understandings of us influence our sense of ourselves. In her discussion of racial identities, Linda Martín Alcoff argues that the histories and ancestral lineage that are taken to be the criteria of racial identity actually take on material form in the ways in which we interpret the visible aspects of human beings: "The processes by which racial identities are produced work through the shapes and shades of human morphology, the size and shape of the nose, the design of the eye, the breadth of the cheekbones, the texture of hair, and the intensity of pigment, and these subordinate other markers such as dress, customs and practices" (Alcoff 2006, 191). In her discussion of the visual categorization on the basis of gender that is as "natural" to our perception as is the recognition of trees and rocks, Simone de Beauvoir says that "to go for a walk with one's eyes open" is enough to see that human beings are divided into two classes: male and female (1989 [1949], xx). What both women draw to our attention is the extent to which we understand particular bodies as carrying different kinds of social meanings. They show us that part of what it is to live among other human beings is to live in a way in which we see racial and gender identity. While the story of what counts as an authentic identity might involve reference to things other than the visual (e.g., in the cases of people of mixed race who pass for white, and of transgendered people), nevertheless, identity ascriptions are usually initially based on visual aspects of human bodies—gaits, facial expressions, clothing, and mannerisms allow us to "see" identities, and compel others to ascribe identities to us, even if those ascriptions do not sit comfortably with what we know about our-selves.[13] Identities are part of our experience of the world—we perceive them, and we live them out, sometimes easily, sometimes with discomfort when our self-descriptions are in tension with the ways in which others see us, sometimes rebelliously. Identities are affordances of the environment, too—they allow us to interpret ourselves and our places in history or in social structures; for better and for worse, they are part of our experience of the world.

The discursivist model of humans is a reaction to (and rejection of) the empiricist model of knowledge, but like the old-fashioned empiricist, the discursivist essentially accepts the idea that what we get from the world in perception is thin input. As a result, the discursivist dismisses experience from the realm of the meaningful. The premise about the thin input of sensation is either an a priori claim (as it seems to be for the dis-cursivist), or it is one based on a particular model of perception operative in some subfields of cognitive psychology (as it appears to be in Quinean-inspired versions of naturalized epistemology). If we understand human beings as actors, rather than as instruments for the reception of stimuli, we come to see our cognitive lives—and the role of experience in them—very differently. We come to see, in Rouse's words, that "the world is the setting within which we encounter meaningful possibilities; but it is the world that is meaningful, and not just our inner experience or our values" (1990, 66). That is, we come to see experience as part of what it is to be in the world as an agent or actor. Perhaps I should say, more accurately, that we are reminded that we are agents and actors.

The model of human beings as actors is the one that the early prag-matists emphasized. In his criticism of empiricism, Dewey says that "to eyes not looking through ancient spectacles, [experience] assuredly appears as an affair of the intercourse of a living being with its physical and social environment," and to the tendency to understand experience as a "psychi-cal" thing, he objects that "what experience suggests about itself is a genu-inely objective world which enters into the actions and sufferings of men and undergoes modifications through their responses" (Dewey 1981, 61). Thus, we can see that the role of appeals to experience is to acknowledge the ways in which we must be accountable to a world that constrains our theorizing and our activity. Rorty objects that this is just a truism; to say that we are accountable to the world is either to say something trivial, or, if not trivial, then unacceptably Kantian, invoking "things in themselves." But to tell a story about how an experience changed us, as in the case of Samuel Delany's epiphany, is to tell a story about our relationship to the world. It is a way of staking a claim to a particular self-understanding and authority. Knowledge based on experience is, then, an achievement, rather than a state that the subject is in. It is a way of saying: "the grounds for my confidence are not just based on the logical relations between this claim and other claims; the grounds for my confidence in this claim are based on a know-how, a way of getting around in the world, that cannot be captured entirely by a syllogism." Of course, our ability to construct arguments, to link claims logically, is part of the story about what kind of beings we are, but to understand ourselves as living beings is to understand ourselves also as agents.

"Where there is experience, there is a living being"

The temptations of reductivism are strong: to reduce experience to stimuli or to discourse seems to be demanded either by our recognition of our status as biological entities, or by our recognition of our status as meaning-making and cultural creatures.[14] The hope that we could use experience as a bulwark against philosophical excesses, as James and Dewey thought it might be used, is surely naïve. We have a better understanding of the intricacies of our perceptual experience and of our lived experience as a result of the debates about anti-foundationalism, theories of identity, and ideology, and this leads us, rightly, to think of experience as a more complicated phenomenon than James and Dewey thought it was.

Nevertheless, the attempt to reduce experience to stimuli or to discourse is also symptomatic of something that James and Dewey resisted: a bifurcated model of human beings. An essential element in the pragmatic revolt against traditional approaches to philosophy was pragmatism's emphasis on the fact that human beings are both natural and social beings, and that these ways of seeing ourselves could—and should—be brought together in an attempt to understand our ways of being in the world. Coupled with this, too, was the more capacious understanding of science and the scientific outlook that pragmatism assumed. For Dewey and James the intermingling of organism and environment, rather than a focus on the context-independent human body, was the hallmark of naturalism. The concomitant emphasis on agency and activity they advocated holds promise for us, in the early twenty-first century, as we reframe our epistemological projects in light of the destabilization of the nature/culture dichotomy that comes out of feminist theory, philosophy of science, and philosophy of mind-body. While Rorty is right that the early pragmatists set themselves against a representationalist model of mind and knowledge, he fails to recognize the extent to which they also set themselves against the assumptions about the human body as a dumb, blind natural object. The focus on the organism-environment dyad that Dewey in particular never tired of emphasizing is antithetical to the strong nature/culture dichotomy expressed in the reduction of experience to stimuli or to discourse.

With the development of feminist analyses of lived experience and the lived body, we can see that the pragmatist model of inquiry in which the natural and the cultural are intertwined can be reintroduced, now supplemented by analyses of the ways in which history, economics, identity categories, and gender and race hierarchies influence the organism-environment dyad. The attempt to reduce experience to stimuli is a way of recognizing our natural, bodily being and our connection to the world; the attempt to reduce experience to discourse is a way of paying homage to our ways of finding the world meaningful, and a recognition of the extent to which that meaning is intertwined with social systems and grounded in our connections with other human beings. But the lesson we learn from the early pragmatists is that understanding ourselves as organisms and agents with things to do, with goals and strivings, including the goal of understanding ourselves and our place in the world, brings these two aspects of our being back together. We are ourselves examples of the intertwining of the natural and the cultural, the biological and the discursive. What we mean by experience is this intertwining.

Notes

INTRODUCTION

1. Goodman 1978, 6n4. See also Goodman 1960.

2. My colleague Katheryn Doran makes the point here clearer: "The way that anything is is relative to a perspective. That there is a world is not" (private correspondence).

3. A "view from nowhere" is Thomas Nagel's (1986) characterization of the ideal of objectivity.

4. Popper 1959, 52n4. Popper is himself quoting from Heinrich Gomperz's 1905 *Weltanschauungslehre I*.

5. See William James, "The Subjective Effects of Nitrous Oxide," Mind 7 (1882), http://ebooks.adelaide.edu.au/j/james/william/nitrous (accessed 17 February 2012). This seems to have been meant as a joke, though, especially given James's well-known antipathy to Hegel and Hegelianism. Graham Bird cites a passage in a letter from James to the editor of *Mind* to show both James's wry sense of humor and his distaste for Hegelianism: "'Why don't you have a special neo-Hegelian department in *Mind*, like the agricultural department or the children's department in our newspapers, which educated readers can skip?'" (Bird 1986, 195n17).

6. James was writing before positivists like Schlick, Carnap, and Ayer, of course. But his work on these themes comes after the positivism of Comte and John Stuart Mill and is contemporaneous with early Russell.

7. For a thorough examination of the ways in which American pragmatism and the verificationism of logical positivism overlap and diverge, see Misak 1995.

8. This term is a difficult one, and in twentieth-century philosophy has become almost meaningless, since almost every philosopher seems to want to label him- or herself a "naturalist." Hilary Putnam points out that "naturalism" is rarely defined, and when it is, the definition offered does not usually shed much light. Putnam says that philosophers often begin an essay or talk by announcing that they are "naturalists" or that the account that follows is a naturalistic one, but "this announcement, in its placing and emphasis, resembles the placing of the announcement in articles written in Stalin's Soviet Union that a view was

in agreement with Comrade Stalin's; as in the case of the latter announcement, it is supposed to be clear that any view that is not 'naturalist' . . . is anathema, and could not possibly be correct" (Putnam 2004, 59). I think that Putnam is right about this, and I take this issue up later in this book. My characterization of James as a naturalist is meant to contrast his outlook with the prescriptivism of the logical positivists as well as the rationalism of transcendental idealists. James's claim to the title is, to my mind, based on his emphasis on human beings as animals, his confidence in scientific inquiry to help illuminate and improve human life, and his attitude of experimentalism. And while this might not be a controversial position for contemporary Anglo-American philosophers, it seems to have been a departure from the ruling orthodoxies in James's time.

9. See, e.g., Dewey's account of his intellectual development in Dewey 1981, 1–13.

10. Dewey uses "the organism" instead of the more common terms "person" or "individual," or the more philosophical "subject." "The organism" is, it seems, meant to emphasize an individual living biological system pursuing its goals. I think that this is a significant rhetorical choice on Dewey's part, meant to connect his projects to a naturalistic understanding of human beings, without being reductive.

11. A word now about the difficulty of writing about any of Quine's positions: when I was in graduate school, we liked to play a game in which we tried to find two passages from Quine that seemed to contradict each other. This was amazingly easy. Needless to say, Quine fans in the department were incensed by this game. But the more time I've spent with Quine's work, as I've read him and taught him, the more convinced I have become that Quine's stated positions have deep and perhaps irreconcilable tensions, if not outright contradictions. Depending on what you focus on—*Word and Object*, "Epistemology Naturalized," the essays in *From a Logical Point of View*—you can come out with a slightly different—or dramatically different— reading of his positions. Perhaps this is to be expected of someone who wrote philosophy for sixty or so years, while also saying that philosophy of science was philosophy enough. My version of Quine draws heavily on his work from 1978 on, focusing most on his version of naturalism and his criticisms of Rorty, Kuhn, and Hanson.

CHAPTER I

1. For a slightly different critique of foundationalism, see Sellars 1997. The idea that there are self-authenticating nonverbal episodes (observations) whose authority is conferred on verbal performances (justifications) by following the semantic rules of a language is the heart of what Sellars calls "the Myth of the Given." Rorty's version of anti-foundationalism owes much of its formulation to

Sellars's discussion of discourse and the given, but as we will see, it takes on a rather different slant.

2. See, e.g., Kuhn 1996 [1962], 158: "The man who embraces a new paradigm at an early stage must often do so in defiance of the evidence provided by problem-solving. He must, that is, have faith that the new paradigm will succeed with the many large problems that confront it, knowing only that the older paradigm has failed with a few. A decision of that kind can only be made on faith."

3. Kuhn 1977, 310. Alert readers might be wondering how well this story of learning to label birds squares with Kuhn's extended discussion of the elements of practical engagement that are required for an appropriate education in a paradigm. I think that it does not fit that well with his discussion of that process in *The Structure of Scientific Revolutions*, and it might be an interesting exercise in history of philosophy of science to try to figure out why Kuhn did think these stories went so well together. I will suggest an explanation later. For an interesting discussion, see Rouse 1990.

4. Quine 1993, 108. In this passage, Quine is going over the history of logical positivism and its struggle to define "protocol sentences," called "observation sentences" in Quine's vocabulary (and in this chapter).

5. This relationship, which I've characterized as "undergirding," is not, Quine emphasizes, a relationship of confirmation; rather it is meant to simply correlate causal inputs with utterances. See, e.g., Quine 1990. I discuss Quine's disagreements with Kuhn and Hanson in more depth in chapter 3, as well as his commitment to behaviorism.

6. Rorty 1982. Rorty's argument extends to "truth," "the world," "reality," and other terms that he regards as equivalent to "experience."

7. Rorty's characterization of "foundationalism," and that of other critics of this tradition, is to some extent a moving target. The foundationalism that Rorty attacks owes as much to Locke as it does to Descartes, combining Descartes's search for immediately justified beliefs with Locke's insistence that all of knowledge comes from experience. Cartesian approaches to foundationalism are often taken to be antithetical to the more empiricist version of it that we find in Locke and in later foundationalists (e.g., William Alston), because Cartesian foundationalism depends on the assumption of innate ideas that are discoverable through introspection. For the purposes of this initial exposition, I will not quibble with Rorty's lumping together of these different approaches. However, as I shall show, the issue becomes more complicated when we investigate the question of the extent to which experience is "biased" by theory or "worldviews."

8. This argument is laid out in detail, with accompanying diagrams, in Rorty 1991a, 113–25.

9. And what counts as a properly scientific psychology is, as we will see, an important issue. Quine's reliance on behaviorism, and his endorsement of

linguistic anthropology, imply that he does not limit the natural sciences to physical science. Thus, in all subsequent mentions of Quine's naturalism, and the empirical sciences, the reader should not assume that "empirical science" = "physical science." I shall have more to say about this when I discuss naturalism in chapter 5.

10. Rorty 2003, 15. This is a distinction that Rorty borrows from Robert Brandom. See Brandom 2009, esp. chaps. 2 and 5.

11. For Rorty, sapience also distinguishes us from computers, which cannot engage in cultural practices. Brandom is silent about the status of computers in his elaboration of the distinction, focusing only on what distinguishes us from animals: "Taking something to be subject to appraisals of its reasons, holding it rationally responsible, is treating it as some*one*: as one of *us* (rational beings). . . . Adopting that attitude is acknowledging a certain kind of *community* with the one recognized. It is the fellowship of those we acknowledge not only as *sentient* (a factual matter of biology) but also as *sapient* (a normative matter of responsibility and authority. It is attributing a kind of rational personhood, treating others as *selves*, in the sense of knowers and agents, ones who are *responsible* for their doings and attitudes" (Brandom 2009, 3).

12. For Mackie, the supposition that moral values are objective in the way that the properties of physical objects are objective would mean that we would have to make room in our ontology for "queer" properties that, he argues, are too different from the ordinary kinds of properties with which we are familiar to make them plausible candidates for being real. I suspect that Quine is committed to this Mackie-ish ontology, but, on the other hand, he seems not to want to engage in the kind of metaphysical argument that would support such an ontological claim. The closest he comes is when he argues for the indispensability of certain entities for scientific theories (e.g., mathematical entities). The problem with this, though, is that it either assumes, without actually looking at scientific theories, that moral values are not indispensable, or it calls into question the status of evaluative properties more generally. Since evaluative properties do seem to be indispensable to our best scientific theories (e.g., parsimony, elegance, coherence), then the question arises: why think that evaluative properties that are moral properties are any "queerer"? I discuss this issue in more detail in chapter 5.

13. See, e.g., the final chapter of Quine 1992.

14. In more recent work, Harman has been drawing on social psychology to emphasize the mythological aspect of moral character, and the extent to which moral judgments are situational. It is unclear to me the extent to which he would still hold that the observer's "psychological set" is fully explanatory in the case of putative moral observations, given this emphasis on the (presumably objective) character of situations. The invocation of the observer's "psychological set" remains vague nonetheless.

15. Nelson 1990 has a very illuminating discussion of these aspects of Quine's epistemology.

CHAPTER 2

1. Much of the discussion in this section derives from Janack 2010.

2. I set aside, for the moment, the acceptability of attributing to subpersonal brain processes the intentional processes of assessment and evaluation, as well as the slide from talk of brain processes to talk of knowledge.

3. Hein and Held 1963. I owe the catchy name "kitten gondola experiment" to my colleague Jon Vaughan, but don't know whether it originated with him.

4. McCauley and Henrich cite Berry 1968, 1971; Porac and Coren 1981; Segall et al. 1966; Stewart 1973; Walters 1942; Wapner and Werner 1957; Wapner et al. 1960; Wohlwill 1960.

CHAPTER 3

1. After I had already written a good deal of this chapter, I read Lorraine Code's critical discussion of childhood development theories—in particular Piagetian theories—in chapter four of her book *Ecological Thinking: The Politics of Epistemic Location* (2006). Code gives very good cautionary advice about attempts to theorize childhood cognitive development in isolation from the social and cultural contexts in which children develop. She also gives a very detailed account of the Piagetian legacy, what it has contributed, and what is wrong with it.

2. In his discussion of what he takes to be Dewey's mistaken attachment to the concept of experience, Rorty implies that, had Dewey been familiar with "intelligent but insensate machines" (Rorty 1998, 296), he would not have been so eager to blur the distinction between reasons and causes for beliefs, and would not have felt that intentionality, intelligence, and consciousness had to stand or fall together. For Dewey, "experience" is the combination of consciousness and intelligence that pins beliefs and intelligence to the causal realm, Rorty assumes. Had Dewey recognized the ability of things to be intelligent without being conscious, in the manner of contemporary machine intelligence, Rorty claims, he might have been more willing to eschew the term "experience" and replace it with "discourse." See "Dewey Between Hegel and Darwin" in Rorty 1998.

3. Jerome Bruner (1990) argues that computationalism—which explicitly invokes programming—and behaviorism—which emphasizes the relationship between inputs and outputs—are related to each other, rather than constituting rival versions of psychological theory. Both share a distrust, Bruner argues, of mentalistic concepts like "belief" and of agency.

4. An occasion sentence is a sentence whose meaning depends on the context in which it is uttered. Occasion sentences usually contain indexicals ("this," "that"). Quine includes observation sentences in the class of occasion sentences.

5. Gary Kemp (2006, 94) argues that for Quine's account of language learning to work, the child cannot be a completely blank slate, since it requires programmed "racial memory" dictated by natural selection in the form of "innate similarity spaces" in the "normal" child. Mia Gosselin (2000) points out that a problem with Quine's story is that it implies that children learn "stuff" nouns before proper names for individuals, whereas they in fact learn the latter first (e.g., "Mama," "Gaga," "Daddy").

6. This may sound unfair to Quine, since he might be said to draw on empirical studies in *Word and Object* (Quine 1960). So some might say that it is fairer to say that Quine stopped drawing on empirical studies of language learning some time in the 1950s. Nevertheless, Quine continued to publish into the 1990s, and never, as far as I know, published a correction of his views based on more up-to-date studies. The question of whether appealing to out-of-date empirical data counts as appealing to empirical data is a discussion that is beyond the scope of this book.

7. Note, however, that reading accounts of psychological experiments shows us how ambiguous this term is, even in scientific contexts. In some accounts, "the stimulus" refers to an object in the experimental context; sometimes it is intended to pick out something less concrete or articulated (e.g., a visual presentation or pattern). It seems, then, that "stimulus" might itself be defined differently in different subfields of psychology.

8. I discuss the question of naturalism, and what counts as an adequately naturalistic approach, in more detail in chapter 5.

9. Although I do not draw on Edward Hutchins's book *Cognition in the Wild* (Cambridge, MA: MIT Press, 1996), its title suggested a way to me of characterizing the set of studies of cognition that Code contrasts with laboratory studies of cognition.

CHAPTER 4

1. See, e.g., Lloyd 1984.

2. Epistemically salient identities are understood by feminist philosophers to be a function of the political nature of identities. How fine-grained one takes these categories to be is a matter of dispute: is the category "woman" comprehensive enough, or do we need to further subdivide it according to race, sexual orientation, class, etc? This is a huge debate in feminist theory, but for present purposes, the reader should assume that "identity" here primarily means gender identity.

3. Haack 1993. If reproduction is any evidence of the popularity of a view, Haack's argument seems to have a lot of traction. It has been reprinted in Pojman 1998 [1993], Haack 1998, several other collections of papers, and several journals.

4. For very useful discussions of feminist attempts to develop empiricist models, see Potter 2006 and Tanesini 1999.

5. The term "natural" in Scott's argument invokes both the idea of "given" (that is, not constructed) and of biological/bodily. I will have more to say about the issue of the natural and the process that Scott refers to as "naturalizing" later in this chapter.

6. Scott sometimes implies that the "natural" and the "real" are synonymous; this implied synonymy could be the subject of book of its own. These terms need not be synonymous, but I cannot address this here. I hope that the rest of this chapter and subsequent chapters will give the reader a sense of what is wrong with running the two together.

7. In addition to "The Evidence of Experience" (Scott 1991), Scott wrote a number of essays and responses to her objectors, including "On 'Experience'" (Scott 1992, an abridged and slightly modified version of "The Evidence of Experience") and "A Rejoinder to Thomas Holt" (Scott 1994).

8. Uma Narayan (1997) presents a very good analysis of the ways that charges of false consciousness and inauthenticity are tied up with ethnic identities and colonialism.

9. See, in particular, Scott's argument in "A Rejoinder to Thomas Holt" (Scott 1994), esp. 399ff.

10. Jay sees similarities between this trend in critiques of experience and those of feminist psychoanalysts like Juliet Mitchell, for whom the structure of the mind makes certain kinds of self-knowledge impossible and self-reports of experience unreliable (Jay 2005, 245–46).

11. To be fair, Haraway's real aim is to get us to see the extent to which the distinctions between human, animal, and machine blur when we think about the real processes of vision. So her aim of recapturing the visual metaphor is not trying to get it to work as a metaphor for "worldviews." Yet, since I am sympathetic to the goal of reconceiving vision on the basis of a truly naturalistic account of it, Haraway's account, as one of the few such attempts, is a necessary stop on the way to developing that reconceptualization.

12. I also make this argument in Janack 2010.

CHAPTER 5

1. Again, let me emphasize that this is Quine's account of language learning with respect to his discussion of scientific theorizing and observation sentences. Turning a different lens on Quine's account of language learning would probably

yield a slightly different account. I would refer readers who are skeptical of my reading to the citations of Quine's claims in chapters 1 and 3.

2. There is a huge literature on the extent to which natural entities are, in fact, "constructed." See, e.g., Ian Hacking (2000) and Karen Barad (1999) for some sample discussions. Nevertheless, natural entities are understood in common parlance as given in ways that social institutions or other artifactual entities are not. Barad characterizes this as the assumption that natural entities have properties independently of our attempts to come to know them or to interact with them. For the moment, I am positing the idea of naturalism in which natural entities are said to be "just there" and real in ways that contrast with social entities like class or gender. It is this sense of "the natural" that Scott objects to and thinks is operative in appeals to experience.

3. "Nomothetic" has a number of distinct meanings, and it is not entirely clear which one McDowell wants to invoke. I am assuming, in this discussion, that McDowell means to draw on the distinction between "explanation" (characterized as an attempt to identify causal relationships) and "understanding" (having to do with particularity and meaning), and that "nomothetic" is roughly analogous to an explanatory approach and is meant to contrast with broadly "hermeneutic" approaches, more typical of the humanities.

4. See, e.g., Krüger 1998.5. Where the term is equivocally used to mean both "part of the natural order" and "correct or appropriate."

6. For thorough, insightful accounts of how this happens, see Fausto-Sterling 1985 and 2000.

7. Linguistics is the only remotely "social" science in the list of sciences Maddy provides (see esp. Maddy 2001, 50), unless, contrary to the dominant practice in the United States, psychology is grouped among the social sciences. But both linguistics and psychology admit of more or less social-scientific content, depending on which subfield(s) one focuses on, so neither falls clearly as a discipline into the social sciences.

8. This might be what William James had in mind in talking about the affective aspect of experience—a felt quality of truth. See Janack 2004.

9. I leave aside the question of whether we can understand computers as language users. If computers could be seen as language users, I would argue that they would not then be understood in purely mechanistic terms.

10. Some literary works, like fiction, might not involve avowals, and thus might not require that we understand their authors as making avowals in order to take them seriously. For interesting discussion of this and related topics, see *Intention and Interpretation*, ed. Gary Iseminger (Philadelphia: Temple University Press, 1995), and *Literary Philosophers: Borges, Calvino, Eco*, ed. Jorge J. E. Gracia, Carolyn Korsmeyer, and Rodolphe Gasché (New York: Routledge, 2002).

11. Much of this next section on impersonal and first-person perspectives borrows from Janack 2010.

12. Reflecting on his own discipline of anthropology, Edward Bruner says: "Traditionally, anthropologists have tried to understand the world as seen by the 'experiencing subject,' striving for an inner perspective . . . [but] we systematically remove the personal and the experiential in accordance with our anthropological paradigms; then we reintroduce them so as to make our ethnographies more real, alive" (Turner and Bruner 1986, 9).

13. For a similar argument about the ways in which third-person and first-person stances interact with attributions of agency, see Appiah 2005, 60.

14. See, e.g., Moran 2001 and a slightly orthogonal, but still relevant argument in Dennett 1978, 253–55, which argues that I cannot but see myself as a person, and thus as a subject, in Scott's terminology.

15. Dennett 1978 actually says that I cannot ever really treat myself as merely behaving, or at least not consistently. Similarly, I suspect that I cannot come to see my own first-person perspective as just a discursive effect, or my own textual production as disconnected from my intentional activity.

CHAPTER 6

1. The chapter 6 epigraph is from Reed 1996, 5.

2. See, e.g., Robbins and Aydede 2009.

3. This is also why Gibsonian approaches would be unfriendly to the claim that all the sciences should be able to be reduced to physics, and to the goal of so reducing them.

4. McDowell 1996, lecture 6, distinguishes between an environment and a world, a distinction borrowed from Hans-Georg Gadamer. I think that Gibson's "environment" is Gadamer's and McDowell's "world."

5. Batswana is the term for the people who live in Botswana.

6. The dynamics of the attempted Boer takeover of Botswana were also intermingled with the racial politics and the politics of urbanization and agriculture of southern Africa. See Louw 2004 for a very interesting account of the battles waged by Boers against British rule and the establishment of the Black Homelands in South Africa.

7. Rhodes scholarships, the first international study program, were a bequest of Cecil Rhodes, the founding chairman of the diamond-mining company De Beers Consolidated Mines.

8. The classical source is Gibson 1979, but see also Noë 2004, Hurley 1998, and Reed 1996.

9. For a detailed analysis of the ways in which the border between subjects and objects is more permeable in an ecological approach, see Thompson 2007.

10.   E.g., Lakoff and Johnson 1999.

11.   There is also experimental evidence to support the enactivist claims. See Hein and Held 1963 and Noë 2004, 9. The extent to which the Hein and Held experiments and experiments with inverting lenses support enactivism is, however, disputed by Prinz 2009 .

12.   Research on infant development shows that young infants reach for three-dimensional objects but not two-dimensional representations of them. See Legerstee 1999.

13.   There are a number of interesting empirical studies of the extent to which people can reliably judge the sex of an actor simply from an abstract, lightpoint pattern of movement. See Kozlowski and Cutting 1977. For further discussion of the variations in reliability in such judgments, see Crawley et al. 2000.

14.   The subheading to this section is a quotation from Dewey's essay "The Need for a Recovery of Philosophy" (1917), www.brocku.ca/MeadProject/Dewey /Dewey_1917b.html (accessed 24 February 2012); also in Dewey 1981.

References

Alcoff, Linda Martín. 2000. "Phenomenology, Post-structuralism, and Feminist Theory on the Concept of Experience." In *Feminist Phenomenology*, ed. Linda Fisher and Lester E. Embree, 39–56. Boston: Kluwer Academic.

———. 2006. *Visible Identities: Race, Gender, and the Self.* New York: Oxford University Press.

Appiah, Kwame Anthony. 2005. *The Ethics of Identity.* Princeton, NJ: Princeton University Press.

Barad, Karen. 1999. "Agential Realism." In *The Science Studies Reader,* ed. Mario Biagioli, 1–11. New York: Routledge.

———. 2007. *Meeting the Universe Halfway: Quantum Physics and the Entanglement of Matter and Meaning.* Durham, NC: Duke University Press.

Beauvoir, Simone de. 1989 [1949]. *The Second Sex.* Translated by H. M. Parshley. New York: Vintage Books.

Bennett, M. R., and P. M. S. Hacker. 2003. *Philosophical Foundations of Neuroscience.* Malden, MA: Blackwell.

Berry, J. W. 1968. "Ecology, Perceptual Development and the Mueller-Lyer Illusion." *British Journal of Psychology* 59: 205–10.

———. 1971. "Mueller-Lyer Susceptibility: Culture, Ecology or Race?" *International Journal of Psychology* 6: 193–97.

Bird, Graham. 1986. *William James.* New York: Routledge and Kegan Paul.

Blackburn, Simon. 2006. "Julius Caesar and George Berkeley Play Leapfrog." In *McDowell and His Critics*, ed. Cynthia Macdonald and Graham Macdonald, 203–17. Malden, MA: Blackwell.

Boyd, Richard, Philip Gasper, and J. D. Trout, eds. 1991. *The Philosophy of Science.* Cambridge, MA: MIT Press.

Brandom, Robert. 2000. *Articulating Reasons: An Introduction to Inferentialism.* Cambridge, MA: Harvard University Press.

———. 2009. *Reason in Philosophy.* Cambridge, MA: Belknap Press of Harvard University Press.

Bruner, Jerome. 1986. *Actual Minds, Possible Worlds.* Cambridge, MA: Harvard University Press.

———. 1990. *Acts of Meaning*. Cambridge, MA: Harvard University Press.

Carnap, Rudolf. 1967. *The Logical Structure of the World and Pseudoproblems in Philosophy*. Translated by Rolf A. George. London: Routledge and Kegan Paul.

Churchland, Paul. 1979. *Scientific Realism and the Plasticity of Mind*. Cambridge: Cambridge University Press.

———. 1988. "Perceptual Plasticity and Theoretical Neutrality: A Reply to Jerry Fodor." *Philosophy of Science* 55 (June): 167–87.

Code, Lorraine. 1991. *What Can She Know? Feminist Theory and the Construction of Knowledge*. Ithaca, NY: Cornell University Press.

———. 1993. "Taking Subjectivity into Account." In *Feminist Epistemologies*, ed. Linda Alcoff and Elizabeth Potter, 15–48. New York: Routledge, 1993.

———. 1995. *Rhetorical Spaces: Essays on Gendered Locations*. New York: Routledge.

———. 1996. "What is Natural About Epistemology Naturalized?" *American Philosophical Quarterly* 33, no. 1: 1–22.

———. 2006. *Ecological Thinking: The Politics of Epistemic Location*. New York: Oxford University Press.

Crawley, Rosalind A., et al. 2000. "Perception of Sex from Complex Body Movement in Young Children." *Ecological Psychology* 12, no. 3: 231–40.

Creighton, J. E. 1902. "The Purposes of a Philosophical Association." *Philosophical Review* 11, no. 3: 219–37.

Davidson, Donald, and Jaako Hintikka, eds. 1975 [1969]. *Words and Objections: Essays on the Work of W. V. Quine*. Rev. ed. Dordrecht: D. Reidel.

Delany, Samuel R. 1993. *The Motion of Light in Water: Sex and Science Fiction Writing in the East Village, 1960–1965*. New York: Masquerade.

Dennett, Daniel Clement. 1978. "Mechanism and Responsibility." In *Brainstorms: Philosophical Essays on Mind and Psychology*, 233–55. Montgomery, VT: Bradford Books.

Dewey, John. 1981. *The Philosophy of John Dewey*. Vol. 1, *The Structure of Experience*. Vol. 2, *The Lived Experience*. Edited by John J. McDermott. Chicago: University of Chicago Press.

Eagleton, Terry. 2006. *Criticism and Ideology: A Study in Marxist Literary Theory*. New York: Verso.

Fausto-Sterling, Anne. 1985. *Myths of Gender: Biological Theories About Men and Women*. New York: Basic Books.

———. 2000. *Sexing the Body: Gender Politics and the Construction of Sexuality*. New York: Basic Books.

Fodor, Jerry. 1984. "Observation Reconsidered." *Philosophy of Science* 51, no. 1: 23–43.

————. 1988. "A Reply to Churchland's Perceptual Plasticity and Theoretical Neutrality." *Philosophy of Science* 55, no. 2: 188–98.

Gibson, James J. 1979. *The Ecological Approach to Visual Perception*. Boston: Houghton Mifflin.

Gilman, Daniel J. 1990. "Observation: An Empirical Discussion." *PSA (1990): Proceedings of the Biennial Meeting of the Philosophy of Science Association* 1: 355–64.

————. 1992. "What's a Theory to Do . . . with Seeing? Or Some Empirical Considerations for Observation and Theory." *Brit. J. Phil. Sci.* 43, no. 3: 287–309.

Goodman, Nelson. 1960. "The Way the World Is." *Review of Metaphysics* 14: 48–56.

————. 1978. *Ways of Worldmaking*. New York: Hackett.

Gosselin, Mia. 2000. "Quine's Hypothetical theory of Language Learning: A Comparison of Different Conceptual Schemes and Their Logic." In *Quine: Naturalized Epistemology, Perceptual Knowledge and Ontology*, ed. Lieven Decock and Leon Horsten, 57–77. Atlanta, GA: Rodopi.

Haack, Susan. 1991. "What Is the Problem of the Empirical Basis, and Does Johnny Wideawake Solve It?" *British Journal of the Philosophy of Science* 42: 369–89.

————. 1993. "Epistemological Reflections of an Old Feminist." *Reason Papers* 18: 31–43.

————. 1998. *Manifesto of a Passionate Moderate: Unfashionable Essays*. Chicago: University of Chicago Press.

Hacking, Ian. 2000. *The Social Construction of What?* Cambridge, MA: Harvard University Press.

Hanson, N. Russell. 1958. *Patterns of Discovery: An Inquiry into the Conceptual Foundations of Science*. New York: Cambridge University Press.

————. 1969. *Perception and Discovery: An Introduction to Scientific Inquiry*. San Francisco: Freeman, Cooper.

Harman, Gilbert. 1975. "An Introduction to 'Translation and Meaning', Chapter Two of *Word and Object*." In *Words and Objections: Essays on the Work of W. V. Quine*, ed. Donald Davidson and Jaako Hintikka. Dordrecht: D. Reidel.

————. 1977. *The Nature of Morality*. New York: Oxford University Press.

Haraway, Donna. 1988. "Situated Knowledges: The Science Question in Feminism and the Privilege of Partial Perspective." *Feminist Studies* 14, no. 3: 575–99.

Heck, Richard. 2006. "Reason and Language." In *McDowell and His Critics*, ed. Cynthia Macdonald and Graham Macdonald, 22–44. Malden, MA: Blackwell.

Hein, Alan, and Richard Held. 1963. "Movement-Produced Stimulation in the Development of Visually Guided Behavior." *Journal of Comparative and Physiological Psychology* 56, no. 5: 872–76.

Hurley, Susan. 1998. *Consciousness in Action*. Cambridge, MA: Harvard University Press.

James, William. 1885 [1884]. "The Meaning of Truth." *Mind* 10; www.authorama .com/meaning-of-truth-1.html (accessed 17 February 2012).

———. 1950 [1890]. *Principles of Psychology*. 2 vols. New York: Dover.

———. 1977 [1896]. *The Writings of William James*. Edited by John J. McDermott. Chicago: University of Chicago Press.

Janack, Marianne. 2004. "Changing the Subject of Epistemology and Psychology: William James's Psychology Without Borders." *Metaphilosophy* 35, no. 1–2: 160–77.

———. 2010. "The Politics and the Metaphysics of Experience." In *Feminist Metaphysics: Explorations in the Ontology of Sex, Gender, and the Self*, ed. Charlotte Witt. Dordrecht: Springer.

Jay, Martin. 2005. *Songs of Experience: Modern American and European variations on a Universal Theme*. Berkeley: University of California Press.

Kemp, Gary. 2006. *Quine: A Guide for the Perplexed*. New York: Continuum International.

Kozlowski, L. T., and J. E. Cutting. 1977. "Recognizing the Sex of a Walker from a Dynamic Point-Light Display." *Perception & Psychophysics* 21: 575–80.

Krüger, Hans-Peter. 1998. "The Second Nature of Human Beings." *Philosophical Explorations* 1, no. 2: 107–19.

Kruks, Sonia. 2001. *Retrieving Experience: Subjectivity and Recognition in Feminist Politics*. Ithaca, NY: Cornell University Press.

Kuhn, Thomas. 1970. "Logic of Discovery or Psychology of Research." In *Criticism and the Growth of Knowledge: Proceedings of the International Colloquium in the Philosophy of Science, London, 1965*, ed. Imre Lakatos and Alan Musgrave, 4: 1–24. New York: Cambridge University Press.

———. 1977. *The Essential Tension*. Chicago: University of Chicago Press.

———. 1996 [1962; 2nd ed., enl., 1969]. *The Structure of Scientific Revolutions*. Chicago: University of Chicago Press.

Kukla, Rebecca. 2009. "The Phrenological Impulse and the Morphology of Character." In *Embodiment and Agency*, ed. Sue Campbell, Letitia Meynell, and Susan Sherwin, 76–99. University Park, PA: Pennsylvania State University Press.

Lakoff, George, and Johnson, Mark. 1999. *Philosophy in the Flesh: The Embodied Mind and Its Challenge to Western Thought*. New York: Basic Books.

Legerstee, Maria. 1999. "Mental and Bodily Awareness in Infancy." In *Models of the Self*, ed. Shaun Gallagher and Jonathan Shear, 213–30. Exeter, UK: Imprint Academic Press.

Lichtenberg, Judith. 1994. "Moral Certainty." *Philosophy: The Journal of the Royal Institute of Philosophy* 69, no. 268: 181–204.

Lloyd, Genevieve. 1984. *The Man of Reason: "Male" and "Female" in the History of Western Philosophy*. Minneapolis: University of Minnesota Press.

Louw, P. Eric. 2004. *The Rise, Fall, and Legacy of Apartheid*. Westport, CT: Praeger.

Maddy, Penelope. 2001. "Naturalism: Friends and Foes." *Philosophical Perspectives 15*, *Metaphysics 2001*: 37–67

Mackie, John. 1991 [1977]. *Inventing Right and Wrong*. New York: Penguin Publishers.

McCauley, R. N., and J. Henrich. 2006. "Susceptibility to the Müller-Lyer Illusion, Theory-Neutral Observation, and the Diachronic Penetrability of the Visual Input System." *Philosophical Psychology* 19, no. 1: 79–101.

McDowell, John. 1996. *Mind and World*. Cambridge, MA: Harvard University Press.

———. 1998. "Comment on Hans-Peter Krüger's Paper." *Philosophical Explorations*, no. 2: 120–25.

———. 2002 "Knowledge and the Internal Revisited." *Philosophy and Phenomenological Research* 64, no. 1: 97–105.

McNaughton, David. 1991. *Moral Vision: An Introduction to Ethics*. Malden, MA: Blackwell.

Meltzoff, Andrew. 2002. "Imitation as a Mechanism of Social Cognition: Origins of Empathy, Theory of Mind, and the Representation Action." In *Blackwell Handbook of Childhood Cognitive Development*, ed. Usha Goswami, 6–25. Malden, MA: Blackwell.

Misak, Cheryl. 1995. *Verificationism: Its History and Prospects*. New York: Routledge.

Moran, Richard. 2001. *Authority and Estrangement: An Essay on Self-Knowledge*. Cambridge, MA: Harvard University Press, 2001.

Moya, Paula, and Michael Hames-Garcia, eds. 2000. *Reclaiming Identity: Realist Theory and the Predicament of Postmodernism*. Berkeley: University of California Press.

Nagel, Thomas. 1986. *The View from Nowhere*. New York: Oxford University Press.

Narayan, Uma. 1997. *Dislocating Cultures: Identities, Traditions, and Third World Feminism*. New York: Routledge.

Nelson, Lynn Hankinson. 1990. *Who Knows: From Quine to a Feminist Empiricism*. Philadelphia: Temple University Press.

Nelson, Lynn Hankinson, and Jack Nelson, eds. 2003. *Feminist Interpretations of W. V. Quine*. University Park: Pennsylvania State University Press.

Nicholson, Linda, ed. 1997. *The Second Wave: A Reader in Feminist Theory*. New York: Routledge.

Noë, Alva. 2004. *Action in Perception*. Cambridge, MA: MIT Press.

————. 2009. *Out of Our Heads: Why You Are Not Your Brain, and Other Lessons from the Biology of Consciousness*. New York: Hill & Wang.

Pojman, Louis, ed. 1998 [1993]. *Theory of Knowledge: Classic and Contemporary Readings*. 2nd ed. Belmont, CA: Wadsworth.

Popper, Karl. 1959. *The Logic of Scientific Discovery*. New York: Basic Books.

————. 1972. *Objective Knowledge: An Evolutionary Approach*. Oxford: Oxford University Press.

Porac, C., and S. Coren. 1981. "Life-Span Age Trends in the Perception of the Mueller-Lyer: Additional Evidence for the Existence of Two Illusions." *Canadian Journal of Psychology* 35, no. 1: 58–62.

Potter, Elizabeth. 2006. *Feminism and Philosophy of Science: An Introduction*. New York: Routledge

Prinz, Jesse. 2009. "Is Consciousness Embodied?" In *The Cambridge Handbook of Situated Cognition*, ed. Philip Robbins and Murat Aydede, 419–36. New York: Cambridge University Press.

Putnam, Hilary. 2004. "The Content and Appeal of 'Naturalism.'" In *Naturalism in Question*, ed. Mario DeCaro and David Macarthur. Cambridge, MA: Harvard University Press.

Quine, W. V. 1960. *Word and Object*. Cambridge, MA: Technology Press of the Massachusetts Institute of Technology.

————. 1964 [1953]. *From a Logical Point of View: 9 Logico-Philosophical Essays*. 2nd ed. rev. Cambridge, MA: Harvard University Press.

————. 1969. "Epistemology Naturalized." In *Ontological Relativity and Other Essays*. New York: Columbia University Press.

————. 1975a. "The Nature of Natural Knowledge." In *Mind and Language*, ed. Samuel Guttenplan. Oxford: Clarendon Press.

————. 1975b. "Replies." In *Words and Objections: Essays on the Work of W. V. Quine*, ed. Donald Davidson and Jaako Hintikka. Dordrecht: D. Reidel.

————. 1990. "Let Me Accentuate the Positive." In *Reading Rorty: Critical Responses to Philosophy and the Mirror of Nature (and Beyond)*, ed. Alan Malachowski and Jo Burrows. Oxford: Basil Blackwell.

———. 1992 [1990]. *Pursuit of Truth.* Rev. ed. Cambridge, MA: Harvard University Press.

———. 1993. "In Praise of Observation Sentences." *Journal of Philosophy* 90, no. 3: 107–16.

Reed, Edward. 1996. *Encountering the World: Toward an Ecological Psychology.* New York: Oxford University Press.

Robbins, P., and M. Aydede. 2009. *The Cambridge Companion to Situated Cognition.* New York: Cambridge University Press.

Rock, Irving. 1984. *Perception.* New York: Scientific American Books.

Rooney, Phyllis. 2003. "Feminist Epistemology and Naturalized Epistemology: An Uneasy Alliance." In *Feminist Interpretations of W. V. Quine,* ed. Lynn Hankinson Nelson and Jack Nelson, 205–39. University Park: Pennsylvania State University Press.

Rorty, Richard. 1972. "The World Well Lost." *Journal of Philosophy* 69, no. 19: 649–65.

———. 1979. *Philosophy and the Mirror of Nature.* Princeton, NJ: Princeton University Press.

———. 1982. "Dewey's Metaphysics." In *Consequences of Pragmatism,* 73–89. Minneapolis: University of Minnesota Press.

———. 1991a. *Objectivity, Relativism and Truth: Philosophical Papers I.* New York: Cambridge University Press.

———. 1991b. "Pragmatism and Feminism." *Michigan Quarterly Review* 30, no. 2 (Spring): 231–58.

———. 1998. *Truth and Progress: Philosophical Papers III.* New York: Cambridge University Press.

———. 2003. "Analytic Philosophy and Narrative Philosophy." MS.

Rouse, Joseph. 1990. *Knowledge and Power: Toward a Political Philosophy of Science.* Ithaca, NY: Cornell University Press.

———. 2002. *How Scientific Practices Matter: Reclaiming Philosophical Naturalism.* Chicago: University of Chicago Press.

Rowe, Shawn M., and James Wertsch. 2002. "Vygotsky's Model of Cognitive Development." In *Blackwell Handbook of Childhood Cognitive Development,* ed. Usha Goswami, 538–54. Malden, MA: Blackwell, 2002.

Schlick, Moritz. 1991. "Positivism and Realism." In *The Philosophy of Science,* ed. Richard Boyd, Philip Gasper, and J. D. Trout. Cambridge, MA: MIT Press.

Scott, Joan. 1991. "The Evidence of Experience." *Critical Inquiry* 17, no. 4: 773–97.

———. 1992. "On 'Experience.'" In *Feminists Theorize the Political,* ed. Judith Butler and Joan Wallach Scott, 22–40. New York: Routledge.

———. 1994. "A Rejoinder to Thomas Holt." In *Questions of Evidence: Proof, Practice, and Persuasion Across the Disciplines*, ed. James Chandler, Arnold Davidson, and Harry Harootunian, 397–400. Chicago: University of Chicago Press.

Seigfried, Charlene Haddock. 1990. *William James's Radical Reconstruction of Philosophy*. Albany: State University of New York Press.

Segall, Marshall H., Donald T. Campbell, and Melville J. Herskovits. 1966. *The Influence of Culture on Visual Perception*. New York: Bobbs-Merrill.

Sellars, Wilfrid. 1997 [1956]. *Empiricism and the Philosophy of Mind*. Cambridge, MA: Harvard University Press.

Sokal, Michael M. 2006. "The Origins of the New Psychology." *Physis* 43, no. 1: 273–300.

Stansell, Christine. 1987. "A Response to Joan Scott." *International Labor and Working Class History*, no. 31.

Stewart, V. Mary. 1973. "Tests of the 'carpentered world' Hypothesis by Race and Environment in America and Zambia." *International Journal of Psychology* 8, no. 2: 83–94.

Tanesini, Alessandra. 1999. *An Introduction to Feminist Epistemologies*. Malden, MA: Blackwell.

Thompson, Evan. 2007. *Mind in Life: Biology, Phenomenology, and the Sciences of Mind*. Cambridge, MA: Harvard University Press.

Turner, Victor, and Edward Bruner. 1986. *The Anthropology of Experience*. Champagne-Urbana, IL: University of Illinois Press.

Vasta, Ross, ed. 1982. *Strategies and Techniques of Child Study*. New York: Academic Press.

Walters, Annette. 1942. *A Genetic Study of Geometrical-Optical Illusions*. Genetic Psychology Monographs, 25. Provincetown, MA: Journal Press.

Wapner, Seymour, and Heinz Werner. 1957. *Perceptual Development: An Investigation Within the Framework of Sensory-Tonic Field Theory*. Worcester, MA: Clark University Press.

Wapner, S., H. Werner, and P. W. Comalli. 1960 "Perception of Part-Whole Relationship in Middle and Old Age." *Journal of Gerontology*, no. 15: 412–16.

Watkins, J. N. 1984. *Science and Skepticism*. Princeton, NJ: Princeton University Press.

Waxman, Sandra. 2002. "Early Word-Learning and Conceptual Development: Everything Had a Name, and Each Name Gave Birth to a New Thought." In *Blackwell Handbook of Childhood Cognitive Development*, ed. Usha Goswami, 102–26. Malden, MA: Blackwell.

Williams, Bernard. 1978. *Descartes: The Project of Pure Enquiry*. Atlantic Highlands, NJ: Humanities Press.

Wohlwill, J. F. 1960. "Developmental Studies of Perception." *Psychological Bulletin* 57: 249–88.

Zammito, John H. 2000. "Reading 'Experience': The Debate in Intellectual History Among Scott, Toews, and LaCapra." In *Reclaiming Identity: Realist Theory and the Predicament of Postmodernism,* ed. Paula Moya and Michael Hames-Garcia, 279–311. Berkeley: University of California Press.

———. 2008. "Kant and Naturalism Reconsidered." *Inquiry* 51, no. 5: 532–58.

Index